Economic Policy Issues
of the New Economy

Economic Policy Issues
of the New Economy

Springer
Berlin
Heidelberg
New York
Barcelona
Hong Kong
London
Milan
Paris
Tokyo

Horst Siebert (Ed.)

Economic Policy Issues of the New Economy

 Springer

Professor Horst Siebert
President
Kiel Institute for World Economics
D-24100 Kiel
http://www.uni-kiel.de/ifw/

ISBN 3-540-43698-7 Springer-Verlag Berlin Heidelberg New York

Library of Congress Cataloging-in-Publication Data applied for
Die Deutsche Bibliothek – CIP-Einheitsaufnahme

Economic policy issues of the new economy / Horst Siebert (ed.). – Berlin ;
Heidelberg ; New York ; Barcelona ; Hongkong ; London ; Mailand ; Paris ;
Singapur ; Tokio : Springer, 2002
    ISBN 3-540-43698-7

Springer-Verlag Berlin Heidelberg New York
a member of BertelsmannSpringer Science+Business Media GmbH

http://www.springer.de

© Springer-Verlag Berlin Heidelberg 2002
Printed in Germany

The use of general descriptive names, registered names, trademarks, etc. in this publication
does not imply, even in the absence of a specific statement, that such names are exempt
from the relevant protective laws and regulations and therefore free for general use.

Cover-Design: Erich Kirchner, Heidelberg

SPIN 10880444   42/2202-5 4 3 2 1 0 – Printed on acid-free paper

CONTENTS

Preface HORST SIEBERT VII

Macro- and Microeconomic Policy in the
New Economy: Introduction and Overview JÜRGEN STEHN VIII

I. Macroeconomics in the New Economy

New and Old Economics in the New Economy KEVIN J. STIROH 3

Comment DOMINIQUE FORAY 29

Information Technology and the U.S. Economy DALE W. JORGENSON 37

The New Economy: End of the Welfare State? CATHERINE L. MANN 81

Comment RÜDIGER SOLTWEDEL 98

II. Microeconomics in the New Economy

Labor Market Policy in the New Economy NORBERT BERTHOLD/
RAINER FEHN 105

Comment MICHAEL C. BURDA 137

A WTO-Framework for the New Economy AADITYA MATTOO/
LUDGER SCHUKNECHT 143

Cyberspace, Governance and the New Economy:
How Cyberspace Regulates Us and
How Should We Regulate Cyberspace ELI M. SALZBERGER 169

Comment PETER JOHNSTON 209

Financial Intermediaries in the New Economy:
Will Banks Lose Their Traditional Role? DAVID T. LLEWELLYN 215

Comment RALPH P. HEINRICH 243

LIST OF CONTRIBUTORS 250

Preface

As modern societies become increasingly dependent on information and communications technologies (ICT), public and private interest in the economic impacts of these technologies is growing. There are many labels that have been found for the new information and communications phenomenon: new economy, internet economy, network economy, virtual economy, weightless economy, e-business, e-lance economy, knowledge economy, and information society. Many of the issues related to ICT-based industries pose new challenges to economic theory and economic policy. Thus, there is a growing body of both theoretical and empirical literature concentrating on these issues.

The objective of the international conference on *Economic Policy in the 'New Economy'*, held in Paderborn in May 2001, was to explore the economic essence of the new economy both from a macroeconomic and a microeconomic perspective. The conference was part of a broad research project on *The New Economy — Trends, Causes and Consequences*. The project as well as the conference greatly benefited from the encouragement and financial support of the Heinz Nixdorf Foundation, which is gratefully acknowledged.

The Kiel Institute is indebted to all the participants in the conference for having presented interesting and challenging papers and for conducting stimulating discussions. We owe thanks to the staff of the Heinz Nixdorf MuseumsForum, where the conference took place, for their valuable organizational support during the conference. At the Kiel Institute, Almut Hahn-Mieth and Jürgen Stehn prepared and organized the conference, Dietmar Gebert and Paul Kramer prepared the conference volume for publication.

Kiel, June 2002   Horst Siebert

Jürgen Stehn

Macro- and Microeconomic Policy in the New Economy: Introduction and Overview

Enthusiasm and expectations about the new economy led to formerly unknown high tides in the stock market in the year 2000. At times, the stock market value of Akamai Technologies, an U.S. internet firm, was 21,000 times higher than its yearly turnover. The dot.coms of the new economy seemed to promise the king's road to easy wealth and fortune without caring about sophisticated business strategies, appropriate price-earnings ratios, positive cash flows, or other hard facts of business life.

Enthusiasm for the new economy abruptly turned into depression with the subsequent turn of the tide at the NASDAQ and other new markets. Nowadays, some observers go as far as to call the new economy just a giant speculative bubble with no solid economic substance. Again, this might be an overshooting of expectations because there is almost no doubt that the information and communications technologies of the new economy will lead to a gradual transition of economic structures that goes well beyond mere stock market fluctuations.

The new economy is mainly driven by modern information and communications technologies which give access to almost any kind of information in an ubiquitous manner on a truly global scale. These general-purpose technologies boost the efficiency of conventional activities and pave the way for creating entirely new activities and products. The evolution of the new economy is not a sectoral phenomenon, but is concerned with fundamental redesign and restructuring of products and production technologies throughout the economy. It is not so much the displacement of old by new industries which establishes the new economy, but the rise in the information content of goods and in the information intensity of production processes throughout the economy. Change may take place at different speed in different industries, but it will eventually affect all parts of the economy (Klodt 2000).

Information has turned into a cheap and ubiquitous production factor which increasingly replaces traditional production factors (Siebert 2000). Thus, the transition to the new economy is associated with fundamental shifts in the relative scarcity of factors: in the agricultural economy, land was scarce and labor was abundant. In the industrial society, physical capital was (is) scarce and raw materials (including environment) were abundant. In the new economy, information is abundant and human capital or the capacity to learn might become the new scarce factor.

Moreover, the properties of information as an economic good are significantly dissimilar from the properties of typical goods produced in the old economy: information is a public good (no consumption rivalry), is an experience good (contrast to inspection goods), and is subject to extreme economies of scale in production (negligible cost of duplication and dissemination) and in consumption (network externalities). Hence, there is ample space for any kind of market failure to arise.

The challenges of modern information and communications technologies also raise important questions with regard to economic policy in the new economy: Does the new economy require new economic text books? Will the new economy lead to the demise of business cycles and inflation? Will the new economy raise the growth rate of productivity? Does the new economy lead to a fatter or leaner welfare state? How to make sure that the opportunities of the new economy are shared and spread among the many rather than being enjoyed by a happy few? Does the new economy require a new international framework for trade and investment? How does the new economy affect the corporate governance of firms? Will the international mobility of capital be raised in the new economy?

The objective of this conference volume is to give at least some first answers to these pending questions. In the first part of the volume ("Macroeconomics of the New Economy"), Kevin J. Stiroh ("New and Old Economics in the New Economy") discusses the pros and cons of two distinct interpretations of the new economy. A moderate interpretation acknowledges that the new information and communications technologies are contributing to recent economic gains, albeit in ways consistent with conventional economic theory. New economy extremists, on the other hand, believe that something more profound has happened, arguing that the new economy follows a new set of economic rules. With special regard to the recent success of the U.S. economy, Stiroh concludes that much of the new economy discussion is not really new and remains squarely based on old economic theories and models. A moderate interpretation of the new economy can recognize the important contributions of technology, globalization, and competitive forces to the success of the U.S. economy without mandating radical changes to our understanding of how the economy actually works.

In the second paper of the first part, Dale W. Jorgenson ("Information Technology and the U.S. Economy") analyzes whether information technologies (IT) have produced a fundamental change in the U.S. economy, leading to a permanent improvement in growth prospects. He shows that the foundation of the American growth resurgence is the development and deployment of semiconductors resulting in a decline in IT prices. This technology has also reduced the cost of a wide variety of other products. The accelerated IT price decline in the 1990s signals faster productivity growth in IT-producing industries. In fact, IT-producing industries have accounted for about half the upsurge in productivity growth since 1995. However, faster growth is not limited to these industries.

In the last paper of the first part, Catherine L. Mann ("The New Economy: End of the Welfare State?") sketches out the forces on two dimensions of government business and government relationships: (1) Tax and expenditure systems, and (2) the issue of privacy and use of personal information. She shows that transaction-based tax regimes will be stressed by the forces of the new economy and will need to evolve in response to the more complex and global nature of production. More-over, the extent to which public expenditures focus on moderating the outcomes of structural change versus supporting the transformation of activities will have to change in order to gain from the dynamics of the new economy. With regard to pri-vacy, she concludes that in this area government intervention is required but must preserve the private sector's incentive to innovate.

In the second part of the volume ("Microeconomics in the New Economy"), Norbert Berthold and Rainer Fehn ("Labor Market Policy in the New Economy") analyze the challenges of the new economy for labor market policy. They argue that the IT revolution and the omnipresence of computers in firms have fundamen-tally transformed the production process in favor of flexibility, teamwork, and multitasking. Specialization of employees on certain well-defined tasks as in the Tayloristic or Fordistic mode of production is increasingly obsolete. Thus, in the age of the new economy, labor market policy must primarily be aimed at two key objectives. First, the institutional framework in the labor market must be designed to at least come close to fully exploiting the potential for productivity and employ-ment growth which is created by the new economy. This affects in particular the degree of centralization of wage bargaining and decision-making within firms. Second, it is sometimes argued that the new economy could trigger a digital divide between those who are successful in the new economy and those who are not up to mastering its challenges. Labor market policy should aim at preventing such a damaging development. However, providing people with the respective skills and qualifications via active labor market policies is at most a second-best policy in-strument. The foundations for being successful in the new economy are laid much earlier, namely, when children are attending the education system and when being educated by one's parents.

Aaditya Mattoo and Ludger Schuknecht ("A WTO-Framework for the New Economy") address two broad questions: (1) What categories of international trade are particularly conducive to realizing the benefits of the new economy and how important is such trade already? (2) How well developed and liberal is the in-ternational trade regime, and what are the main challenges ahead? Their analysis elucidates that trade in new-economy-related products is large, accounting for 15-20 percent of world trade in goods and services, and growing rapidly. As regards trade in goods, the Information Technology Agreement (ITA) has secured far-reaching liberalization of market access. The rules governing trade in goods are well developed and contingency protection is not being applied much against new economy products. As regards software and other digitizable media products, a decision needs to be taken on whether to treat internet-based trade in such products as services or as goods. In the services domain, market access commitments and rules need to be further strengthened so as to provide a secure and liberal environment for international trade.

The main objective of the paper by Eli M. Salzberger ("Cyberspace, Governance, and the New Economy: How Cyberspace Regulates Us and How Should We Regulate Cyberspace") is to examine the characteristics of markets in cyberspace and to analyze possible market failures in comparison to market failures in the nonvirtual world. He shows that, on the one hand, some of the nonvirtual market failures induced by the lack of information and by the existence of externalities or transaction costs are of diminishing importance in cyberspace. On the other hand, cyberspace creates some new market deficiencies that are almost unknown in traditional markets. Costs in verifying information as well as the technological race between distinct enforcement measures are prominent examples for virtual market failures.

David T. Llewellyn ("Financial Intermediaries in the New Economy: Will Banks Lose Their Traditional Role?") poses a series of fundamental questions about the future of banking in the new economy. He shows that the related pressures of competition, declining entry barriers, deregulation, financial innovation, and technology have eroded some of the comparative advantages of banks. With the exponential development of information, trading and delivery technology, the value added in the banking business is increasingly passing away from banks to specialist technology companies. Moreover, banks are no longer the exclusive suppliers of banking services: there are many traditional activities of banks that can now be undertaken equally well by markets and other types of financial and nonfinancial companies. Banks face competition from a wider variety of competitors (including niche players) whose underlying economics are different from established firms. Smaller firms and new entrants are also able to challenge the scale advantages of incumbents through outsourcing.

References

Klodt, H. (2001). The Essence of the New Economy. Kiel Discussion Papers 375. Kiel Institute for World Economics, Kiel.

Siebert, H. (2000). The New Economy — What Is Really New? Kiel Working Papers 1000. Kiel Institute for World Economics, Kiel.

I.
Macroeconomics
in the New Economy

Kevin J. Stiroh

New and Old Economics in the New Economy

1. Introduction

The surprising success of the U.S. economy in the late 1990s has led to a growing suspicion that it has changed in fundamental ways, that there is "new economy," that we are in a "new era," and that there is need for a "new paradigm" for economic analysis. While the strength of the U.S. economy should not be easily dismissed, the "new economy" phrase is a vacuous one that may generate more heat than light. Before throwing out the old economy, we must carefully consider what is truly new about the new economy and make an effort to separate the rhetoric from the reality.

The new economy is typically characterized as the recent productivity, inflation, and unemployment gains resulting from three new economy forces – technology, globalization, and increased competitive pressures. Broadly speaking, new economy proponents fall into two camps. A moderate interpretation readily acknowledges that these forces are contributing to recent economic gains, albeit in ways consistent with conventional economic theory. New economy extremists, on the other hand, believe that something more profound has happened, arguing that these forces have changed the structure of the economy, so that it now follows a new set of rules. This essay examines the recent performance of the U.S. economy with an eye toward differentiating the moderate explanations from the more extreme ones.

It is difficult to refute a moderate interpretation of the new economy. A consensus is now emerging, for example, that information technology has played a critical role in the U.S. productivity revival. Similarly, there is evidence that U.S. inflation and unemployment improved in part due to positive supply shocks associated with technology, globalization, and increased competitiveness. While these forces are often highlighted in new economy discussions, they have always af-

Remark: I thank Dominique Foray, Rob Rich, Charles Steindel, Lauren Stiroh, and Meredith Walker-Tsui for helpful comments on an earlier draft, John Eller for helpful discussions, and Paul Edelstein for excellent research assistance. All views expressed in this paper are those of the author only and do not necessarily reflect those of the Federal Reserve Bank of New York or the Federal Reserve System.

fected economic performance and the moderate view simply emphasizes their recent contributions. In this sense, the new economy is more evolutionary than revolutionary as new realizations of familiar forces continuously shape the economy.

Extreme new economy proponents, on the other hand, claim that the economy has experienced deeper and more fundamental changes in how it operates. For example, some argue that technology-driven increasing returns and network effects are now the most appropriate model for the U.S. economy. Others claim that increased global competition has rendered the Phillips curve obsolete or that productivity gains have permanently lowered the natural rate of unemployment. This more extreme interpretation suggests that basic economic relationships have changed and calls for a reworking of economic theory.

A broad reading of the new economy literature suggests that most economists fall into the moderate new economy camp and link technology, globalization, and competition to traditional economic theories. Radical does not necessarily mean wrong, however, and there may still be room for some extreme new economy ideas. Why, for example, has total factor productivity growth apparently accelerated outside of manufacturing? Has the Internet improved job matching and permanently lowered the natural rate of unemployment? Why did conventional forecasting models fail to predict the success of the 1990s? Potential answers from the extreme new economy proponents exist, but they require more conceptual work and stronger empirical evidence to achieve widespread acceptance.

The recent success of the U.S. economy is beyond debate, so economists and the business press have now turned their attention to differentiating "new" economy explanations from "old" economy ones. This is a difficult and somewhat artificial distinction, however, since most new economy explanations are squarely built on old economic foundations. That is, technology, globalization, and competitive forces are indeed contributing to the success of the U.S. economy, but in ways quite consistent with conventional economic theory and models. The blurring of the lines between old and new economics and the hype of new economy extremists, however, should not cause us to dismiss the recent success of the U.S. economy.

2.   What Is the New Economy?

> Parameters such as normal rates of unemployment and potential growth have surely changed. But the basic laws of supply and demand and the verities of human psychology have not. (Summers 2000b)
> In textbook economics the supply of products would only increase if their price went up; in the new economics the supply increases as price goes down. (Kelly 1998: 55)

The new economy is a broad topic that often means different things to different people. For the purposes of this paper, I define the new economy as the productivity gains, unemployment declines, and inflation moderation in the late 1990s that resulted from technology, globalization, and increased competitive pressures.

This definition is broadly representative of the new economy literature, e.g., Broadbent and Walton (2000), Council of Economic Advisors (CEA 2001), Greenspan (1998), McTeer (1999), Gundlach (2001), Madrick (1999), Nakamura (2000), Pakko (1999), Shepard (1997), Stiroh (1999), Summers (2000a), and Wadhwani (2001) provide very similar descriptions. Bosworth and Triplett (2000), Centre for the Study of Living Standards (CSLS 2000), Gordon (2000), Nordhaus (2000), and Van Ark (2000) focus more narrowly on the role of information technology (IT) as a source of accelerating output and productivity growth. Mandel (1998a) and OECD (2000a) broaden the IT topic to include determinants of innovation, research and development, and venture capital, while Summers (2000b) identifies the fundamental change as the move from production of physical goods to the production of knowledge.

Others offer a more sweeping view. Shepard (1997) calls IT a "transcendent technology" that affects virtually everything, while Kelly (1998) claims the new economy is a "tectonic upheaval," where the penetration of vast networks drive business activity as the economy becomes more global, intangible, and interlinked. Cohen et al. (2000) begin with the productivity gains in IT, and then argue that IT represents a "new tool" that completely transforms business and opens new organizational possibilities. These broader characterizations are in the minority, however, and it is useful to distinguish between a "moderate" and an "extreme" interpretation of the new economy.[1]

The moderate view, espoused by most economists, readily acknowledges that new economy forces, e.g., technology, globalization, and competition, are affecting the economy. There is no argument, however, that the underlying economic relationships themselves have changed. Rather, familiar economic forces are simply operating through different channels. This interpretation is apparent in the broad new economy survey by Wadhwani (2001) and Woodall (2000), work on information technology and productivity by Bosworth and Triplett (2000), Jorgenson (2001), Jorgenson and Stiroh (2000), Oliner and Sichel (2000), Stiroh (2002, forthcoming), and Triplett (1999). It also reflects the inflation/unemployment work of Gordon (1998), Katz and Krueger (1999), and Rich and Rissmiller (2000). Since

---

[1] Stiroh (1999) outlined three versions of the new economy – a long-run growth version that emphasizes faster productivity, a short-run business cycle version that emphasizes an improved inflation/unemployment trade-off, and a sources-of-growth version that emphasizes alternative forces driving growth. Broadly speaking, the third version is most consistent with the extreme new economy.

these forces have always mattered, the real question is whether they are now affecting the economy in ways that are profoundly different than in the past.

In this extreme view – "techno-visionaries" according to *The Economist* (1999) – the same new economy forces are fundamentally changing the way the economy and businesses operate. This moves past the moderate view to identify a radically new economy. Kelly (1998), for example, points to increasing returns and network externalities as fundamentally altering the way businesses compete and interact. Cox and Alm (1999) discusses the end of scarcity and pervasiveness of increasing returns to scale as hallmarks of the new economy. Summers (2000b) describes a switch from an old economy world of negative feedback to a new economy world of positive feedback, while Nakamura (2000) points to creativity as the driving force in the new economy, which moves economics away from the standard model of perfect competition.

Other economists have raised the possibility of extreme new economy effects, although typically as speculation rather than as firmly held beliefs. DeLong (1998), for example, wonders whether the information age will reduce the importance of traditional economic concepts like excludability, rivalry, and transparency, which will lessen the effectiveness of the market system. OECD (2000a, 2000b), Schreyer (2000), and Van Ark (2000) raise the possibility that IT is not a "normal" good because it may create production spillovers or serve as a general purpose technology that facilitates complementary innovations. Both of these features are not handled easily by conventional productivity analysis.

The remainder of this paper examines two fundamental features of the new economy debate: the resurgence of productivity growth and the apparent improvement in the inflation/unemployment trade-off.[2] I examine the explanations provided by conventional economics and the moderate new economy view, and then look for evidence of more extreme new economy positions. The analysis focuses on the U.S. experience in the 1990s, but also draws some evidence from Europe.

3.   Productivity Growth in the New Economy

The revolution starts this summer. … The management planning behind the acquisition of the first UNIVAC to be used in business may eventually be recorded by historians as the foundation of the second industrial revolution. (Osborn 1954: 99) We argue that the rewards from new technology accrue to the direct participants: first, to the innovating industries producing the high-technology assets, and sec-

---

[2]   I focus on macroeconomic indicators and do not examine the stock market effects. See Brynjolfsson and Yang (1997), Greenwood and Jovanvic (1999), and Hall (2000) for alternative interpretations of the new economy impact on the stock market.

ond, to the industries that restructure to implement the latest technology. ... The empirical record provides little support for the "new economy" picture of spill-overs cascading from IT producers onto the users of this technology. (Jorgenson and Stiroh 2000: 128–129)

a.   The Recent Productivity Experience

The revival in U.S. productivity growth in the mid-1990s is a cornerstone of the new economy. After more than two decades of relatively slow growth, both labor productivity and total factor productivity accelerated after 1995. The long-awaited gains occurred contemporaneously with massive amounts of investment in infor-mation technology (IT), so the productivity revival has become a critical piece of evidence for the technology component of the new economy.

The U.S. Bureau of Labor Statistics (BLS) compiles the official U.S. produc-tivity estimates and reports that average labor productivity growth (ALP) for the nonfarm business sector jumped to 2.48 percent per year for the period 1995–2000 compared to 1.35 percent 1973–1995 (Figure 1). Total factor productivity (TFP) also showed strong improvement, rising from 0.42 percent for 1973–1995 to

Figure 1: U.S. Labor Productivity Growth, 1947–2000

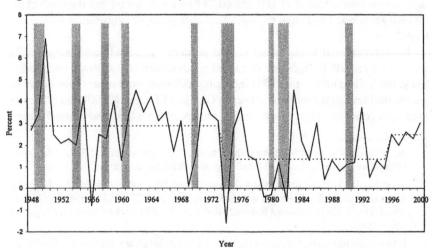

Note: Recession bars according to the NBER U.S. Business Cycle Expansion and Contraction dates. Productivity growth is for the nonfarm business sector from BLS (2001b). Solid line is average annual growth; dotted line is period average, for 1947–1973, 1973–1995, 1995–2000.

1.10 percent for 1995–1999 (BLS 2001a).[3] While the rate of labor productivity growth has not yet returned to the "golden age" of the 1950s and 1960s, the improvement is quite impressive nonetheless.[4]

An interesting feature of this productivity revival is that it has occurred very late into the U.S. economic expansion. The stylized fact is that productivity is procyclical due to some combination of input utilization, technological shocks, or increasing returns to scale; Figure 1 shows that productivity typically slows as the economy enters recessions and accelerates as it exits recessions. In contrast, the productivity boom of the late 1990s began very late into the economic expansion, leading some to believe that this productivity revival is fundamentally different.

b.   Is This a New Economy?

In the moderate view of the new economy, the answer is yes. A consensus is now emerging that both the *production* and the *use* of IT have contributed substantially to the U.S. aggregate productivity revival in the late 1990s, e.g., CEA (2001), Jorgenson (2001), Jorgenson and Stiroh (2000), Oliner and Sichel (2000), Stiroh (forthcoming), and Whelan (2000).[5] Gordon (2000), a leading IT skeptic, assigns a larger role to cyclical forces, and thus only finds productivity gains from the production of IT. Table 1 summarizes growth-accounting results from several of these studies. The growing contribution from the use of IT (IT-related capital deepening) and the production of IT (IT-related TFP) are substantial, but they reflect traditional economic forces like technological change, input substitution, and investment.[6]

The international evidence on IT and productivity growth also supports this view. Schreyer (2000) finds that IT capital goods contribute to growth and productivity, but little evidence that IT is inherently different from other types of capital goods. Building on the work of Schreyer, Gust and Marquez (2000) find that countries with relatively high IT-producing sectors like Finland and Ireland experi-

---

[3]   According to Gust and Marquez (2000), neither ALP growth nor TFP growth appears to have accelerated as much in most other industrialized countries.

[4]   Note that the ALP estimates reflect the multiyear GDP revisions by the U.S. Bureau of Economic Analysis (BEA) that were announced on July 27, 2001, while the TFP estimates do not. These revisions lowered GDP growth, and therefore productivity growth was reduced.

[5]   Information technology typically includes computer hardware, computer software, and telecommunications equipment, although definitions vary across studies. Note that these studies do not reflect the multiyear BEA revisions.

[6]   This section focuses on aggregate IT evidence. See Brynjolfsson and Hitt (2000) for a broad survey from a more microeconomic perspective.

Tabelle 1: Alternative Estimates of the Productivity Impact of IT

	BLS	CEA	Gordon	Jorgenson & Stiroh	Oliner & Sichel
ALP revival period, 1995–1999	2.40	3.01	2.75	2.37	2.57
ALP early period, 1973–1995	1.39	1.39	1.42	1.42	1.41
Acceleration	1.01	1.62	1.33	0.95	1.16
Capital deepening	0.30	0.38	0.33	0.29	0.33
IT-related	0.48	0.62	-na-	0.34	0.50
Other	−0.21	−0.23	-na-	−0.05	−0.17
Labor quality	0.06	0.00	0.05	0.01	0.04
TFP	0.70	1.19	0.31	0.65	0.80
IT-related		0.18	0.29	0.24	0.31
Other		1.00	0.02	0.41	0.49
Cyclical effect		0.04	0.50		
Price measurement			0.14		

Note: Revival period is 1995–2000 for CEA and 1995–1998 for Jorgenson and Stiroh. BLS, CEA, Oliner and Sichel, and Gordon examine nonfarm business sector; Jorgenson and Stiroh include business sector plus private households. Gordon compares the revival period to trend productivity growth for the early period. IT-related capital deepening refers to information processing equipment and software for BLS and CEA; computer hardware, software and telecommunications equipment for Jorgenson and Stiroh and Oliner and Sichel. IT-related TFP is from computer and communications production for CEA, from computer plus computer-related semiconductors for Gordon and Oliner and Sichel, and from computer hardware, software, and telecommunications for Jorgenson and Stiroh. Numbers may not add up due to rounding.

Source: CEA (2001), BLS (2001a), Gordon (2000), Jorgenson and Stiroh (2000), Oliner and Sichel (2000).

enced relatively fast TFP growth, although the capital deepening effects from IT use appear to be smaller than in the United States. This likely reflects smaller IT investment shares in Europe through 1996, when the studies end. For a sample of 15 European countries, Daveri (2001) reports that a sizable fraction of cross-country growth differences can be attributed to variation in IT adoption and accumulation. The European Central Bank (2001) shows that the growth contribution of IT increased in the late 1990s for the Euro area, although they report few spillover effects from ICT use.

This conventional IT/productivity story is largely one of technological progress and capital deepening. Technological progress in the sector that produces IT leads to lower and lower prices for IT capital goods, which, in turn, induces profit-maximizing firms to substitute between heterogeneous inputs and rapidly accumulate

IT. IT capital deepening then contributes to increased labor productivity in the IT-using industries. There is nothing new about fundamental technological progress in leading sectors and input substitution in response to relative price changes; this is very old economics dating back to at least Solow (1957).

The fact that productivity accelerated very late in the economic expansion, however, is one aspect of the recent productivity revival that appears different. CEA (2000) shows that, in contrast to the expansions of the 1960s and 1980s, productivity growth accelerated after the fourth year of the current expansion, which they attribute to investment, technology, and skill enhancement. Basu et al. (2000) conclude the recent productivity surge reflects technological phenomenon, rather than cyclical forces, which is supported by the aggregate growth accounting of CEA (2001) and the cross-industry evidence of Stiroh (forthcoming). Gordon (2000) offers an opposing view and argues that much of the productivity boom is cyclical in nature. Whether one believes that cyclical forces, capital deepening, or technology has played the dominant role, however, these explanations are quite mainstream in nature.

What about more extreme new economy views? The data suggest that there is room for extreme new economy explanations like production spillovers and network externalities, although there is relatively little evidence to date. The potential for new economy effects lies in the apparent acceleration of TFP growth outside of the industries that produce IT. CEA (2001) reports that TFP growth, excluding the computer industry and controlling for cyclical effects, accelerated by 1 percentage point when 1995–2000 is compared to 1973–1995 (Table 1). Basu et al. (2000) report a surge in technological progress in the nonmanufacturing sector after accounting for adjustment costs and utilization effects. If one believes that it is not a cyclical artifact, this acceleration remains unexplained by conventional economics and could reflect extreme new economy forces.

OECD (2000a, 2000b), Schreyer (2000), and Van Ark (2000) all raise the possibility that IT capital is fundamentally different from other forms of capital. Network effects, increasing returns, or production spillovers associated with IT could, in principle, explain the rise in TFP growth throughout the U.S. economy. Early research on IT, e.g., Bresnahan (1986), Brynjolfsson and Hitt (1995), and Lichtenberg (1995), concluded that IT generates nonpecuniary externalities that were measured as excess returns to IT and TFP growth.

More recent work at both the micro level (Brynjolfsson and Hitt (2000) and the macro level (Gordon (2000) and Stiroh (1998, 2002)), however, finds little evidence that IT investment leads to TFP growth; the early results could reflect omitted variables and measurement errors. Thus, linking TFP growth to the use of information technology remains an important empirical objective for the extreme new economy proponents.

It is also useful to remember that IT in general and the computer in particular is not that new anymore. The first stored-program electronic computer for a nongovernment entity was installed by General Electric (GE) in 1954.[7] Roddy Osborn, manager of the Business Procedures Section at GE, lists four business tasks that this early computer could undertake: "handling payroll, material scheduling and inventory control, order service and billing, and general and cost accounting" (Osborn 1954: 101). These tasks are virtually the same as those touted by modern new economy and IT enthusiasts! Thus, the recent productivity revival could be more associated with the quantity, speed, and the diffusion of IT services, rather than new functionality or special characteristics of IT itself.

The observation that IT played a substantial role in the resurgence of U.S. productivity growth does not constitute a new economy in the deeper, more extreme sense. The recent productivity gains largely reflect familiar economic forces like technological progress, input substitution, and capital deepening, and there is little evidence that the gains reflect extreme new economy concepts like spillovers, increasing returns, or network effects. This is not to say that IT does not matter; it does. Rather, the evidence to date suggests that IT-related technology and capital accumulation affect the economy in the same way that technology and capital accumulation have always affected the economy.

4.   Unemployment and Inflation in the New Economy

> The "natural rate of unemployment," in other words, is the level that would be ground out by the Walrasian system of general equilibrium equations ... including market imperfections, stochastic variability in demands and supplies, the cost of gathering information about job vacancies and labor availability, the cost of mobility, and so on. (Friedman 1968: 8)
> One would expect the Internet to permit superior job matching between the unemployed and the available vacancies – this effect should lead to a fall in the NAIRU. (Wadhwani 2000: 7)

a.   The Recent Experience

A second cornerstone of the new economy is the apparent improvement in the short-run inflation/unemployment trade-off in the United States and in Europe. Since 1995, both the unemployment rate and the inflation rate have dropped substantially. This has led some to argue that there have been fundamental changes in the dynamics of price and wage inflation that imply a lower natural rate or a lower nonaccelerating inflation rate of unemployment (NAIRU) in a new economy. In

---

[7]   See Ceruzzi (2000) for a detailed history of early computing.

Figure 2: U.S. Inflation/Unemployment Experience, 1978–2000

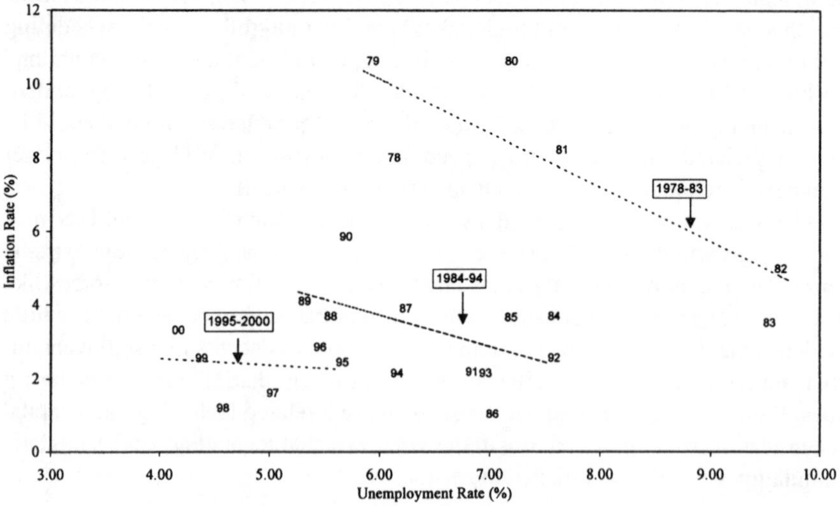

Note: Inflation based on the CPI-U-RS and unemployment rates are civilian unemployment rates. Both are from BLS and seasonally adjusted. Inflation is December–December annual rate and unemployment is average of monthly estimates. See text for details.

addition, there is a notion that new economy forces, particularly technology-led productivity gains, have permanently lowered unemployment.

Figure 2 presents a scatter plot of annual inflation and unemployment rates for 1978 to 2000 using BLS data.[8] This figure is a standard "Phillips curve" representation familiar from most macroeconomic textbooks and shows a negative, short-run relationship between unemployment and inflation. For example, during the late 1970s and early 1980s the U.S. economy experienced moderating inflation as unemployment rates increased. Conversely, the late 1980s saw rising inflation and declining unemployment. This is the conventional short-run Phillips curve relationship.

---

[8]   The annual inflation rate is the December-December growth of the seasonally adjusted BLS CPI-U-RS series, which is a methodologically consistent estimate of the consumer price index for all urban consumers. The unemployment rate is the average of monthly figures for the civilian labor force of adults 16 years and older, seasonally adjusted. Both series are from BLS. The dotted lines represent fitted values from OLS regressions of inflation on a constant and the unemployment rate for the periods 1978–1983, 1984–1994, and 1995–2000.

Figure 3: U.S. Monthly Unemployment and Inflation Rates, 1990–2000

Note: Inflation rates based on the CPI-U-RS and unemployment rates are civilian unemployment rates. Both are from BLS and seasonally adjusted. Inflation is annualized monthly rate. See text for details.

Beginning in the early 1990s, however, the picture looks somewhat different. Unemployment fell from 7.5 percent during 1992 to 4.5 percent in 1998, even as inflation moderated from 2.6 percent to 1.4 percent. In the most recent years, 1999 and 2000, there seems to be a return to the traditional short-run Phillips curve relationship as inflation accelerated while unemployment continued to fall. Figure 3 plots the time paths of these two series, on a monthly frequency during the 1990s, and shows the steady downward trend in both until 1999, when inflation picked up in response to cyclical pressures and energy prices.

European countries show a similar phenomenon during the mid and late 1990s. Figure 4 plots the inflation/unemployment relationship for the United States and the European Union during the 1990s.[9] While the level of European unemployment remains considerably higher than the U.S. level, both data show large declines in inflation and some moderation in unemployment after 1993. In addition, OECD (2000c) reports a decline in the NAIRU for the late 1990s in most European countries, e.g., OECD estimates that the NAIRU fell from 9.2 percent in

---

[9]   The inflation rate is based on the annual CPI reported in OECD (2000c: Annex Table 16). The unemployment rate is a standardized unemployment rate reported in OECD (2000c: Annex Table 22).

Figure 4: Inflation and Unemployment in the European Union and the United States, 1991–1999

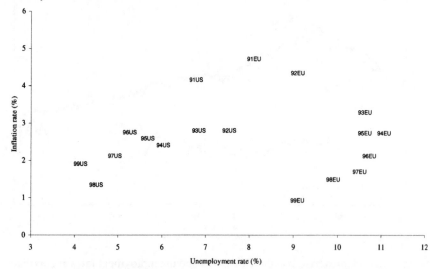

Source: Inflation is based on annual CPI and unemployment is a standardized rate calculated by OECD (2000c).

1995 to 8.8 percent in 1999 for the Euro area and from 5.3 percent to 5.2 percent for the United States. While there are sizable standard errors around these estimates, the point estimates suggest that the NAIRU has fallen in both Europe and the United States.

b.   Is This a New Economy?

The contemporaneous decline in unemployment and inflation in the United States and in Europe through much of the 1990s has fueled many new economy arguments, since it seems inconsistent with the simplest Phillips curve with a constant NAIRU. This is somewhat of a straw man comparison, however, and the real comparison is between any new economy explanation and the modern econometric formulations of inflation dynamics that allow for supply shocks, inflation inertia, and a slow evolution of the NAIRU itself.[10] Gordon (1998) provides a useful characterization of three alternative explanations – new economy advocates who point

---

[10]   This modern characterization follows the "triangle model," reviewed in Gordon (1997).

to IT as removing previous supply constraints and globalization as providing lower-priced low-tech goods; Phillips curve nonbelievers; and Phillips curve defenders who argue that the NAIRU has shifted downward.

Recent econometric work suggests that traditional models offer a reasonable explanation for these trends. Gordon (1998), for example, argues that the U.S. experience reflects a series of positive supply shocks. These include traditional shocks like changes in real food prices and import prices, as well as new ones that include an acceleration in computer price declines, declines in medical care inflation, and improved measurement techniques. While falling computer prices and import prices have a new economy flavor, they are conventional supply shocks and fit easily into the standard inflation model.[11]

Rich and Rissmiller (2000) also estimate a supply shock-augmented Phillips curve. They argue that conventional economic factors and favorable supply shocks, most notably a decline in import prices, explain the low U.S. inflation in recent years. They conclude there is no evidence that the fundamental dynamics have changed. Staiger et al. (1997) estimate that the NAIRU has fallen by about 1 percentage point, although they emphasize the substantial imprecision in this type of exercise and do not provide specific explanations.

These interpretations of the recent unemployment/inflation experience suggest traditional explanations. While there is some disagreement about how far the NAIRU may have shifted, all reject the notion that the short-run Phillips curve has vanished altogether. The positive supply shocks allow for temporarily lower unemployment and inflation, but the underlying relationship remains intact. In this view, there is nothing fundamentally new about this as the positive supply shocks of the 1990s can be seen as the mirror image of the negative supply shocks of the 1970s.

What about the more extreme new economy view? As with the productivity debate, there may be room for extreme new economy explanations, since the supply shock story is largely about short-run dynamics. That is, positive supply shocks explain why inflation and unemployment were *temporarily* low, but some argue that new economy forces may have *permanently* lowered the natural rate of unemployment. Going back to the formulation of the natural rate in Friedman (1968), that is ultimately a story about the structure of the labor market.[12]

---

[11]   Gordon estimates a "time-varying NAIRU," which is essentially a short-term NAIRU concept. OECD (2000 c: 157) characterizes a short-term NAIRU as the rate of unemployment consistent with stable inflation given any supply and demand shocks. A medium-term NAIRU is the rate to which unemployment converges in the absence of temporary supply shocks. A long-term NAIRU is the long-term unemployment equilibrium after the NAIRU has adjusted to all supply and policy influences. This long-term NAIRU is most consistent with the natural rate formulation of Friedman (1968) and Phelps (1968).

[12]   Stock (1998) raises a similar point.

Wadhwani (2000) and CEA (2000), for example, argue that IT and the Internet lower labor market search costs, effectively altering the structural parameters of the labor market in a way consistent with a permanently lower long-run natural rate. Krueger (2000) reports that Internet job boards cost 5 percent of a help-wanted ad in a major newspaper; lower search costs speed up job matching and lower unemployment. Similarly, Gomme (1998) shows how an improvement in matching technology could lower the long-run unemployment rate, although he concludes that this is not the channel that new economy proponents have in mind. Potential gains from better matching via the Internet or IT are certainly possible, but the evidence on the actual impact of the Internet on labor markets remains limited.

Alternatively, Stiglitz (1997) raises the possibility that increased competitiveness and globalization, two new economy forces, contributed to the decline of the NAIRU, although he is not precise about the mechanism. Osterman (1999) discusses fundamental labor market changes like increased worker turnover, a new emphasis on "pay-for-performance," and reduced union power that result from new economy forces. In principle, these explanations could change labor market dynamics permanently and lower the long-run natural rate.

There are competing labor market explanations for a decline in the long-term NAIRU, however, that are decidedly less new economy in spirit. Gordon (1997), for example, points to the decline in unions, while Katz and Krueger (1999) emphasize demographic changes, an increased prison population, more efficient labor market matching, and a weak-backbone hypothesis. Otoo (1999) identifies the rise of the temporary help industry as a source of downward pressure on the natural rate. Of these explanations, only the more efficient labor market matching explanation has a clear new economy interpretation. Katz and Krueger (1999), however, emphasize job search assistance programs and a growing temporary help sector as the underlying forces, rather than Internet job boards or the like.

Finally, there is a question of whether productivity gains can, even in principle, affect the long-run unemployment rate. Gomme (1998) interprets the new economy extremists as arguing that favorable technology shocks *permanently* lowered the NAIRU. There seems to be little evidence for this, either theoretically or empirically. Stiglitz (1997), for example, argues that both the level and rate of change of productivity have no long-run effect on the unemployment rate, while Blanchard and Katz (1997) conclude that the long-run natural rate appears insensitive to productivity changes. Altig and Gomme (1998) and CEA (2000) conclude that productivity shocks are likely to have only a short-run impact on unemployment due to worker misperceptions, while Meyer (2000) reaches a similar conclusion based on sticky wages. In these cases, productivity shocks temporarily lower both inflation and unemployment, but they will have no long-run effect.

It appears that there is little justification for the apparent new economy belief that technology and productivity shocks can permanently lower the unemployment rate. There can be temporary effects, either through worker misperceptions or slow wage adjustments, but these will dissipate as the economy and workers adjust to faster trend productivity growth.

The best hope of the new economy side, therefore, seems to be a story of IT-driven improvements in labor-matching technology, since Internet job boards and online resume banks have the potential to permanently lower the natural rate. The main impact of these forces, however, is likely to be in the future and not as an explanation of the past. In 1998, for example, Kuhn and Skuterud (2000) estimate that only 13 percent of the unemployed used the Internet. It remains to be seen whether this innovation will be large enough to change the structure of the labor market and lower the natural rate of unemployment.

5.   Questions for the New Economy

I now turn to a series of questions about the new economy. Whether one accepts the moderate new economy explanation or is sympathetic to the more extreme new economy view, these questions should be of interest. Moreover, answers to these questions will help us to better understand which new economy argument is the most appropriate.

a.   What Changed in 1995?

The economic gains in the U.S. economy seem to have begun in 1995.[13] An important issue, therefore, is to understand what exactly changed in 1995. If the recent success is more than a series of random shocks, economists should be able to identify the smoking gun and trace the changes to something tangible in the economy.

In his Presidential Address to the American Economic Association, Jorgenson (2001; see also this volume) points to the development and deployment of semiconductors as the foundation of the U.S. economic resurgence. In this view, Moore's law, which states the complexity of a state-of-the-art semiconductor doubles every 18 to 24 months, accelerated and drove the economy with it. The pace of technological change, measured as the decline in quality-adjusted prices of

---

[13]   Stiroh (forthcoming) finds a trend-break in the aggregate U.S. labor productivity series in 1995:Q3.

computer hardware accelerated to 25.0 percent per year for 1995–2000 from only 12.2 percent per year for 1987–1995, which Jorgenson attributes to a switch from a three-year to a two-year product cycle for semiconductors. This implies that the key driver was technological progress, which accelerated in response to intensifying competitive pressures in the semiconductor industry.

Other explanations include the widespread commercialization of the Internet (OECD 2000a and Nordhaus 2000), the emergence of open-source software and continued deregulation (DeLong 2000b), a growing role of e-commerce, and increased IT-related standards. These explanations, however, seem to be less important as explanations of the past than as predictions for the future. For example, Litan and Rivlin (2000) report that the annual volume of e-commerce in the United States is $100–$200 billion, which is much too small to have a large impact on the economy, while Oliner and Sichel (2000) estimate that e-commerce has had a negligible effect on TFP growth. Since e-commerce and business-to-business applications are projected to grow considerably, the Internet will likely affect the future performance of the economy, but is less likely to be able to explain past performance.

The best answer seems to be one of increasing speed, power, and diffusion of IT-related forces. Early studies by Oliner and Sichel (1994) and Jorgenson and Stiroh (1999) reported a smaller role of IT than more recent studies simply because IT was a much smaller part of the economy and state-of-the-art IT was much less powerful in earlier years. The current-cost net stock of information procession equipment and software, for example, increased from $663 billion in 1990 to $1,182 billion in 1999 (Herman 2000). When one factors in the enormous quality improvements across successive vintages of IT equipment, the gains in both the quantity and the quality of IT equipment are enormous.[14] Thus, one can reasonably conclude that IT had a much bigger impact in the late 1990s than in the 1980s and early 1990s simply because a much larger amount of much more powerful IT equipment is currently in use.

b.   Can IT Continue to Drive the Economy?

If one accepts that the increased power of IT plays a critical role in the resurgence of the U.S. economy, the next question is: can these performance gains, epitomized by Moore's law, continue? This is really a question for the engineer and not

---

[14]   Ceruzzi (2000) provides an example of the IT power issue. In the 1960s, IBM used couriers to transport data on electronic storage tapes from its data-entry centers throughout the country to a single 7070 processor in West Virginia. Ceruzzi estimates that the speed of this manual transfer was approximately equal to what a home PC could handle over telephone wires in the 1990s.

the economist, but it is worth pointing out that the engineers seem to be split between optimists and pessimists.

Mann (2000) argues that the end of Moore's law is fast approaching as engineers face the physical limits on how many features can be crammed onto a single computer chip. Others, however, point to improvements in both the existing technology and fundamentally new technologies that could continue to drive rapid advances. Fisher (2000), for example, points to the recent development of a microprocessor that operates at one gigahertz (a billion cycles per second), which could lead to feasible advances like true interactive voice recognition and video. Stix (2001) shows how the pace of improvement in fiber-optic technology greatly surpasses those in chips, e.g., utilization of different wavelengths over a given fiber-optic network, so-called "dense wavelength division multiplexing," greatly increases the bandwidth of existing networks. As deployment of the Internet continues, developments in communications technology will become increasingly important. Others are even more optimistic; Reed and Tour (2000) discuss the potential of "molecular-scale electronics," where individual molecules could be built to perform the functions of the today's microelectronics, but with greatly enhanced speed and power.

Predicting the future of IT is not a place where an economist has a comparative advantage. Nonetheless, this is a very important question, since it directly affects the current performance of the U.S. economy and impacts our assessment of the future. The U.S. Congressional Budget Office (CBO 2001), for example, points to IT-related productivity gains as a primary reason for the steady increases in its growth projections in recent years.[15] The potential for continued technological gains in the production of IT certainly raises the possibility of continued IT-driven productivity gains throughout the economy.

c.   **Why Did TFP Growth Accelerate outside of IT Production?**

The traditional models described above explain much of the U.S. productivity revival in terms of IT-related technological progress and capital deepening. This decomposition, however, cannot entirely explain the U.S. productivity revival. CEA (2001), Jorgenson and Stiroh (2000), and Oliner and Sichel (2000) all report large increases in total factor productivity in the non-IT-producing industries. While Gordon (2000) views this gain as largely cyclical in nature, CEA (2001) disagrees, which leaves a potential channel for extreme new economy effects.

One way to search for the new economy effects like production spillovers and network effects is to compare measured TFP growth to investment in IT. Schreyer

---

[15]   CBO (2001) reports that its current 10-year projection for annual GDP growth is 3.0 percent per year, up from the 2.1 percent per year forecast that it made in 1997.

(2000) has done this at the aggregate level for European countries and reports little obvious relationship and Stiroh (2002) finds little link for U.S. manufacturing industries. While one could argue that the effects have not been realized yet or that one needs to look more closely at the IT-intensive service industries, analysis to date yields little evidence that IT generates the types of new economy effects that would show up in measured TFP growth. This implies the traditional model is approximately correct, and there is little evidence for new economy effects like spillovers or network externalities. Finding evidence for these types of effects remains an important research question for the new economy proponents.

d.   Why Were Forecasters So Wrong in the New Economy Era?

There are by now many explanations for the recent success of the United States. It is interesting to note, however, that this strong performance appears to have been quite a surprise to the U.S. forecasting community.[16] An interesting question, therefore, is why did the macroeconomists and forecasters fail? Is this a sign that there is something fundamentally new in the economy? Or is it perfectly reasonable to expect that a series of standard, albeit unanticipated, shocks reduced the accuracy of forecasters?

Figure 5 shows these errors by comparing actual growth of United States. GDP to the Blue Chip Indicators consensus forecast one year earlier.[17] The data run from 1984:Q1 to 2000:Q4. For the early part of the sample through 1995:Q3, the Blue Chip forecast runs through the fluctuating GDP series and the mean error (forecast less actual) is –0.1 percentage point. For the new economy period beginning in 1995:Q4, however, the actual GDP growth exceeded forecast GDP growth by a staggering 1.7 percentage points.[18] Indeed, it was not until 2000 that the Blue Chip forecast began to incorporate the recent experience and trend noticeably upward, and this occurred even as actual growth slowed. Figure 6 shows a similar plot for unemployment and reveals that Blue Chip forecast overestimated unemployment by about 0.42 percentage points in the new economy period, but was essentially on target for the earlier period.

These figures are obviously not a rigorous analysis of forecasting accuracy, but they illustrate the simple point that there does seem to be something different

---

[16]   Jorgenson and Stiroh (2000) and Walsh (1999) point this out in regard to the CBO projections.

[17]   The Blue Chip Indicators is a monthly survey of nearly 100 economists. These forecasts are then averaged to generate a consensus forecast. See Blue Chip Indicators (2001) for details.

[18]   The charts begin in 1984 after the recessions of the early 1980s. 1995:Q3 is a breakpoint based on Stiroh (forthcoming).

Figure 5: Actual GDP Growth vs. Blue Chip Forecast, 1984–2000

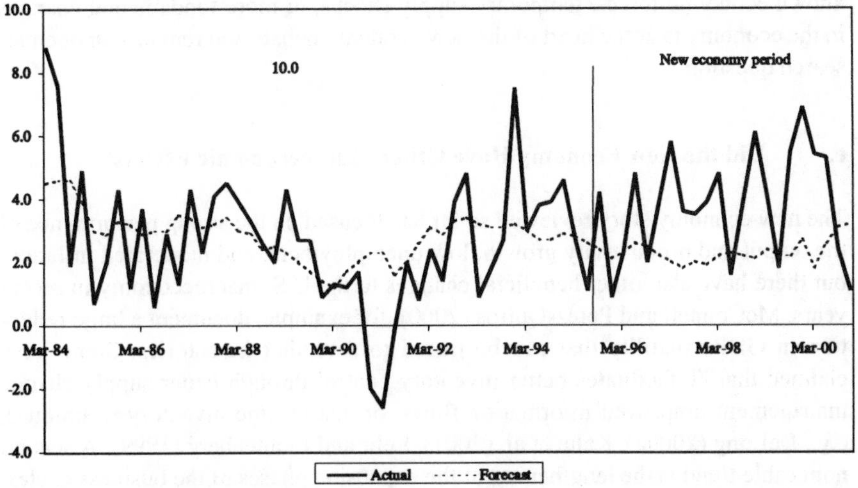

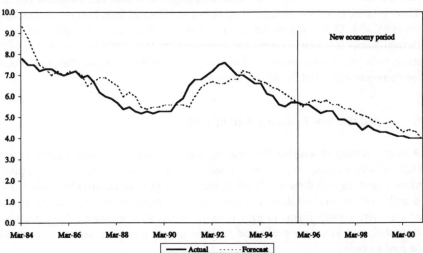

Note: Forecast is Blue Chip Indicators consensus forecast from one year earlier. Actual figures as reported by Blue Chip Indicators. New economy period begins in 1995:Q4.

Figure 6: Actual Unemployment Rate vs. Blue Chip Forecast, 1984–2000

Note: Forecast is Blue Chip Indicators consensus forecast from one year earlier. Actual figures as reported by Blue Chip Indicators. New economy period begins in 1995:Q4.

about the new economy period of the 1995–2000. Whether this reflects well-known economic forces, temporary supply shocks, or more fundamental changes in the economy is at the heart of the new economy debate and remains an open research question.

e.   Did the New Economy Have Other Macroeconomic Effects?

The new economy story reviewed so far has focused on the strong performance of the output and productivity growth, low unemployment, and moderated inflation, but there have also other beneficial changes to the U.S. macroeconomy in recent years. McConnell and Perez-Quiros (2000), for example, document a large reduction in GDP volatility that can be traced to smoother inventories. Some have claimed that IT facilitates better inventory control through better supply change management, improved information flows, or just-in-time inventory techniques, e.g., DeLong (2000a), Kahn et al. (2001), Lehr and Lichtenberg (1999). A second noticeable trend is the lengthening of the expansion phases of the business cycles. The 1982–1990 expansion, for example, lasted 92 months and the current expansion has reached 120 months, compared to a post-war average expansion of 50 months.

Reduced volatility and longer economic expansions are both positive developments for an economy and an interesting question is whether these two trends reflect the new economy forces of technology, globalization, and competitiveness. There is some evidence, both from academic studies and from business-sector discussions, that IT has played an important role in the reduced volatility of GDP through better inventory control and management. Because this type of change is likely to be permanent, understanding this process will help us to better understand the complete impact of the new economy.

f.   Did the New Economy End in 1999?

A final question is whether the new economy has already ended. Recently, real GDP growth slowed, investment in equipment and software declined, unemployment edged up, inflation accelerated, and major U.S. stock markets indices fell sharply. While some of these indicators remain strong by historic standards and productivity growth seems to have held up so far, these indicators have declined from their new economy peaks and raise the question that the new economy may be past its peak.

If the extreme new economy proponents are correct and fundamental changes in how the economy works were responsible for the gains in the late 1990s, then the recent sluggishness can be expected to pass quickly. Alternatively, if the success reflects a series of temporary supply shocks and other cyclical forces, there is no reason to expect a sustained return to the strength of the late 1990s. While most new economy supporters do not believe the business cycle is obsolete (see, e.g., Mandel 1998b, 2000 and Wadhwani 2001), structural changes should be lasting ones; so it seems reasonable that these fundamental forces will reassert themselves in the near future if the extreme new economy views are correct. Thus, the recent economic slowdown represents an important test of the new economy.

6.   Conclusions

The recent success of the U.S. economy has received considerable attention from both academics and the business press. And justifiably so – the performance of output and productivity growth, unemployment rates, and inflation in recent years have surpassed the forecasts of all but the most optimistic practitioners of the dismal science. This robust and surprising strength has led some to believe that the U.S. economy is a new economy. I conclude, however, that much of the new economy discussion is not really so new and remains squarely based on old economic theories and models. A moderate interpretation of the new economy can recognize the important contributions of technology, globalization, and competitive forces to the success of the U.S. economy without mandating radical changes to our understanding of how the economy actually works.

This is not to say that old economics can explain everything about the recent success of the U.S. economy, since important questions remain unanswered and important issues unresolved. More extreme new economy ideas could, at least in principle, provide useful insights into understanding these questions and possible changes in the workings of the modern economy. So far, however, the more extreme new economy ideas remain largely untested and unconfirmed and appear to be more rhetoric than reality.

References

Altig, D., and P. Gomme (1998). In Search of the NAIRU. *Economic Commentary,* May 1. Federal Reserve Bank of Cleveland.

Basu, S., J.G. Fernald, and M.D. Shapiro (2000). Productivity Growth in the 1990s: Technology, Utilization, or Adjustment? Manuscript prepared for the Carnegie-Rochester Conference. November 7.

Blanchard, O., and L.F. Katz (1997). What We Know and Do Not Know about the Natural Rate of Unemployment. *Journal of Economic Perspectives* 11(1): 51–72.

BLS (Bureau of Labor Statistics) (2001a). Multifactor Productivity Trends, 1999. USDL 01–82, April 10.

BLS (Bureau of Labor Statistics) (2001b). Productivity and Costs: Second Quarter 2001. USDL 01–248, August 7.

Blue Chip Economic Indicators (2001). Blue Chip Economic Indicators: Top Analysts' Forecasts of the U.S. Economic Outlook for the Year Ahead. 26(1), January 10.

Bosworth, B.P., and J.E. Triplett (2000). What's New about the New Economy? IT, Economic Growth and Productivity. Mimeo. Brookings Institution, Washington, D.C. December 12.

Bresnahan, T.F. (1986). Measuring the Spillovers from Technical Advance: Mainframe Computers in Financial Services. *American Economic Review* 76(4): 741–755.

Broadbent, B., and D. Walton (2000). How "New" Is the UK Economy? Global Economics Paper 43. Goldman Sachs, New York.

Brynjolfsson, E., and L. Hitt (1995). Information Technology as a Factor of Production: The Role of Differences Among Firms. *Economics of Innovation and New Technology* 3(3/4): 183–200.

Brynjolfsson, E., and L. Hitt (2000). Beyond Computation: Information Technology, Organizational Transformation and Business Practices. *Journal of Economic Perspectives* 14(4): 23–48.

Brynjoflsson, E., and S. Yang (1997). The Intangible Benefits and Costs of Computer Investments: Evidence from the Stock Market. Mimeo. Sloan School of Management, MIT.

CBO (Congressional Budget Office) (2001). *The Budget and Economic Outlook: Fiscal Years 2002–2011.* Washington, D.C.: U.S. Government Printing Office.

CEA (Council of Economic Advisors) (2000). Annual Report of the Council of Economic Advisors. In *Economic Report of the President* (January).

CEA (Council of Economic Advisors) (2001). Annual Report of the Council of Economic Advisors. In *Economic Report of the President* (January).

Ceruzzi, P.E. (2000). *A History of Modern Computing.* Cambridge, Mass.: The MIT Press.

Cohen, S.S., J.B. DeLong, and J. Zysman (2000). Tools for Thought: What Is New and Important about the "E-conomy". BRIE Working Paper 138. UC Berkeley.

Cox, W.M., and R. Alm (1999). The New Paradigm. *Federal Reserve Bank of Dallas Annual Report* 1999: 3–23.

CSLS (Centre for the Study of Living Standards) (2000). Trend Productivity and the New Economy. Mimeo. Centre for the Study of Living Standards, Ottawa Ontario. September.

Daveri, F. (2001). Information Technology and European Growth. Mimeo. University of Parma, May 10.

DeLong, J.B. (1998). How "New" Is Today's Economy? From http://www.j-bradford-delong.net. on August 18.

DeLong, J.B. (2000a). Macroeconomic Implications of the "New Economy. From http://www.j-bradford-delong.net in May.

DeLong, J.B. (2000b). Why Now? Three Factors that Together Have Made Our Age the Age of the Computer Revolution. From http://www.j-bradford-delong.net in May.

The Economist (1999). How Real Is the New Economy? *The Economist*, July 24: 17–18.

European Central Bank (2001). New Technologies and Productivity the Euro Area. *ECB Monthly Bulletin* (July): 37–48.

Fischer, L.M. (2000). New Era Approaches: Gigabyte Chips. *New York Times*, February 7:C8.

Friedman, M. (1968). The Role of Monetary Policy. *American Economic Review* 58(1): 1–17.

Gomme, P. (1998). What Labor Market Theory Tells Us about the "New Economy." *Economic Review* (Federal Reserve Bank of Cleveland) 34(3): 16–24.

Gordon, R.J. (1997). The Time-Varying NAIRU and Its Implications for Economic Policy. *Journal of Economic Perspectives* 11(1): 11–32.

Gordon, R.J. (1998). Foundations of the Goldilocks Economy: Supply Shocks and the Time-Varying NAIRU. *Brookings Papers on Economic Activity* (2): 297–346.

Gordon, R.J. (1999). Has the "New Economy" Rendered the Productivity Slowdown Obsolete? Manuscript. Northwestern University, Evanston, Ill., June 12.

Gordon, R.J. (2000). Does the "New Economy" Measure Up to the Great Inventions of the Past? *Journal of Economic Perspectives* 14(4): 49–74.

Greenspan, A. (1998). Is There a New Economy? Remarks at the Haas Annual Business Faculty Research Dialogue. UC Berkeley, September 4.

Greenwood, J., and B. Jovanovic (1999). The IT Revolution and the Stock Market. NBER Working Paper 6931. National Bureau of Economic Research, Cambridge, Mass.

Gundlach, E. (2001). Interpreting Productivity Growth in the New Economy: Some Agnostic Notes. Kiel Working Paper 1020. Kiel Institute for World Economics, Kiel.

Gust, C., and M. Marquez (2000). Productivity Developments Abroad. *Federal Reserve Bulletin* 86(10): 665–681.

Hall, R.E. (2000). e-Capital: The Link between the Stock Market and the Labor Market in the 1990s. Mimeo. Stanford University, October 11.

Herman, S. (2000). Fixed Assets and Consumer Durable Goods for 1925–1999. *Survey of Current Business* (September): 19–30.

Jorgenson, D.W. (2001). Information Technology and the U.S. Economy. *American Economic Review* 91(1): 1–32.

Jorgenson, D.W., and K.J. Stiroh (1999). Information Technology and Growth. *American Economic Review (Papers and Proceedings)* 89(2): 109–115.

Jorgenson, D.W., and K.J. Stiroh (2000). Raising the Speed Limit: U.S. Economic Growth in the Information Age. *Brookings Papers on Economic Activity* (1): 125–211.

Kahn, J.A., M.M. McConnell, and G. Perez-Quiros (2001). Inventories and the Information Revolution: Implications for Output Volatility. Mimeo. Federal Reserve Bank of New York, January 4.

Katz, L.F., and A.B. Krueger (1999). The High-Pressure U.S. Labor Market of the 1990s. *Brookings Papers on Economic Activity* (1): 1–87.

Kelly, K. (1998). *New Rules for the New Economy.* New York, NY: Penguin Putnam.

Krueger, A.B. (2000). Economic Scene. *New York Times*, July 20: C2.

Kuhn, P., and M. Skuterud (2000). Internet and Traditional Job Search Methods, 1994–1999. Mimeo. University of California at Santa Barbara, April.

Lehr, B., and F. Lichtenberg (1999). Information Technology and Its Impact on Firm-Level Productivity: Evidence from Government and Private Data Sources, 1977–1993. *Canadian Journal of Economics* 32(2): 335–362.

Lichtenberg, F. (1995). The Output Contributions of Computer Equipment and Personnel: A Firm-Level Analysis. *Economics of Innovation and New Technology* 3(3/4): 201–217.

Litan, R.E., and A.M. Rivlin (2000). The Economy and the Internet: What Lies Ahead? The Brookings Institution, Conference Report 4, December.

Madrick, J. (1999). How New Is the New Economy? *Working USA* 3(4): 24–47.

Mandel, M.J. (1998a). Innovation: You Ain't Seen Nothing Yet. *Business Week*, August 31: 60–63.

Mandel, M.J. (1998b). Yes, Virginia, There Will Be Recessions. *Business Week*, August 31: 64.

Mandel, M.J. (2000). The Next Downturn. *Business Week*, October 9: 173–180.

Mann, C.C. (2000). The End of Moore's Law? *Technology Review: MIT's Magazine of Innovation*, May/June.

McTeer, R.D., Jr. (1999). Out on a New-Paradigm Limb. *Federal Reserve Bank of Dallas Annual Report* 1999: 1–2.

McConnell, M.M., and G. Perez-Quiros (2000). Output Fluctuations in the United States: What Has Changed Since the Early 1980s? *American Economic Review* 90(5): 1464–1476.

Meyer, L.H. (2000). The Economic Outlook and the Challenges Facing Monetary Policy. Speech at the Century Club Breakfast Series. Washington University, October 19.

Nakamura, L.I. (2000). Economics and the New Economy: The Invisible Hand Meets Creative Destruction. *Business Review* (Federal Reserve Bank of Philadelphia) (July/August): 15–30.

Nordhaus, W.D. (2000). Policy Rules in the New Economy. Presentation for the Discussion on the New Economy sponsored by the Congressional Budget Committee and the Senate Budget Committee, June 6.

OECD (Organization for Economic Cooperation and Development) (2000a). *A New Economy: The Changing Role of Innovation and Information Technology in Growth.* Paris: OECD.

OECD (Organization for Economic Cooperation and Development) (2000b). *OECD Economic Outlook.* June 2000 (67). Paris: OECD.

OECD (Organization for Economic Cooperation and Development) (2000c). *OECD Economic Outlook.* December 2000 (68). Paris: OECD.

Oliner, S.D., and D.E. Sichel (1994). Computers and Output Growth Revisited: How Big Is the Puzzle? *Brookings Papers on Economic Activity* (2): 273–317.

Oliner, S.D., and D.E. Sichel (2000). The Resurgence of Growth in the Late 1990s: Is Information Technology the Story? *Journal of Economic Perspectives* 14(4): 3–22.

Osborn, R.F. (1954). GE and Univac: Harnessing the High-Speed Computer. *Harvard Business Review* 32(4): 99–107.

Osterman, P. (1999). Securing Prosperity: New Rules for the New Economy. *Working USA* 3(4): 5–8.

Otoo, M.W. (1999). Temporary Unemployment and the Natural Rate of Unemployment. Finance and Economic Discussion Series 1999-66. Board of Governors of the Federal Reserve System, Washington, D.C.

Pakko, M.R. (1999). The U.S. Trade Deficit and the "New Economy." *Review* (Federal Reserve Bank of St. Louis) (September/October): 11–19.

Phelps, E.S. (1968). Money-Wage Dynamics and Labor-Market Equilibrium. *Journal of Political Economy* 76 (4, part 2): 678–711.

Reed, M.A., and J.M. Tour (2000). Computing with Molecules. *Scientific American* 282(6): 86–93.

Rich, R.W., and D. Rissmiller (2000). Understanding the Recent Behavior of U.S. Inflation. *Current Issues in Economics and Finance* (Federal Reserve Bank of New York) 6(8): 1–6.

Schreyer, P. (2000). The Contribution of Information and Communication Technology to Output Growth: A Study of the G7 Countries. STI Working Paper 2000/2; OECD working papers 8(66). OECD: Paris.

Shepard, S.B. (1997). The New Economy: What It Really Means. *Business Week*, November 17.

Solow, R.M. (1957). Technical Change and the Aggregate Production Function. *Review of Economics and Statistics* 39(3): 313–330.

Staiger, D., J.H. Stock, and M.W. Watson (1997). The NAIRU, Unemployment, and Monetary Policy. *Journal of Economic Perspectives* 11(1): 33–49.

Stiglitz, J. (1997). Reflections on the Natural Rate Hypothesis. *Journal of Economic Perspectives* 11(1): 3–10.

Stiroh, K.J. (1998). Computers, Productivity, and Input Substitution. *Economic Inquiry* 36(2): 175–191.

Stiroh, K.J. (1999). Is There a New Economy? *Challenge* 42(4): 82–101.

Stiroh, K.J. (2002). Are ICT-Spillovers Driving the New Economy? *Review of Income and Wealth* 48(1).

Stiroh, K.J. (forthcoming). Information Technology and the U.S. Productivity Review: What Do the Industry Data Say? *American Economic Review.*

Stix, G. (2001). The Triumph of the Light. *Scientific American* 284(1): 80–87.

Stock, J.H. (1998). Comment on: Foundations of the Goldilocks Economy: Supply Shocks and the Time-Varying NAIRU. *Brookings Papers on Economic Activity* (2): 334–341.

Summers, L.H. (2000a). The United States and India in a New Global Economy. Remarks to the Confederation of Indian Industry, Mumbai India, January 16, 2000.

Summers, L.H. (2000b). The New Wealth of Nations. Remarks at the Hambrecht & Quist Technology Conference, San Francisco CA, May 10, 2000.

Triplett, J.E. (1999). Economic Statistics, the New Economy, and the Productivity Slowdown. *Business Economics* 34(2): 13–17.

Van Ark, B. (2000). Measuring Productivity in the New Economy: Towards a European Perspective. *De Economist* 148(1): 87–105.

Wadhwani, S. (2000). The Impact of the Internet on UK Inflation. Speech delivered at the London School of Business. February 23.

Wadhwani, S. (2001). The New Economy: Myths and Realities. Speech delivered at London Guildhall University. March 20.

Walsh, C.E. (1999). Projecting Budget Surpluses? Federal Reserve Bank of San Francisco, *Economic Letter* (99-27) September 10.

Whelan, K. (2000). Computers, Obsolescence, and Productivity. Finance and Economics Discussion Series 2000–2006. Board of Governors of the Federal Reserve Systems, Washington, D.C.

Woodall, P. (2000). The New Economy Survey. *The Economist*, September 23: 5–40.

Comment on Kevin J. Stiroh

Dominique Foray

The main argument developed by Kevin Stiroh is in favor of a moderate interpretation of the new economy and this is convincing given the empirical evidence and theoretical discussions provided in his paper. New technology, globalization, and increased competition have contributed to recent economic gains in ways which are consistent with conventional economic theory.

The empirical evidence on productivity growth are consistent with such a moderate interpretation, while the phenomena discussed at the analytical level – network effects, increasing returns, knowledge as nonrival good and nonpecuniary externalities – are not that new and conventional theory can deal with the macro- and microeconomic implications of them. Thus, "there is no argument ... that the underlying economic relationships themselves have changed" (Stiroh, this volume, p. 5).

What I would like briefly to stress is the danger of moving too fast from a moderate interpretation of the new economy to a moderate interpretation of new technology (the new information and communications technologies) (ICTs). It is important to show that there is no inconsistency in being both a new economy sceptic and a new technology enthusiast.[1]

1.   An Unfortunate Debate

I believe that macroeconomists (I talk here in general) have been so considerably teased and irritated by the pseudo-economic arguments developed by the "new economy gurus" that they have pushed the pendulum too far towards a very skeptical view about the new ICTs. Such an attitude is, of course, reinforced by the fact that macroeconomists, by training and tradition, do not pay so much attention to the microlevel details of innovation and new technologies.[2]

---

[1]   Most of the tradition in the economics of innovation as well as in the historical economics on technological change could be characterized by such a position. Freeman and Soete (1997) provide the best illustration.

[2]   The well-known example is of course the paper published by Gordon (2000) in the *Journal of Economic Perspectives*.

We have, thus, an unfortunate debate between two camps (Woodall 2000). On the one hand, there is the camp of the "Internet gurus", supporting the idea that Internet is the greatest invention since the wheel and is transforming the world so radically that there is a need for a new economics to understand and analyze those transformations. On the other hand, the camp of ICT sceptics, looking deeply and rigorously at the data, and claiming that, after all, this is a conventional story of a technological revolution and capital deepening, resulting in economic growth. However, some of the ICT skeptics are jumping too fast to a hyperskepticism about technology, claiming that the Internet is an insignificant toy: when the technology bubble bursts on the stock market, its economic benefits will turn out to be no greater than the 17th century tulip bubble (when a mass hysteria of tulip-buying mania occurred in Europe) (Woodall 2000).

We understand, thus, the problem: much evidence for the new economy is anecdotal. There are great stories from business executives (but they just talk about their managerial genius). On the other hand, macroeconomists are not so interested in technology and do not pay enough attention to the fact that executives after executives in industry after industry tell the same story in convincing detail.

The paper written by K. Stiroh does not belong to the category of such a hyperskepticism about the impact of the new ICTs on the economy. Stiroh recognizes several times that information technology plays a substantial role in the resurgence of U.S. productivity growth. It is, however, possible to trace in his paper a line of skeptical argument about the role of new ICTs. For example, are the tasks described as undertaken in 1954 by a computer – inventory control, cost accounting, and so forth – really the same as those undertaken by the new ICT system? Saying yes is quite misleading and shows an inaccurate analysis of the potential for economic changes provided by the new ICT system.

As an economist of innovation, I can only plead for reconciling the moderate and quite reasonable interpretation of the new economy with a more optimistic view about the impact and potential for economic changes of the new ICT system.

2.   On the New ICT System and Its Potential for Creating Economic Changes

It is a revolution of crucial importance in that the system basically involves technologies for knowledge and information production and dissemination. These new technologies, which first emerged in the 1950s and then really took off with the advent of the Internet, have breathtaking potential. They enable remote access to information and even knowledge. In addition to transmitting written texts and other digitizable items (music, pictures), they also allow users to access and work upon knowledge systems from a distance (e.g., remote experimentation), to take distance-learning courses within the framework of interactive teacher-student relations (tele-education), and to have unbelievable quantities of information – a sort of universal library – available on their desktops.

Information technologies can affect knowledge creation in a number of different ways. For a start, the mere fact that one has the capacity to create such a wealth of information is truly revolutionary. Imagine how hard it was for people to obtain instruments of knowledge before the modern age. Apart from a handful of marvellous centers of intellectual life such as the ancient library of Alexandria, such instruments were few and far between. The great eleventh-century thinker, Gerbert d'Aurillac, had a library containing no more than 20 books (although that was quite a lot in those days). Even in the somewhat less perilous times of a couple of decades ago, imagine what a laborious task it was for students to produce a roundup of the "state of the art" in a particular subject or discipline, and the uphill struggle involved in remaining abreast of the latest findings in their study field.

Development here has been a long, drawn-out process punctuated by the invention of the codex and the book (which took over from scrolls), the perfecting of paper, the book's transformation into a knowledge tool (indexes, tables, footnotes, and endnotes), improvements in the productivity of material copymaking (from the "industrial" organization of the scriptorium through to the invention of the printing press), the proliferation of modern libraries and, finally, the advent of increasingly high-performance access and communications networks. Do new technologies signal an end to that evolution? Clearly not, for an enormous amount of progress remains to be made in such areas as information search systems. But they could almost be said to be curtailing what the French medievalist Georges Duby once called the "relentless pursuit of instruments of knowledge" that has preoccupied humankind since the dark ages.

Second, information technologies enhance creative interaction between product designers, suppliers, and the end customers, for example. The creation of virtual objects that can be modified ad infinitum and are instantly accessible to one and all, serves to facilitate collective work and learning. In this respect, the new possibilities opened up by numerical simulation represent a key factor.

Third, the new technologies enable the processing of gigantic databases, which is in itself a potent means of knowledge enhancement (in natural, human and social sciences, and management alike). Research stimulated by such possibilities has a strong influence in some areas of managerial work.

Finally, the above three ways in which information technologies affect knowledge creation can be combined in the development of large-scale decentralized systems for data gathering and calculation and the sharing of findings. Such systems characterize the research being done these days in the fields of astronomy, oceanography, and so on.

3.   Beyond ICTs

Beyond these various kinds of impacts, one should stress the rapid growth of the codified knowledge base. David and Foray (1995) and Cowan and Foray (1997) analyze to what extent the cost of codification falls with the new ICTs and how these new ICTs generate new economic opportunities to increase further the codified knowledge base.

Knowledge can be codified: so articulated and clarified that it can be expressed in a particular language and recorded on a particular medium. Codification involves the exteriorization of memory. It hinges on a range of increasingly complex actions, such as using a natural language to write a cooking recipe, applying industrial design techniques to draft a scale drawing of a piece of machinery, building a system expert from the formalized rules of inference underlying the sequence of stages geared to problems, and so on. As such, knowledge is detached from the individual and the memory and communication capacity created is independent of human beings (as long as the medium upon which the knowledge is stored is safeguarded and the language in which it is expressed is remembered). With the emergence of codification, "the problem of memory ceases to dominate intellectual life" (Goody 1977: 143). Learning programs are then produced that partially replace the person who holds and teaches knowledge. "Partially" is the key word here, for codification amounts to the mutilation of knowledge. What is expressed and recorded is not complete knowledge. It is a learning program that helps to reproduce knowledge. When a young technician receives a user's manual, he or she is not directly given knowledge on "how to run the machine." That said, the manual is helpful and will serve to reduce the costs of knowledge reproduction.

In many cases, when technicians have "learned to learn" and are dealing with more or less standard machines, knowledge reproduction becomes almost instantaneous and assumes characteristics close to those of information reproduction.

There is, it must be stressed, a second and, in my view, crucial function of codification. Codification consists in translating knowledge into symbolic representations so that it can be stored on a particular medium. This creates new cognitive potentialities that remain inconceivable so long as the knowledge is attached to the individual and, hence, only heard (when spoken) or seen (when put it into practice). Codifying (through writing, graphics, modeling, virtuality) makes it possible to examine and arrange knowledge in different ways and to isolate, classify, and combine different components. This leads to the creation of new knowledge objects such as lists, tables, formulae, etc. These are fundamentally important in that they open up new cognitive possibilities (classification, taxonomy, tree networks, simulation) that can provide a framework for the rapid production of new knowledge (Goody 1977). But they are only possible when people consider the matter of codifying and, hence, the symbolic representation of knowledge. Advances in information technology-based recording methods are crucial here, for they allow representations of knowledge to progress from the so-called "preliterate" stage (gestures and words) to the literate (writing and drawing) and then postliterate stages (modeling structured interactions).

Codification thus plays a central role in the knowledge economy because it serves to further memorization, communication and learning, and forms a sound basis for the creation of new knowledge objects.

4.   And Beyond Beyond

An example of a secondary effect resulting from the various technological evolutions discussed above is that of the great opportunities of spatial reorganization of economic and social activities. An evolution which is notoriously neglected by the new technology/economy skeptics.

Given how efficiently knowledge and information can travel and the fact that the costs involved in moving people are still so high (and even rising with the growth in size of urban areas), one may well have grounds for believing that increasing numbers of people are going to be working at home now that the technological capacity is available for knowledge-sharing, remote access and teamwork, and organizing and coordinating tasks over wide areas. Does this herald the end of geography or, at the very least, of the influence of geographical distance over how activities are organized? Clearly, the influence of geographical distance is waning. Many different kinds of transactions now take place within the framework of location strategies "unconstrained by distance." And many customers have not the slightest idea where (geographically speaking) their transaction is being processed.

But whether or not this marks a trend of work returning to the home is rather less clear. Historical perspectives are still too sketchy to ascertain whether there really is some tendency for the pendulum to start swinging back (Mokyr 2001), thus ending the centuries-long development of a factory system that has compelled workers in industry and then services, trade, and education to commute to work. The costs involved, though impossible to quantify, have certainly been huge. Cairncross (1997: 12) suggests that in "half a century's time it may well seem extraordinary that millions of people once trooped from one building (their home) to another (their office) each morning, only to reverse procedure each evening. ... Commuting wastes time and building capacity. One building – the home – stands empty all day; another – the office – stands empty all night. All this might strike our grandchildren as bizarre." Mokyr (2001) makes a sound case for considering some development of a home-production economy in light of the fact that it costs less to transport knowledge than people.

For sure, many activities cannot be coordinated by virtual means alone. The emulation and spontaneity generated by physical presence and groupings often remain crucial. Likewise, direct face-to-face exchanges are important when they enable other forms of sensorial perception to be stimulated than those used within the framework of electronic interaction. On the whole, individuals now have far more room to choose between working at home (and cutting commuting costs) and traveling to the collective workplace (to benefit from the advantages of interacting with a "real" group).

However, all these evolutions are still a long way off as an economy-wide phenomenon. This is why this particular aspect of ICTs is often overlooked by the new-economy skeptics. These evolutions are likely to continue being impeded by all manner of apathy for some time to come, which leaves much to be done as regards the redesigning of space in line with the opportunities offered by the knowledge economy. These evolutions are also conditional on current technology, especially on the supply of bandwidth. Finally, issues of trust and social capital are still to be addressed. "Trust" represents the whole complex of (social) issues surrounding interpersonal (and therefore interorganizational) transactions under the following emergent conditions of the knowledge economy: increasing specialization, increasing asymmetry in the distribution of information and expertise, increasing personal anonymity, and increasing facilities for masquerade and misappropriation of identities (David et al. 2001).

And this great potential for economic changes is only relevant for situations in which the main object of the transaction can be digitalized (knowledge and information), and that covers potentially a very large part of the economy. On the other hand, Gordon (2000) is right when claiming that where the main object of the transaction is not digitalizable, there are severe limitations to the full realization of the potential for economic changes offered by the new ICT systems. You can, of course, order potatoes on Internet. But much of the transaction will still be dependent upon the traditional ways of delivering goods and the efficiency of the transaction is still dependent upon "a truck and a driver."

5.   Conclusion

Now that the emergence of knowledge-based economies has been put into historical perspective, the new economy debate can only be viewed with a degree of amusement, as it focuses on the possible radical reform of economics because economics would have failed to account for the American economy's performance over the last half-decade of an entire millennium. Overall, this debate will mainly be remembered for the clash between the ultra-optimists and their relatively crude economic thinking, and the skeptical macroeconomists who, despite their usual rigor and prudence, have an extremely partial and truncated view of the impacts of new technologies. Yet, is not what the United States and, more recently, European and other Western countries have been experiencing just an accelerating transition to the knowledge-based economy, a process that began quite some time ago but which only started gathering momentum fairly recently owing to the slow maturation of the technological revolution (David and Foray 2002)?

References

Cairncross, F. (1997). *The Death of Distance: How the Communication Revolution Will Change Our Lives?* Boston: Harvard Business School Press.

Cowan, R., and D. Foray (1997). The Economics of Codification and Diffusion of Knowledge. *Industrial and Corporate Changes* 6(3): 595–622.

David, P.A., and D. Foray (1995). Accessing and Expanding the Science and Technology Knowledge Base. *STI Review (OECD)* 16: 13–67.

David, P.A., and D. Foray (2002). An Introduction to the Knowledge Economy and Society. Published in a special issue of the *International Social Science Journal*, March.

David, P.A., D. Foray, and J. Mairesse (2001). Public Dimensions of the Knowledge-Driven Economy. Working Paper. Center for Educational Research and Innovation. OECD, Paris.

Freeman, C., and L. Soete (1997). *The Economics of Industrial Innovation.* London: Pinter.

Goody, J. (1977). *The Domestication of the Savage Mind.* Cambridge: Cambridge University Press.

Gordon, B. (2000). Does the "New Economy" Measure Up to the Great Inventions of the Past? *Journal of Economic Perspectives* 14(4): 49–74.

Mokyr, J. (2001). The Rise and Fall of the Factory System: Technology, Firms, and Households Since the Industrial Revolution. *Carnegie Rochester Conference on Public Policy.* 55 (December): 1–45.

Stiroh, K.J. (2001). New and Old Economics in the New Economy. This volume.

Woodall, P. (2000). Untangling e-Economics. In *The Economist: A Survey of the New Economy.* September 23rd.

Dale W. Jorgenson

Information Technology and the U.S. Economy

The resurgence of the American economy since 1995 has outrun all but the most optimistic expectations. Economic forecasting models have been seriously off track and growth projections have been revised to reflect a more sanguine outlook only recently.[1] It is not surprising that the unusual combination of more rapid growth and slower inflation in the 1990's has touched off a strenuous debate among economists about whether improvements in America's economic performance can be sustained.

The starting point for the economic debate is the thesis that the 1990's are a mirror image of the 1970's, when an unfavorable series of "supply shocks" led to stagflation – slower growth and higher inflation (Gordon 1998, 2000; Bosworth and Triplett 2000). In this view, the development of information technology (IT) is one of a series of positive, but *temporary*, shocks. The competing perspective is that IT has produced a fundamental change in the U.S. economy, leading to a *permanent* improvement in growth prospects (Greenspan 2000).

The relentless decline in the prices of information technology equipment has steadily enhanced the role of IT investment as a source of American economic growth. Productivity growth in IT-producing industries has gradually risen in importance and a productivity revival is now under way in the rest of the economy. Despite differences in methodology and data sources, a consensus is building that the remarkable behavior of IT prices provides the key to the surge in economic growth.

Remark: This paper was previously delivered at the one-hundred thirteenth meeting of the American Economic Association, January 6, 2001, New Orleans, LA, and subsequently published in the *American Economic Review.*

I am indebted to the Program on Technology and Economic Policy at Harvard University which provided financial support. I am also indebted to Kevin J. Stiroh for our joint research and his helpful comments, Jon Samuels for excellent research assistance, Mun S. Ho for the labor data, as well as useful comments. J. Steven Landefeld, Clinton McCully, and David Wasshausen of the Bureau of Economic Analysis provided valuable data on information technology. Colleagues far too numerous to mention have contributed useful suggestions and advice. I am grateful to all of them but retain sole responsibility for any remaining deficiencies.

[1]   See Congressional Budget Office (2000) on official forecasts and Economics and Statistics Administration (2000: 60) on private forecasts.

In the following section I show that the foundation for the American growth resurgence is the development and deployment of semiconductors. The decline in IT prices is rooted in developments in semiconductor technology that are widely understood by technologists and economists. This technology has found its broadest applications in computing and communications equipment, but has reduced the cost of a wide variety of other products.

A substantial acceleration in the IT price decline occurred in 1995, triggered by a much sharper acceleration in the price decline of semiconductors in 1994. Although the decline in semiconductor prices has been projected to continue for at least another decade, the recent acceleration could be temporary. This can be traced to a shift in the product cycle for semiconductors from three years to two years that took place in 1995 as the consequence of intensifying competition in markets for semiconductor products.

In Section 2 I outline a framework for analyzing the role of information technology in the American growth resurgence. Constant-quality price indexes separate the change in the performance of IT equipment from the change in price for a given level of performance. Accurate and timely computer prices have been part of the U.S. National Income and Product Accounts (NIPA) since 1985. Unfortunately, important information gaps remain, especially on trends in prices for closely related investments, such as software and communications equipment.

The cost of capital is an essential concept for capturing the economic impact of information technology prices. Swiftly falling prices provide powerful economic incentives for the substitution of IT equipment for other forms of capital and for labor services. The rate of the IT price decline is a key component of the cost of capital, required for assessing the impacts of rapidly growing stocks of computers, communications equipment, and software.

In Section 3 I analyze the impact of the 1995 acceleration in the information technology price decline on U.S. economic growth. I introduce a production possibility frontier that encompasses substitutions between outputs of consumption and investment goods, as well as inputs of capital and labor services. This frontier treats IT equipment as part of investment goods output and the capital services from this equipment as a component of capital input.

Capital input has been the most important source of U.S. economic growth throughout the postwar period. More rapid substitution toward information technology has given much additional weight to components of capital input with higher marginal products. The vaulting contribution of capital input since 1995 has boosted growth by nearly a full percentage point. The contribution of IT accounts for more than half of this increase. Computers have been the predominant impetus to faster growth, but communications equipment and software have made important contributions as well.

The accelerated information technology price decline signals faster productivity growth in IT-producing industries. In fact, these industries have been the source of most of aggregate productivity growth throughout the 1990's. Before 1995 this was due to the decline of productivity growth elsewhere in the economy. The IT-producing industries have accounted for about half the surge in productivity growth since 1995, but faster growth is not limited to these industries.

I conclude that the decline in IT prices will continue for some time. This will provide incentives for the ongoing substitution of IT for other productive inputs. Falling IT prices also serve as an indicator of rapid productivity growth in IT-producing industries. However, it would be premature to extrapolate the recent acceleration in productivity growth in these industries into the indefinite future, since this depends on the persistence of a two-year product cycle for semiconductors.

In Section 4 I outline research opportunities created by the development and diffusion of information technology. A voluminous and rapidly expanding business literature is testimony to the massive impact of IT on firms and product markets. Highest priority must be given to a better understanding of the markets for semiconductors. Although several models of the market for semiconductors already exist, none explains the shift from a three-year to a two-year product cycle.

The dramatic effects of information technology on capital and labor markets have already generated a substantial and growing economic literature, but many important issues remain to be resolved. For capital markets the relationship between equity valuations and growth prospects merits much further study. For labor markets more research is needed on investment in information technology and substitution among different types of labor.

1.   The Information Age

The development and deployment of information technology is the foundation of the American growth resurgence. A mantra of the "new economy" – *faster, better, cheaper* – captures the speed of technological change and product improvement in semiconductors and the precipitous and continuing fall in semiconductor prices. The price decline has been transmitted to the prices of products that rely heavily on semiconductor technology, like computers and telecommunications equipment. This technology has also helped to reduce the cost of aircraft, automobiles, scientific instruments, and a host of other products.

Modern information technology begins with the invention of the transistor, a semiconductor device that acts as an electrical switch and encodes information in binary form. A binary digit or *bit* takes the values zero and one, corresponding to the off and on positions of a switch. The first transistor, made of the semiconductor germanium, was constructed at Bell Labs in 1947 and won the Nobel Prize in Physics in 1956 for the inventors – John Bardeen, Walter Brattain, and William Shockley.[2]

The next major milestone in information technology was the coinvention of the *integrated circuit* by Jack Kilby of Texas Instruments in 1958 and Robert Noyce of Fairchild Semiconductor in 1959. An integrated circuit consists of many, even millions, of transistors that store and manipulate data in binary form. Integrated circuits were originally developed for data storage and retrieval and semiconductor storage devices became known as *memory chips*.[3]

The first patent for the integrated circuit was granted to Noyce. This resulted in a decade of litigation over the intellectual property rights. The litigation and its outcome demonstrate the critical importance of intellectual property in the development of information technology. Kilby was awarded the Nobel Prize in Physics in 2000 for discovery of the integrated circuit; regrettably, Noyce died in 1990.[4]

a.   Moore's Law

In 1965 Gordon E. Moore, then Research Director at Fairchild Semiconductor, made a prescient observation, later known as *Moore's Law*.[5] Plotting data on memory chips, he observed that each new chip contained roughly twice as many transistors as the previous chip and was released within 18–24 months of its predecessor. This implied exponential growth of chip capacity at 35–45 percent per year! Moore's prediction, made in the infancy of the semiconductor industry, has tracked chip capacity for 35 years. He recently extrapolated this trend for at least another decade (Moore 1997).

In 1968 Moore and Noyce founded Intel Corporation to speed the commercialization of memory chips (Moore 1996). Integrated circuits gave rise to microprocessors with functions that can be programmed by software, known as *logic chips*. Intel's first general purpose microprocessor was developed for a calculator produced by Busicom, a Japanese firm. Intel retained the intellectual property rights and released the device commercially in 1971.

---

[2]   On Bardeen, Brattain, and Shockley, see: *http://www.nobel.se/physics/laureates/1956/*.

[3]   Petzold (1999) provides a general reference on computers and software.

[4]   On Kilby, see: *http://www.nobel.se/physics/laureates/2000/*. On Noyce, see Wolfe (2000).

[5]   Moore (1965). Ruttan (2001) provides a general reference on the economics of semiconductors and computers. On semiconductor technology, see: *http://euler.berkeley.edu/~esrc/csm*.

The rapidly rising trends in the capacity of microprocessors and storage devices illustrate the exponential growth predicted by Moore's Law. The first logic chip in 1971 had 2,300 transistors, while the Pentium 4 released on November 20, 2000, had 42 million! Over this 29-year period the number of transistors increased by 34 percent per year. The rate of productivity growth for the U.S. economy during this period was slower by two orders of magnitude.

b.   Semiconductor Prices

Moore's Law captures the fact that successive generations of semiconductors are *faster* and *better*. The economics of semiconductors begins with the closely related observation that semiconductors have become *cheaper* at a truly staggering rate! Figure 1 gives semiconductor price indexes constructed by Grimm (1998) of the U.S. Bureau of Economic Analysis (BEA) and employed in the U.S. National Income and Product Accounts since 1996. These are divided between memory chips and logic chips. The underlying detail includes seven types of memory chips and two types of logic chips.

Between 1974 and 1996 prices of memory chips *decreased* by a factor of 27,270 times or at 40.9 percent per year, while the implicit deflator for the gross domestic product (GDP) *increased* by almost 2.7 times or 4.6 percent per year! Prices of logic chips, available for the shorter period 1985 to 1996, *decreased* by a factor of 1,938 or 54.1 percent per year, while the GDP deflator *increased* by 1.3 times or 2.6 percent per year! Semiconductor price declines closely parallel Moore's Law on the growth of chip capacity, setting semiconductors apart from other products.

Figure 1 also reveals a sharp acceleration in the decline of semiconductor prices in 1994 and 1995. The microprocessor price decline leapt to more than 90 percent per year as the semiconductor industry shifted from a three-year product cycle to a greatly accelerated two-year cycle. This is reflected in the *2000 Update* of the International Technology Road Map for Semiconductors,[6] prepared by a consortium of industry associations.

c.   Constant-Quality Price Indexes

The behavior of semiconductors prices is a severe test for the methods used in the official price statistics. The challenge is to separate observed price changes between changes in semiconductor performance and changes in price that hold per-

---

[6]   On International Technology Road Map for Semiconductors (2000), see: *http://public.itrs.net/*.

Figure 1: Relative Prices of Computers and Semiconductors, 1959–1999

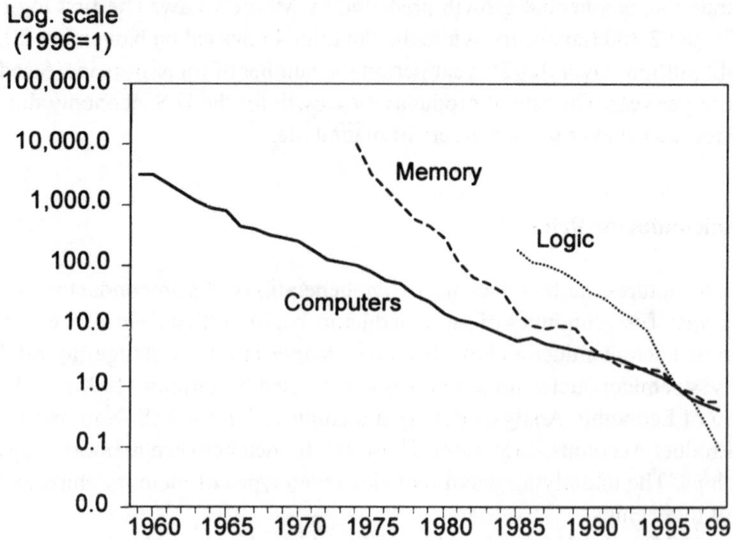

Log. scale
(1996=1)

Note: All price indexes are divided by the output price index.

formance constant. Achieving this objective has required a detailed understanding of the technology, the development of sophisticated measurement techniques, and the introduction of novel methods for assembling the requisite information.

Dulberger (1993) of IBM introduced a "matched model" index for semiconductor prices. A matched model index combines price relatives for products with the same performance at different points of time. Dulberger presented constant quality price indexes based on index number formulas, including the [Irving] *Fisher* (1922) *ideal index* used in the U.S. national accounts (Landefeld and Parker 1997). The Fisher index is the geometric average of the familiar Laspeyres and Paasche indexes.

Diewert (1976) defined a *superlative* index number as an index that exactly replicates a *flexible* representation of the underlying technology (or preferences). A flexible representation provides a second-order approximation to an arbitrary technology (or preferences). Konus and Byushgens (1926) first showed that the Fisher ideal index is superlative in this sense. Laspeyres and Paasche indexes are not superlative and fail to capture substitutions among products in response to price changes accurately.

Grimm (1998) combined matched model techniques with hedonic methods, based on an econometric model of semiconductor prices at different points of time. A hedonic model gives the price of a semiconductor product as a function of the characteristics that determine performance, such as speed of processing and storage capacity. A constant-quality price index isolates the price change by holding these characteristics of semiconductors fixed.

Beginning in 1997, the U.S. Bureau of Labor Statistics (BLS) incorporated a matched model price index for semiconductors into the Producer Price Index (PPI) and since then the national accounts have relied on data from the PPI. Reflecting long-standing BLS policy, historical data were not revised backward. Semiconductor prices reported in the PPI prior to 1997 do not hold quality constant, failing to capture the rapid semiconductor price decline and the acceleration in 1994.

d.   Computers

The introduction of the Personal Computer (PC) by IBM in 1981 was a watershed event in the deployment of information technology. The sale of Intel's 8086–8088 microprocessor to IBM in 1978 for incorporation into the PC was a major business breakthrough for Intel (Moore 1996). In 1981 IBM licensed the MS-DOS operating system from the Microsoft Corporation, founded by Bill Gates and Paul Allen in 1975. The PC established an Intel/Microsoft relationship that has continued up to the present. In 1985 Microsoft released the first version of Windows, its signature operating system for the PC, giving rise to the Wintel (Windows-Intel) nomenclature for this ongoing collaboration.

Mainframe computers, as well as PC's, have come to rely heavily on logic chips for central processing and memory chips for main memory. However, semiconductors account for less than half of computer costs and computer prices have fallen much less rapidly than semiconductor prices. Precise measures of computer prices that hold product quality constant were introduced into the NIPA in 1985 and the PPI during the 1990's. The national accounts now rely on PPI data, but historical data on computers from the PPI, like the PPI data on semiconductors, do not hold quality constant.

Chow (1967) pioneered the use of hedonic techniques for constructing a constant quality index of computer prices in research conducted at IBM. Chow documented price declines at more than 20 percent per year during 1960–1965, providing an initial glimpse of the remarkable behavior of computer prices.[7] In 1985 the Bureau of Economic Analysis incorporated constant-quality price indexes for computers and peripheral equipment constructed by Cole et al. (1986) of IBM into the NIPA. Triplett (1986) discussed the economic interpretation of these indexes, bringing the rapid decline of computer prices to the attention of a very broad audience.

---

[7]   Further details are given by Berndt (1991: 102–149).

Figure 2: Relative Prices of Computers, Communications, Software, and Services, 1948–1999

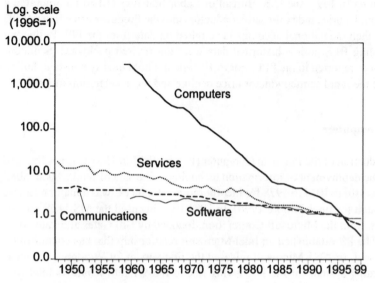

Note: All price indexes are divided by the output price index.

The BEA-IBM constant-quality price index for computers provoked a heated exchange between BEA and Denison (1989), one of the founders of national accounting methodology in the 1950's and head of the national accounts at BEA from 1979 to 1982. Denison sharply attacked the BEA-IBM methodology and argued vigorously against the introduction of constant-quality price indexes into the national accounts.[8] Young (1989), then Director of BEA, reiterated BEA's rationale for introducing constant-quality price indexes.

Dulberger (1989) presented a more detailed report on her research on the prices of computer processors for the BEA-IBM project. Speed of processing and main memory played central roles in her model. Triplett (1989) provided an exhaustive survey of research on hedonic price indexes for computers. Gordon (1989, 1990) gave an alternative model of computer prices and identified computers and communications equipment, along with commercial aircraft, as assets with the highest rates of price decline.

Figure 2 gives BEA's constant-quality index of prices of computers and peripheral equipment and its components, including mainframes, PC's, storage devices,

---

[8]   Denison cited his 1957 paper, "Theoretical Aspects of Quality Change, Capital Consumption, and Net Capital Formation," as the definitive statement of the traditional BEA position.

other peripheral equipment, and terminals. The decline in computer prices follows the behavior of semiconductor prices presented in Figure 1, but in much attenuated form. The 1995 acceleration in the computer price decline parallels the acceleration in the semiconductor price decline that resulted from the changeover from a three-year product cycle to a two-year cycle in 1995.

e.   Communications Equipment and Software

Communications technology is crucial for the rapid development and diffusion of the Internet, perhaps the most striking manifestation of information technology in the American economy.[9] Flamm (1989) was the first to compare the behavior of computer prices and the prices of communications equipment. He concluded that the communications equipment prices fell only a little more slowly than computer prices. Gordon (1990) compared Flamm's results with the official price indexes, revealing substantial bias in the official indexes.

Communications equipment is an important market for semiconductors, but constant-quality price indexes cover only a portion of this equipment. Switching and terminal equipment rely heavily on semiconductor technology, so that product development reflects improvements in semiconductors. Grimm's (1997) constant-quality price index for digital telephone switching equipment, given in Figure 3, was incorporated into the national accounts in 1996. The output of communications services in the NIPA also incorporates a constant-quality price index for cellular phones.

Much communications investment takes the form of the transmission gear, connecting data, voice, and video terminals to switching equipment. Technologies such as fiber optics, microwave broadcasting, and communications satellites have progressed at rates that outrun even the dramatic pace of semiconductor development. An example is dense wavelength division multiplexing (DWDM), a technology that sends multiple signals over an optical fiber simultaneously. Installation of DWDM equipment, beginning in 1997, has doubled the transmission capacity of fiber-optic cables every 6–12 months.[10]

Both software and hardware are essential for information technology and this is reflected in the large volume of software expenditures. The eleventh comprehensive revision of the national accounts, released by BEA on October 27, 1999, reclassified computer software as investment.[11] Before this important advance,

---

[9]   A general reference on the Internet is Choi and Whinston (2000). On Internet indicators, see: *http://www.internetindicators.com/*.

[10]   Rashad (2000) characterizes this as the "demise" of Moore's Law. Hecht (1999) describes DWDM technology and provides a general reference on fiber optics.

[11]   Moulton (2000) describes the eleventh comprehensive revision of NIPA and the 1999 update.

Figure 3: Relative Prices of Computers, Communications, and Software, 1959–1999

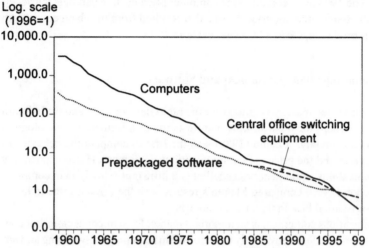

Note: All price indexes are divided by the output price index.

business expenditures on software were treated as current outlays, while personal and government expenditures were treated as purchases of nondurable goods. Software investment is growing rapidly and is now much more important than investment in computer hardware.

Parker and Grimm (2000) describe the new estimates of investment in software. BEA distinguishes among three types of software – prepackaged, custom, and own-account software. Prepackaged software is sold or licensed in standardized form and is delivered in packages or electronic files downloaded from the Internet. Custom software is tailored to the specific application of the user and is delivered along with analysis, design, and programming services required for customization. Own-account software consists of software created for a specific application. However, only price indexes for prepackaged software hold performance constant.

Parker and Grimm (2000) present a constant-quality price index for prepackaged software, given in Figure 3. This combines a hedonic model of prices for business applications software and a matched model index for spread-sheet and word-processing programs developed by Oliner and Sichel (1994). Prepackaged software prices decline at more than 10 percent per year over the period 1962–1998. Since 1998 the BEA has relied on a matched model price index for all prepackaged software from the PPI; prior to 1998 the PPI data do not hold quality constant.

BEA's prices for own-account software are based on programmer wage rates. This implicitly assumes no change in the productivity of computer programmers, even with growing investment in hardware and software to support the creation of new software. Custom software prices are a weighted average of prepackaged and own-account software prices with arbitrary weights of 75 percent for own-account and 25 percent for prepackaged software. These price indexes do not hold the software performance constant and present a distorted picture of software prices, as well as software output and investment.

f.   Research Opportunities

The official price indexes for computers and semiconductors provide the paradigm for economic measurement. These indexes capture the steady decline in IT prices and the recent acceleration in this decline. The official price indexes for central office switching equipment and prepackaged software also hold quality constant. BEA and BLS, the leading statistical agencies in price research, have carried out much of the best work in this area. However, a critical role has been played by price research at IBM, long the dominant firm in information technology (Chandler 2000: 26 [Table 1.1]).

It is important to emphasize that information technology is not limited to applications of semiconductors. Switching and terminal equipment for voice, data, and video communications has come to rely on semiconductor technology and the empirical evidence on prices of this equipment reflects this fact. Transmission gear employs technologies with rates of progress that far outstrip those of semiconductors. This important gap in our official price statistics can only be filled by constant-quality price indexes for all types of communications equipment.

Investment in software is more important than investment in hardware. This was essentially invisible until BEA introduced new measures of prepackaged, custom, and own-account software investment into the national accounts in 1999. This is a crucial step in understanding the role of information technology in the American economy. Unfortunately, software prices are another statistical blind spot, with only prices of prepackaged software adequately represented in the official system of price statistics. The daunting challenge that lies ahead is to construct constant-quality price indexes for custom and own-account software.

2.   The Role of Information Technology

At the aggregate level IT is identified with the outputs of computers, communications equipment, and software. These products appear in the GDP as investments by businesses, households, and governments along with net exports to the rest of the world. The GDP also includes the services of IT products consumed by households and governments. A methodology for analyzing economic growth must capture the substitution of IT outputs for other outputs of goods and services.

While semiconductor technology is the driving force behind the spread of IT, the impact of the relentless decline in semiconductor prices is transmitted through falling IT prices. Only net exports of semiconductors, defined as the difference between U.S. exports to the rest of the world and U.S. imports, appear in the GDP. Sales of semiconductors to domestic manufacturers of IT products are precisely offset by purchases of semiconductors and are excluded from the GDP.

Constant-quality price indexes, like those reviewed in the previous section, are a key component of the methodology for analyzing the American growth resurgence. Computer prices were incorporated into the NIPA in 1985 and are now part of the PPI as well. Much more recently, semiconductor prices have been included in the NIPA and the PPI. Unfortunately, evidence on the prices of communications equipment and software is seriously incomplete, so that the official price indexes are seriously misleading.

a.   Output

The output data in Table 1 are based on the most recent benchmark revision of the national accounts, updated through 1999.[12] The output concept is similar, but not identical, to the concept of gross domestic product used by the BEA. Both measures include final outputs purchased by businesses, governments, households, and the rest of the world. Unlike the BEA concept, the output measure in Table 1 also includes imputations for the service flows from durable goods, including IT products, employed in the household and government sectors.

The imputations for services of IT equipment are based on the cost of capital for IT described in more detail below. The cost of capital is multiplied by the nominal value of IT capital stock to obtain the imputed service flow from IT products. In the business sector this accrues as capital income to the firms that employ these products as inputs. In the household and government sectors the flow of capital income must be imputed. This same type of imputation is used for housing in the NIPA. The rental value of renter-occupied housing accrues to real estate firms as

---

[12]   See Jorgenson and Stiroh (2000b: Appendix A) for details on the estimates of output.

Table 1: Information Technology Output and Gross Domestic Product

Year	Computer		Software		Communications		IT services		Total IT		Gross domestic product	
	Value	Price	Value	Price	Value	Price	Value	Price	Value	Price	Value	Price
1948					1.8	0.81	0.4	3.26	2.3	2.47	307.7	0.19
1949					1.7	0.81	0.4	2.19	2.0	2.29	297.0	0.18
1950					1.9	0.83	0.6	2.38	2.5	2.38	339.0	0.19
1951					2.2	0.86	0.8	2.30	3.0	2.43	370.6	0.19
1952					2.7	0.84	1.1	2.50	3.9	2.43	387.4	0.19
1953					3.0	0.80	1.5	2.56	4.5	2.38	418.2	0.20
1954					2.7	0.81	1.3	1.86	3.9	2.15	418.3	0.20
1955					3.0	0.81	1.8	2.25	4.7	2.30	461.3	0.20
1956					3.7	0.82	2.0	2.27	5.7	2.33	484.7	0.21
1957					4.3	0.85	1.9	1.79	6.2	2.22	503.6	0.21
1958					3.8	0.86	2.1	1.84	5.9	2.25	507.2	0.22
1959	0.0	662.98			4.7	0.86	2.7	2.14	7.4	2.37	551.9	0.22
1960	0.2	662.98	0.1	0.58	5.1	0.84	2.8	1.99	8.2	2.28	564.9	0.22
1961	0.3	497.23	0.2	0.59	5.6	0.82	2.8	1.88	9.0	2.19	581.8	0.22
1962	0.3	350.99	0.2	0.59	6.2	0.82	3.3	1.99	10.0	2.20	623.3	0.22
1963	0.8	262.69	0.5	0.59	6.2	0.81	3.3	1.81	10.8	2.08	666.9	0.23
1964	1.0	218.30	0.6	0.57	6.9	0.79	3.6	1.76	12.1	2.01	726.5	0.24
1965	1.3	179.45	0.9	0.58	8.1	0.78	4.7	1.99	15.0	2.03	795.1	0.25
1966	1.9	126.16	1.2	0.54	9.7	0.76	5.2	1.85	18.0	1.88	871.3	0.25
1967	2.1	102.41	1.5	0.58	10.7	0.76	5.0	1.50	19.3	1.75	918.2	0.26
1968	2.1	87.48	1.6	0.58	11.6	0.78	5.4	1.40	20.7	1.71	973.0	0.26
1969	2.7	79.16	2.3	0.63	13.0	0.79	5.8	1.31	23.8	1.70	1,045.8	0.27
1970	3.0	71.13	3.1	0.70	14.4	0.81	6.7	1.34	27.1	1.73	1,105.2	0.29
1971	3.1	54.17	3.2	0.69	14.7	0.83	8.1	1.47	29.0	1.73	1,178.8	0.30
1972	3.9	43.67	3.7	0.70	15.6	0.85	9.0	1.48	32.2	1.72	1,336.2	0.32
1973	3.9	41.39	4.3	0.72	18.2	0.86	12.1	1.78	38.4	1.82	1,502.5	0.34
1974	4.3	33.80	5.3	0.77	19.9	0.90	10.9	1.45	40.4	1.73	1,605.9	0.37
1975	4.0	31.27	6.6	0.83	21.3	0.96	12.0	1.46	43.9	1.79	1,785.8	0.41
1976	4.9	26.12	7.1	0.85	23.8	0.98	14.2	1.58	50.0	1.83	2,017.5	0.44
1977	6.3	22.72	7.5	0.87	28.1	0.97	22.5	2.28	64.4	2.02	2,235.7	0.46
1978	8.5	15.44	9.2	0.90	32.7	0.99	20.3	1.86	70.6	1.85	2,517.7	0.49
1979	11.4	12.81	11.9	0.94	38.4	1.02	26.5	2.18	88.2	1.92	2,834.9	0.54
1980	14.0	9.97	14.5	1.00	43.9	1.07	23.5	1.73	95.9	1.80	2,964.5	0.57
1981	19.2	8.75	17.8	1.08	48.6	1.13	22.4	1.46	108.0	1.76	3,285.2	0.62
1982	22.0	7.80	21.1	1.12	50.9	1.17	25.6	1.49	119.5	1.77	3,445.4	0.66
1983	28.8	6.44	24.9	1.13	55.0	1.17	29.5	1.50	138.1	1.71	3,798.8	0.70
1984	37.4	5.24	30.4	1.15	62.9	1.18	33.3	1.44	163.9	1.63	4,288.1	0.74
1985	39.6	4.48	35.2	1.15	69.9	1.17	38.5	1.44	183.1	1.57	4,542.6	0.75
1986	45.9	4.45	38.5	1.13	72.7	1.17	42.7	1.36	199.7	1.54	4,657.4	0.74
1987	48.6	3.93	43.7	1.14	74.9	1.15	50.3	1.37	217.5	1.50	5,078.1	0.78
1988	54.1	3.72	51.2	1.15	82.1	1.14	59.3	1.40	246.7	1.48	5,652.0	0.83
1989	56.9	3.52	61.4	1.13	85.1	1.13	63.0	1.31	266.3	1.43	5,988.8	0.85
1990	52.4	3.09	69.3	1.12	86.5	1.12	68.5	1.28	276.6	1.38	6,284.9	0.88
1991	52.6	2.85	78.2	1.13	83.9	1.12	67.5	1.13	282.2	1.32	6,403.3	0.90
1992	54.9	2.44	83.9	1.06	88.1	1.11	77.3	1.15	304.1	1.27	6,709.9	0.92
1993	54.8	2.02	95.5	1.06	92.6	1.09	84.7	1.11	327.6	1.21	6,988.8	0.93
1994	57.6	1.80	104.6	1.04	102.6	1.07	96.6	1.12	361.4	1.17	7,503.9	0.96
1995	70.5	1.41	115.7	1.03	112.4	1.03	108.7	1.10	407.2	1.11	7,815.3	0.97
1996	78.3	1.00	131.0	1.00	120.1	1.00	115.1	1.00	444.5	1.00	8,339.0	1.00
1997	86.0	0.73	158.1	0.97	131.5	0.98	123.0	0.90	498.7	0.91	9,009.4	1.04
1998	86.9	0.53	193.3	0.94	140.4	0.95	131.9	0.79	552.5	0.82	9,331.1	1.03
1999	92.4	0.39	241.2	0.94	158.1	0.92	140.9	0.69	632.6	0.75	9,817.4	1.04

Notes: Values are in billions of current dollars. Prices are normalized to one in 1996. Information technology output is gross domestic product by type of product.

Table 2: Growth Rates of Outputs and Inputs

	1990–1995		1995–1999	
	Prices	Quanti-ties	Prices	Quanti-ties
Outputs				
Gross domestic product	1.99	2.36	1.62	4.08
Information technology	−4.42	12.15	−9.74	20.75
Computers	−15.77	21.71	−32.09	38.87
Software	−1.62	11.86	−2.43	20.80
Communications equipment	−1.77	7.01	−2.90	11.42
Information technology services	−2.95	12.19	−11.76	18.24
Noninformation technology investment	2.15	1.22	2.20	4.21
Noninformation technology consumption	2.35	2.06	2.31	2.79
Inputs				
Gross domestic income	2.23	2.13	2.36	3.33
Information technology capital services	−2.70	11.51	−10.46	19.41
Computer capital services	−11.71	20.27	−24.81	36.36
Software capital services	−1.83	12.67	−2.04	16.30
Communications equipment capital services	2.18	5.45	−5.90	8.07
Noninformation technology capital services	1.53	1.72	2.48	2.94
Labor services	3.02	1.70	3.39	2.18

Note: Average annual percentage rates of growth.

capital income, while the rental value of owner-occupied housing is imputed to households.

Current dollar GDP in Table 1 is $9.8 trillions in 1999, including imputations, and real output growth averaged 3.46 percent for the period 1948–1999. These magnitudes can be compared to the current dollar value of $9.3 trillions in 1999 and the average real growth rate of 3.40 percent for the period 1948–1999 for the official GDP. Table 1 presents the current dollar value and price indexes of the GDP and IT output. This includes outputs of investment goods in the form of computers, software, communications equipment, and non-IT investment goods. It also includes outputs of non-IT consumption goods and services as well as imputed IT capital service flows from households and governments.

The most striking feature of the data in Table 1 is the rapid price decline for computer investment, 17.1 percent per year from 1959 to 1995. Since 1995 this decline has almost doubled to 32.1 percent per year. By contrast the relative price of software has been flat for much of the period and began to fall only in the late 1980's. The price of communications equipment behaves similarly to the software price, while the consumption of capital services from computers and software by households and governments shows price declines similar to computer investment.

Figure 4: Output Shares of Information Technology by Type, 1948–1999

Percent of current dollar GDP

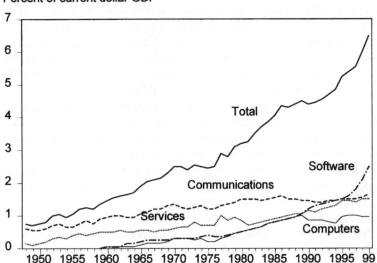

The top panel of Table 2 summarizes the growth rates of prices and quantities for major output categories for 1990–1995 and 1995–1999. Business investments in computers, software, and communications equipment are the largest categories of IT spending. Households and governments have also spent sizable amounts on computers, software, communications equipment and the services of information technology. Figure 4 shows that the output of software is the largest IT category as a share of GDP, followed by the outputs of computers and communications equipment.

b.   Capital Services

This subsection presents capital estimates for the U.S. economy for the period 1948 to 1999.[13] These begin with BEA investment data; the perpetual inventory method generates estimates of capital stocks and these are aggregated, using service prices as weights. This approach, originated by Jorgenson and Griliches (1996), is based on the identification of service prices with marginal products of

---

[13]   See Jorgenson and Stiroh (2000b: Appendix B) for details on the estimates of capital input.

different types of capital. The service price estimates incorporate the cost of capital.[14]

The cost of capital is an annualization factor that transforms the price of an asset into the price of the corresponding capital input (Jorgenson and Yun 1991: 7). This includes the nominal rate of return, the rate of depreciation, and the rate of capital loss due to declining prices. The cost of capital is an essential concept for the economics of information technology (Jorgenson and Stiroh 1995: 300–303), due to the astonishing decline of IT prices given in Table 1.

The cost of capital is important in many areas of economics, especially in modeling producer behavior, productivity measurement, and the economics of taxation.[15] Many of the important issues in measuring the cost of capital have been debated for decades. The first of these is incorporation of the rate of decline of asset prices into the cost of capital. The assumption of perfect foresight or rational expectations quickly emerged as the most appropriate formulation and has been used in almost all applications of the cost of capital.[16]

The second empirical issue is the measurement of economic depreciation. The stability of patterns of depreciation in the face of changes in tax policy and price shocks has been carefully documented. The depreciation rates presented by Jorgenson and Stiroh (2000b) summarize a large body of empirical research on the behavior of asset prices.[17] A third empirical issue is the description of the tax structure for capital income. This depends on the tax laws prevailing at each point of time. The resolution of these issues has cleared the way for detailed measurements of the cost of capital for all assets that appear in the national accounts, including information technology.[18]

The definition of capital includes all tangible assets in the U.S. economy, equipment and structures, as well as consumers' and government durables, land, and inventories. The capital service flows from durable goods employed by households and governments enter measures of both output and input. A steadily rising proportion of these service flows are associated with investments in IT. Invest-

---

[14]   Jorgenson (2000) presents a model of capital as a factor of production. BLS (U.S. Bureau of Labor Statistics 1983) describes the version of this model employed in the official productivity statistics. For a recent update, see: *http://www.bls.gov/news. release/prd3.nr0.htm*. Hulten (2001) surveys the literature.

[15]   Lau (2000) surveys applications of the cost of capital.

[16]   See, for example, Jorgenson et al. (1987: 40–49) and Jorgenson and Griliches (1996).

[17]   Jorgenson and Stiroh (2000b: 196–197 [Table B4]) give the depreciation rates employed in this study. Fraumeni (1997) describes depreciation rates used in the NIPA. Jorgenson (2000) surveys empirical studies of depreciation.

[18]   See Jorgenson and Yun (2001). Diewert and Lawrence (2000) survey measures of the price and quantity of capital input.

ments in IT by business, household, and government sectors must be included in the GDP, along with household and government IT capital services, in order to capture the full impact of IT on the U.S. economy.

Table 3 gives capital stocks from 1948 to 1999, as well as price indexes for total domestic tangible assets and IT assets – computers, software, and communications equipment. The estimate of domestic tangible capital stock in Table 3 is $35.4 trillions in 1999, considerably greater than the $27.9 trillions in fixed capital estimated by Herman (2000) of BEA. The most important differences reflect the inclusion of inventories and land in Table 3.

Business IT investments, as well as purchases of computers, software, and communications equipment by households and governments, have grown spectacularly in recent years, but remain relatively small. The stocks of all IT assets combined account for only 4.35 percent of domestic tangible capital stock in 1999. Table 4 presents estimates of the flow of capital services and corresponding price indexes for 1948–1999.

The difference between growth in capital services and capital stock is the *improvement in capital quality*. This represents the substitution toward assets with higher marginal products. The shift toward IT increases the quality of capital, since computers, software, and communications equipment have relatively high marginal products. Capital stock estimates fail to account for this increase in quality and substantially underestimate the impact of IT investment on growth.

The growth of capital quality is slightly less than 20 percent of capital input growth for the period 1948–1995. However, improvements in capital quality have increased steadily in relative importance. These improvements jumped to 44.9 percent of total growth in capital input during the period 1995–1999, reflecting very rapid restructuring of capital to take advantage of the sharp acceleration in the IT price decline. Capital stock has become progressively less accurate as a measure of capital input and is now seriously deficient.

Figure 5 gives the IT capital service flows as a share of gross domestic income. The second panel of Table 2 summarizes the growth rates of prices and quantities of capital inputs for 1990–1995 and 1995–1999. Growth of IT capital services jumps from 11.51 percent per year in 1990–1995 to 19.41 percent in 1995–1999, while growth of non-IT capital services increases from 1.72 percent to 2.94 percent. This reverses the trend toward slower capital growth through 1995.

c.   **Labor Services**

This subsection presents estimates of labor input for the U.S. economy from 1948 to 1999. These incorporate individual data from the *Censuses of Population* for 1970, 1980, and 1990, as well as the annual *Current Population Surveys*. Con-

Table 3: Information Technology Capital Stock and Domestic Tangible Assets

Year	Computer		Software		Communications		Total IT		Total domestic tangible assets	
	Value	Price	Value	Price	Value	Price	Value	Price	Value	Price
1948					4.7	0.81	4.7	1.37	711.7	0.13
1949					5.9	0.82	5.9	1.37	750.5	0.13
1950					7.3	0.84	7.3	1.41	824.5	0.13
1951					9.0	0.87	9.0	1.46	948.1	0.14
1952					10.6	0.84	10.6	1.41	1,017.5	0.14
1953					12.2	0.81	12.2	1.36	1,094.9	0.15
1954					13.7	0.81	13.7	1.37	1,146.9	0.15
1955					15.2	0.81	15.2	1.36	1,238.4	0.15
1956					17.5	0.82	17.5	1.38	1,373.2	0.16
1957					20.7	0.86	20.7	1.44	1,494.1	0.17
1958					22.5	0.86	22.5	1.45	1,562.3	0.17
1959	0.2	752.87	0.1	0.54	24.7	0.86	25.0	1.45	1,655.7	0.18
1960	0.2	752.87	0.1	0.54	26.5	0.84	26.8	1.42	1,755.3	0.18
1961	0.5	564.66	0.3	0.55	28.8	0.83	29.5	1.39	1,854.8	0.18
1962	0.6	398.58	0.4	0.55	31.7	0.83	32.7	1.38	1,982.7	0.19
1963	1.1	298.31	0.8	0.56	33.8	0.81	35.7	1.34	2,088.5	0.19
1964	1.6	247.90	1.1	0.55	36.4	0.79	39.1	1.31	2,177.3	0.19
1965	2.2	203.79	1.6	0.55	40.0	0.78	43.8	1.28	2,315.4	0.20
1966	2.9	143.27	2.3	0.52	44.5	0.76	49.7	1.22	2,512.1	0.20
1967	3.7	116.30	3.2	0.56	50.8	0.77	57.6	1.22	2,693.3	0.21
1968	4.3	99.34	3.8	0.56	57.7	0.79	65.7	1.23	2,986.0	0.22
1969	5.3	89.90	5.1	0.61	65.4	0.80	75.7	1.25	3,319.1	0.24
1970	6.2	80.77	7.0	0.68	74.4	0.83	87.5	1.29	3,595.0	0.25
1971	6.3	61.52	7.9	0.67	82.1	0.84	96.3	1.28	3,922.6	0.26
1972	7.3	49.59	9.1	0.67	90.6	0.86	107.0	1.29	4,396.8	0.28
1973	8.6	47.00	10.7	0.69	99.9	0.88	119.2	1.31	4,960.3	0.31
1974	9.1	38.38	13.2	0.75	112.8	0.91	135.0	1.35	5,391.6	0.32
1975	9.7	35.51	16.3	0.80	128.7	0.98	154.6	1.43	6,200.5	0.36
1976	10.4	29.66	18.3	0.82	142.1	1.01	170.7	1.45	6,750.0	0.38
1977	12.4	25.81	20.4	0.84	152.3	0.99	185.1	1.42	7,574.4	0.41
1978	14.1	17.46	23.5	0.87	171.8	1.02	209.4	1.42	8,644.9	0.46
1979	19.3	14.47	28.7	0.91	195.0	1.04	243.0	1.43	9,996.7	0.51
1980	24.2	11.27	35.3	0.97	225.7	1.09	285.2	1.47	11,371.0	0.56
1981	33.6	9.90	43.6	1.04	260.9	1.15	338.1	1.53	13,002.5	0.63
1982	42.4	8.84	52.0	1.08	290.0	1.19	384.3	1.55	13,964.7	0.66
1983	52.6	7.32	60.6	1.09	314.3	1.20	427.5	1.53	14,526.0	0.68
1984	66.2	5.95	72.3	1.11	344.8	1.20	483.3	1.50	15,831.0	0.71
1985	77.7	5.08	84.2	1.11	375.0	1.20	537.0	1.46	17,548.6	0.77
1986	86.0	4.34	94.9	1.10	404.3	1.18	585.1	1.41	18,844.3	0.80
1987	94.1	3.71	108.5	1.11	434.8	1.17	637.4	1.37	20,216.2	0.84
1988	107.2	3.45	125.2	1.12	467.7	1.16	700.0	1.35	21,880.1	0.89
1989	121.0	3.23	144.4	1.11	499.7	1.15	765.7	1.33	23,618.7	0.93
1990	122.3	2.89	165.2	1.10	527.1	1.14	814.5	1.29	24,335.1	0.94
1991	124.6	2.58	189.9	1.10	548.3	1.13	862.8	1.27	24,825.7	0.95
1992	128.2	2.17	203.8	1.04	569.7	1.11	901.7	1.21	25,146.8	0.95
1993	135.6	1.82	231.8	1.05	589.5	1.10	956.9	1.17	25,660.4	0.95
1994	150.4	1.61	255.8	1.02	612.8	1.07	1,019.0	1.13	26,301.0	0.95
1995	170.3	1.33	286.7	1.03	634.1	1.03	1,091.1	1.07	27,858.4	0.98
1996	181.6	1.00	318.1	1.00	659.3	1.00	1,158.9	1.00	29,007.9	1.00
1997	198.7	0.76	365.2	0.97	695.8	0.98	1,259.7	0.94	30,895.3	1.04
1998	210.0	0.55	431.2	0.95	730.9	0.94	1,372.1	0.87	32,888.5	1.07
1999	232.4	0.41	530.6	0.95	778.5	0.90	1,541.5	0.81	35,406.9	1.11

Notes: Values are in billions of current dollars. Prices are normalized to one in 1996. Domestic tangible assets include fixed assets and consumer durable goods, land, and inventories.

Table 4: Information Technology Capital Services and Gross Domestic Income

Year	Computer		Software		Communications		Total IT		Gross domestic income	
	Value	Price	Value	Price	Value	Price	Value	Price	Value	Price
1948					1.7	1.20	1.7	4.31	307.7	0.14
1949					1.3	0.79	1.3	2.83	297.0	0.14
1950					1.8	0.91	1.8	3.27	339.0	0.15
1951					2.1	0.90	2.1	3.21	370.6	0.15
1952					2.6	0.94	2.6	3.36	387.4	0.15
1953					3.2	0.96	3.2	3.46	418.2	0.15
1954					2.7	0.70	2.7	2.49	418.3	0.15
1955					3.6	0.85	3.6	3.05	461.3	0.16
1956					4.2	0.87	4.2	3.12	484.7	0.17
1957					3.7	0.68	3.7	2.44	503.6	0.17
1958					4.1	0.68	4.1	2.45	507.2	0.17
1959	0.2	444.36	0.1	0.63	5.2	0.80	5.5	2.87	551.9	0.18
1960	0.2	433.59	0.1	0.62	5.4	0.75	5.6	2.68	564.9	0.18
1961	0.3	637.21	0.1	0.58	5.6	0.71	6.0	2.59	581.8	0.18
1962	0.4	508.68	0.2	0.62	6.6	0.76	7.2	2.71	623.3	0.19
1963	0.6	311.81	0.3	0.58	6.5	0.67	7.3	2.34	666.9	0.20
1964	0.8	211.28	0.4	0.60	7.1	0.67	8.3	2.26	726.5	0.21
1965	1.3	182.17	0.6	0.59	9.1	0.78	11.0	2.52	795.1	0.22
1966	2.2	173.57	1.0	0.64	9.6	0.73	12.8	2.40	871.3	0.23
1967	2.3	110.97	1.1	0.50	9.8	0.66	13.2	2.01	918.2	0.23
1968	2.6	87.05	1.6	0.60	10.2	0.61	14.5	1.86	973.0	0.24
1969	2.8	68.23	1.7	0.52	11.3	0.61	15.8	1.76	1,045.8	0.25
1970	3.6	65.38	2.3	0.56	13.3	0.65	19.1	1.83	1,105.2	0.26
1971	5.2	72.48	3.7	0.77	14.9	0.67	23.9	1.99	1,178.8	0.27
1972	4.9	48.57	4.0	0.71	16.6	0.69	25.4	1.85	1,336.2	0.30
1973	4.4	33.06	4.5	0.71	22.8	0.88	31.7	2.04	1,502.5	0.32
1974	6.6	38.82	5.1	0.70	20.3	0.72	32.0	1.84	1,605.9	0.34
1975	5.9	28.43	6.7	0.80	23.2	0.77	35.7	1.85	1,785.8	0.37
1976	6.6	26.07	7.7	0.81	25.0	0.78	39.2	1.84	2,017.5	0.41
1977	7.0	20.69	8.4	0.82	41.8	1.20	57.2	2.40	2,235.7	0.44
1978	11.8	22.49	9.7	0.86	35.5	0.93	57.0	2.07	2,517.7	0.47
1979	11.6	13.33	11.6	0.90	47.9	1.14	71.1	2.15	2,834.9	0.51
1980	16.6	11.81	13.6	0.91	42.0	0.90	72.2	1.82	2,964.5	0.53
1981	17.7	7.89	15.5	0.90	40.5	0.79	73.6	1.53	3,285.2	0.58
1982	19.6	5.93	17.6	0.89	43.1	0.77	80.3	1.41	3,445.4	0.60
1983	26.4	5.46	20.6	0.91	49.4	0.82	96.4	1.43	3,798.8	0.66
1984	36.1	4.87	25.4	0.96	54.3	0.83	115.7	1.41	4,288.1	0.71
1985	39.6	3.70	30.6	0.99	63.1	0.89	133.3	1.35	4,542.6	0.73
1986	43.1	3.04	35.3	0.99	69.3	0.89	147.6	1.27	4,657.4	0.73
1987	53.4	2.93	42.1	1.04	86.5	1.02	181.9	1.36	5,078.1	0.77
1988	52.7	2.31	50.5	1.10	104.1	1.14	207.3	1.36	5,652.0	0.81
1989	57.6	2.08	60.4	1.13	105.8	1.07	223.8	1.29	5,988.8	0.84
1990	64.7	2.01	67.2	1.08	109.8	1.04	241.7	1.25	6,284.9	0.86
1991	64.2	1.76	70.8	1.00	104.2	0.93	239.2	1.12	6,403.3	0.88
1992	71.7	1.66	89.9	1.11	112.2	0.96	273.7	1.16	6,709.9	0.91
1993	77.8	1.45	90.4	0.98	126.9	1.03	295.1	1.11	6,988.8	0.92
1994	80.1	1.19	109.5	1.05	142.4	1.10	331.9	1.10	7,503.9	0.96
1995	99.3	1.12	115.5	0.99	160.7	1.16	375.6	1.09	7,815.3	0.96
1996	123.6	1.00	131.9	1.00	149.0	1.00	404.5	1.00	8,339.0	1.00
1997	134.7	0.76	156.2	1.02	157.1	0.98	448.1	0.92	9,009.4	1.04
1998	152.5	0.59	178.2	0.97	162.0	0.93	492.6	0.82	9,331.1	1.04
1999	157.7	0.42	204.4	0.91	175.3	0.91	537.4	0.72	9,817.4	1.06

Notes: Values are in billions of current dollars. Prices are normalized to one in 1996.

Figure 5: Input Shares of Information Technology by Type, 1949–1999

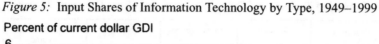

Percent of current dollar GDI

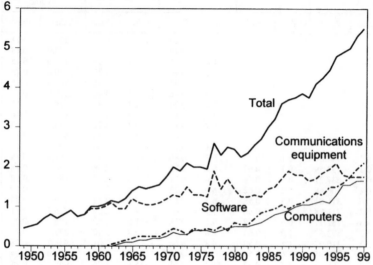

stant-quality indexes for the price and quantity of labor input account for the het-erogeneity of the workforce across sex, employment class, age, and education lev-els. This follows the approach of Jorgenson et al. (1987). The estimates have been revised and updated by Ho and Jorgenson (2000).[19]

The distinction between labor input and labor hours is analogous to the distinc-tion between capital services and capital stock. The growth in labor quality is the difference between the growth in labor input and hours worked. Labor quality re-flects the substitution of workers with high marginal products for those with low marginal products. Table 5 presents estimates of labor input, hours worked, and la-bor quality.

The value of labor expenditures in Table 5 is $5.8 trillions in 1999, 59.3 percent of the value of output. This share accurately reflects the concept of gross domestic income, including imputations for the value of capital services in household and government sectors. As shown in Table 2, the growth rate of labor input acceler-ated to 2.18 percent for 1995–1999 from 1.70 percent for 1990–1995. This is pri-marily due to the growth of hours worked, which rose from 1.17 percent for 1990–

---

[19]   See Jorgenson and Stiroh (2000b: Appendix C) for details on the estimates of labor input. Gollop (2000) discusses the measurement of labor quality.

Table 5: Labor Services

Year	Labor services				Employ-ment	Weekly hours	Hourly compen-sation	Hours worked
	Price	Quantity	Value	Quality				
1948	0.08	1,924.6	156.1	0.75	61,536	39.1	1.2	125,127
1949	0.09	1,860.0	171.5	0.75	60,437	38.5	1.4	121,088
1950	0.09	1,961.0	179.2	0.76	62,424	38.5	1.4	125,144
1951	0.10	2,133.0	214.4	0.78	66,169	38.7	1.6	133,145
1952	0.10	2,197.2	227.2	0.79	67,407	38.5	1.7	135,067
1953	0.11	2,254.3	241.8	0.80	68,471	38.3	1.8	136,331
1954	0.11	2,190.3	243.9	0.81	66,843	37.8	1.9	131,477
1955	0.11	2,254.9	256.7	0.81	68,367	37.8	1.9	134,523
1956	0.12	2,305.0	275.0	0.82	69,968	37.5	2.0	136,502
1957	0.13	2,305.1	295.5	0.83	70,262	37.0	2.2	135,189
1958	0.14	2,245.3	309.1	0.83	68,578	36.7	2.4	130,886
1959	0.14	2,322.1	320.1	0.84	70,149	36.8	2.4	134,396
1960	0.15	2,352.2	344.1	0.84	71,128	36.5	2.5	135,171
1961	0.15	2,378.5	355.0	0.86	71,183	36.3	2.6	134,451
1962	0.15	2,474.1	376.7	0.87	72,673	36.4	2.7	137,612
1963	0.15	2,511.4	386.2	0.88	73,413	36.4	2.8	139,050
1964	0.16	2,578.1	417.6	0.88	74,990	36.3	3.0	141,447
1965	0.17	2,670.6	451.9	0.89	77,239	36.3	3.1	145,865
1966	0.18	2,788.5	500.3	0.89	80,802	36.0	3.3	151,448
1967	0.19	2,842.4	525.5	0.90	82,645	35.7	3.4	153,345
1968	0.20	2,917.0	588.3	0.91	84,733	35.5	3.8	156,329
1969	0.22	2,992.1	646.6	0.91	87,071	35.4	4.0	160,174
1970	0.23	2,938.6	687.3	0.91	86,867	34.9	4.4	157,488
1971	0.26	2,924.9	744.5	0.90	86,715	34.8	4.7	156,924
1972	0.27	3,011.7	817.6	0.91	88,838	34.8	5.1	160,873
1973	0.29	3,135.0	909.4	0.91	92,542	34.8	5.4	167,271
1974	0.31	3,148.2	988.5	0.91	94,121	34.2	5.9	167,425
1975	0.35	3,082.9	1,063.9	0.92	92,575	33.8	6.5	162,879
1976	0.38	3,174.4	1,194.0	0.92	94,922	33.9	7.1	167,169
1977	0.41	3,277.4	1,334.5	0.92	98,202	33.8	7.7	172,780
1978	0.44	3,430.3	1,504.2	0.92	102,931	33.8	8.3	180,842
1979	0.47	3,554.7	1,673.2	0.92	106,463	33.7	9.0	186,791
1980	0.52	3,535.7	1,827.9	0.92	107,061	33.3	9.9	185,591
1981	0.55	3,563.8	1,968.8	0.93	108,050	33.2	10.6	186,257
1982	0.60	3,519.7	2,096.3	0.93	106,749	32.9	11.5	182,772
1983	0.63	3,586.7	2,269.8	0.94	107,810	33.1	12.2	185,457
1984	0.66	3,786.7	2,499.1	0.94	112,604	33.2	12.9	194,555
1985	0.69	3,882.9	2,679.0	0.95	115,205	33.1	13.5	198,445
1986	0.75	3,926.3	2,931.1	0.95	117,171	32.9	14.6	200,242
1987	0.74	4,075.1	3,019.7	0.96	120,474	32.9	14.6	206,312
1988	0.75	4,207.7	3,172.2	0.96	123,927	32.9	15.0	211,918
1989	0.80	4,348.4	3,457.8	0.97	126,755	33.0	15.9	217,651
1990	0.84	4,381.5	3,680.8	0.97	128,341	32.9	16.8	219,306
1991	0.88	4,322.0	3,800.2	0.98	127,080	32.5	17.7	214,994
1992	0.94	4,353.9	4,086.9	0.98	127,238	32.6	19.0	215,477
1993	0.96	4,497.4	4,297.7	0.99	129,770	32.8	19.5	221,003
1994	0.96	4,628.3	4,453.1	0.99	132,799	32.9	19.6	226,975
1995	0.98	4,770.7	4,660.5	1.00	135,672	33.0	20.0	232,545
1996	1.00	4,861.7	4,861.7	1.00	138,018	32.8	20.6	235,798
1997	1.03	4,987.9	5,122.0	1.00	141,184	33.0	21.1	242,160
1998	1.08	5,108.8	5,491.5	1.00	144,305	33.0	22.2	247,783
1999	1.12	5,204.8	5,823.4	1.00	147,036	32.9	23.1	251,683

Notes: Value is in billions of current dollars. Quantity is in billions of 1996 dollars. Price and quality are normalized to one in 1996. Employment is in thousands of workers. Weekly hours is hours per worker, divided by 52. Hourly compensation is in current dollars. Hours worked are in millions of hours.

1995 to 1.98 percent for 1995–1999, as labor-force participation increased and un-employment rates plummeted.

The growth of labor quality has declined considerably in the late 1990's, drop-ping from 0.53 percent for 1990–1995 to 0.20 percent for 1995–1999. This slow-down captures well-known demographic trends in the composition of the work-force, as well as exhaustion of the pool of available workers. Growth in hours worked does not capture these changes in labor quality growth and is a seriously misleading measure of labor input.

3.   The American Growth Resurgence

The American economy has undergone a remarkable resurgence since the mid-1990's with accelerating growth in output, labor productivity, and total factor pro-ductivity. The purpose of this section is to quantify the sources of growth for 1948–1999 and various subperiods. An important objective is to account for the sharp acceleration in the level of economic activity since 1995 and, in particular, to document the role of information technology.

The appropriate framework for analyzing the impact of information technology is the production possibility frontier, giving outputs of IT investment goods as well as inputs of IT capital services. An important advantage of this framework is that prices of IT outputs and inputs are linked through the price of IT capital services. This framework successfully captures the substitutions among outputs and inputs in response to the rapid deployment of IT. It also encompasses costs of adjustment, while allowing financial markets to be modeled independently.

As a consequence of the swift advance of information technology, a number of the most familiar concepts in growth economics have been superseded. The aggre-gate production function heads this list. Capital stock as a measure of capital input is no longer adequate to capture the rising importance of IT. This completely ob-scures the restructuring of capital input that is such an important wellspring of the growth resurgence. Finally, hours worked must be replaced as a measure of labor input.

a.   Production Possibility Frontier

The *production possibility frontier* describes efficient combinations of outputs and inputs for the economy as a whole.[20] Aggregate output Y consists of outputs of in-

---

[20]   The production possibility frontier was introduced into productivity measurement by Jorgenson (1996: 27–28).

vestment goods and consumption goods. These outputs are produced from aggregate input X, consisting of capital services and labor services. Productivity is a "Hicks-neutral" augmentation of aggregate input.

The production possibility frontier takes the form:

(1) $Y(I_n, I_c, I_s, I_t, C_n, C_c) = A \cdot X(K_n, K_c, K_s, K_t, L),$

where the outputs include non-IT investment goods I_n and investments in computers I_c, software I_s, and communications equipment I_t, as well as non-IT consumption goods and services C_n and IT capital services to households and governments C_c. Inputs include non-IT capital services K_n and the services of computers K_c, software K_s, and telecommunications equipment K_t, as well as labor input L.[21] *Total factor productivity (TFP)* is denoted by A.

The most important advantage of the production possibility frontier is the explicit role that it provides for constant-quality prices of IT products. These are used as deflators for nominal expenditures on IT investments to obtain the quantities of IT outputs. Investments in IT are cumulated into stocks of IT capital. The flow of IT capital services is an aggregate of these stocks with service prices as weights. Similarly, constant-quality prices of IT capital services are used in deflating the nominal values of consumption of these services.

Another important advantage of the production possibility frontier is the incorporation of costs of adjustment. For example, an increase in the output of IT investment goods requires forgoing part of the output of consumption goods and non-IT investment goods, so that adjusting the rate of investment in IT is costly. However, costs of adjustment are external to the producing unit and are fully reflected in IT prices. These prices incorporate forward-looking expectations of the future prices of IT capital services.

b.   Aggregate Production Function

The aggregate production function employed by Solow (1957, 1960) and, more recently, by Greenwood et al. (1997, 2000), Harberger (1998), and Hercowitz (1998) is a competing methodology. The production function gives a single output as a function of capital and labor inputs. There is no role for separate prices of investment and consumption goods and, hence, no place for constant-quality IT price indexes for outputs of IT investment goods.

Greenwood et al. employ a price index for consumption to deflate the output of all investment goods, including information technology. Confronted by the fact

---

21   Services of durable goods to governments and households are included in both inputs and outputs.

that constant-quality prices of investment goods differ from consumption goods prices, they borrow the concept of *embodiment* from Solow (1960) in order to convert investment goods output into an appropriate form for measuring capital stock.[22] Investment has two prices, one used in measuring output and the other used in measuring capital stock. This inconsistency can be removed by simply distinguishing between outputs of consumption and investment goods, as in the national accounts and equation (1). The concept of embodiment can then be dropped.

Perhaps inadvertently, Greenwood et al. have revisited the controversy accompanying the introduction of a constant-quality price index for computers into the national accounts. They have revived Denison's (1993) proposal to use a consumption price index to deflate investment in the NIPA. Denison found this appealing as a means of avoiding the introduction of constant-quality price indexes for computers. Denison's approach leads to a serious underestimate of GDP growth and an overestimate of inflation.

Another limitation of the aggregate production function is that it fails to incorporate costs of adjustment. Lucas (1967) presented a production model with internal costs of adjustment. Hayashi (2000) shows how to identify these adjustment costs from Tobin's (1969) Q-ratio, the ratio of the stock market value of the producing unit to the market value of the unit's assets. Implementation of this approach requires simultaneous modeling of production and asset valuation. If costs of adjustment are external, as in the production possibility frontier (1), asset valuation can be modeled separately from production.[23]

c.   **Sources of Growth**

Under the assumption that product and factor markets are competitive, producer equilibrium implies that the share-weighted growth of outputs is the sum of the share-weighted growth of inputs and growth in total factor productivity

$$(2) \quad \overline{w}_{I,n} \Delta \ln I_n + \overline{w}_{I,c} \Delta \ln I_c + \overline{w}_{I,s} \Delta \ln I_s$$
$$+ \overline{w}_{I,t} \Delta \ln I_t + \overline{w}_{C,n} \Delta \ln C_n + \overline{w}_{C,c} \Delta \ln C_c$$
$$= \overline{v}_{K,n} \Delta \ln K_n + \overline{v}_{K,c} \Delta \ln K_c$$
$$+ \overline{v}_{K,s} \Delta \ln K_s + \overline{v}_{K,t} \Delta \ln K_t + \overline{v}_L \Delta \ln L + \Delta \ln A$$

where $\overline{w}$ and $\overline{v}$ denote average value shares. The shares of outputs and inputs add to one under the additional assumption of constant returns, $\overline{w}_{I,n} + \overline{w}_{I,c} + \overline{w}_{I,s}$
$+ \overline{w}_{I,t} + \overline{w}_{C,n} + \overline{w}_{C,c} = \overline{v}_{K,n} + \overline{v}_{K,c} + \overline{v}_{K,s} + \overline{v}_{K,t} + \overline{v}_L = 1$.

---

[22]   Whelan (1999) also employs Solow's concept of embodiment.

[23]   See, for example, Campbell and Shiller (1998).

Table 6: Sources of Gross Domestic Product Growth

	1948–1999	1948–1973	1973–1990	1990–1995	1995–1999
			Outputs		
Gross domestic product	3.46	3.99	2.86	2.36	4.08
Contribution of information technology	0.40	0.20	0.46	0.57	1.18
Computers	0.12	0.04	0.16	0.18	0.36
Software	0.08	0.02	0.09	0.15	0.39
Communications equipment	0.10	0.08	0.10	0.10	0.17
Information technology services	0.10	0.06	0.10	0.15	0.25
Contribution of noninformation technology	3.06	3.79	2.40	1.79	2.91
Contribution of noninformation technology investment	0.72	1.06	0.34	0.23	0.83
Contribution of noninformation technology consumption	2.34	2.73	2.06	1.56	2.08
			Inputs		
Gross domestic income	2.84	3.07	2.61	2.13	3.33
Contribution of information technology capital services	0.34	0.16	0.40	0.48	0.99
Computers	0.15	0.04	0.20	0.22	0.55
Software	0.07	0.02	0.08	0.16	0.29
Communications equipment	0.11	0.10	0.12	0.10	0.14
Contribution of noninformation technology capital services	1.36	1.77	1.05	0.61	1.07
Contribution of labor services	1.14	1.13	1.16	1.03	1.27
Total factor productivity	0.61	0.92	0.25	0.24	0.75

Notes: Average annual percentage rates of growth. The contribution of an output or input is the rate of growth, multiplied by the value share.

Equation (2) makes it possible to identify the contributions of outputs as well as inputs to U.S. economic growth. The growth rate of output is a weighted average of growth rates of investment and consumption goods outputs. The *contribution* of each output is its weighted growth rate. Similarly, the growth rate of input is a weighted average of growth rates of capital and labor services and the contribution of each input is its weighted growth rate. The *contribution* of TFP, the growth rate of the augmentation factor A in equation (2), is the difference between growth rates of output and input.

Table 6 presents results of a growth accounting decomposition, based on equation (2), for the period 1948–1999 and various subperiods, following Jorgenson and Stiroh (1999, 2000b). Economic growth is broken down by output and input categories, quantifying the contribution of information technology to investment and consumption outputs, as well as capital inputs. These estimates identify computers, software, and communications equipment as distinct types of information technology.

Rearranging equation (2), the results can be presented in terms of *average labor productivity* (ALP), defined as $y = Y/H$, the ratio of output Y to hours worked H, and $k = K/H$ is the ratio of capital services K to hours worked:

(3) $\Delta \ln y = \bar{v}_K \Delta \ln k + \bar{v}_L (\Delta \ln L - \Delta \ln H) + \Delta \ln A.$

Equation (3) allocates ALP growth among three sources. The first is *capital deepening*, the growth in capital input per hour worked, and reflects the capital-labor substitution. The second is *improvement in labor quality* and captures the rising proportion of hours by workers with higher marginal products. The third is *TFP growth*, which contributes point-for-point to ALP growth.

d.   Contributions of IT Investments

Figure 5 depicts the rapid increase in the importance of IT services, reflecting the accelerating pace of IT price declines. In 1995–1999 the capital service price for computers fell 24.81 percent per year, compared to an increase of 36.36 percent in capital input from computers. As a consequence, the value of computer services grew substantially. However, the current dollar value of computers was only 1.6 percent of gross domestic income in 1999.

The rapid accumulation of software appears to have different sources. The price of software services has declined only 2.04 percent per year for 1995–1999. Nonetheless, firms have been accumulating software very rapidly, with real capital services growing 16.30 percent per year. A possible explanation is that firms respond to computer price declines by investing in complementary inputs like software. However, a more plausible explanation is that the price indexes used to deflate software investment fail to hold quality constant. This leads to an overstatement of inflation and an understatement of growth.

Although the price decline for communications equipment during the period 1995–1999 is comparable to that of software, investment in this equipment is more in line with prices. However, prices of communications equipment also fail to hold quality constant. The technology of switching equipment, for example, is similar to that of computers; investment in this category is deflated by a constant-quality price index developed by BEA. Conventional price deflators are employed for transmission gear, such as fiberoptic cables. This leads to an underestimate of the growth rates of investment, capital stock, capital services, and the GDP, as well as an overestimate of the rate of inflation.

Figures 6 and 7 highlight the rising contributions of IT outputs to U.S. economic growth. Figure 6 shows the breakdown between IT and non-IT outputs for subperiods from 1948 to 1999, while Figure 7 decomposes the contribution of IT into its components. Although the importance of IT has steadily increased,

Figure 6: Output Contribution of Information Technology

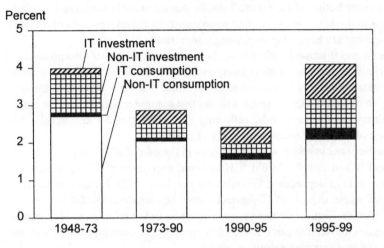

Note: Output contributions are the average annual (percentage) growth rates, weighted by the output shares.

Figure 7: Output Contribution of Information Technology by Type

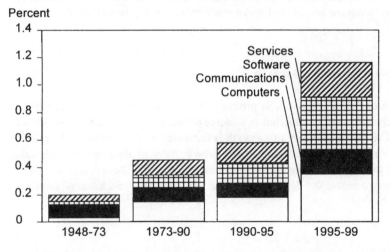

Note: Output contributions are the average annual (percentage) growth rates, weighted by the output shares.

Figure 6 shows that the recent investment and consumption surge nearly doubled the output contribution of IT. Figure 7 shows that software is the largest single IT contributor in the late 1990's, but that investments in computers and communications equipment are becoming increasingly important.

Figures 8 and 9 present a similar decomposition of IT inputs into production. The contribution of these inputs is rising even more dramatically. Figure 8 shows that the contribution of IT now accounts for more than 48.1 percent of the total contribution of capital input. Figure 9 shows that computer hardware is the largest IT contributor on the input side, reflecting the growing share and accelerating growth rate of computer investment in the late 1990's.

Private business investment predominates in the output of IT, as shown by Jorgenson and Stiroh (1999, 2000b).[24] Household purchases of IT equipment and services are next in importance. Government purchases of IT equipment and services, as well as net exports of IT products, must be included in order to provide a complete picture. Firms, consumers, governments, and purchasers of U.S. exports are responding to relative price changes, increasing the contributions of computers, software, and communications equipment.

Table 2 shows that the price of computer investment fell by more than 32 percent per year, the price of software 2.4 percent, the price of communications equipment 2.9 percent, and the price of IT services 11.8 percent during the period 1995–1999, while non-IT prices rose 2.2 percent. In response to these price changes, firms, households, and governments have accumulated computers, software, and communications equipment much more rapidly than other forms of capital.

e.   Total Factor Productivity

The price or "dual" approach to productivity measurement makes it possible to identify the role of IT production as a source of productivity growth at the industry level.[25] The rate of productivity growth is measured as the decline in the price of output, plus a weighted average of the growth rates of input prices with value shares of the inputs as weights. For the computer industry this expression is dominated by two terms: the decline in the price of computers and the contribution of

---

[24]   Bosworth and Triplett (2000) compare the results of Jorgenson and Stiroh (2000b) with those of Oliner and Sichel (2000).

[25]   The dual approach is presented by Jorgenson et al. (1987: 53–63).

Figure 8: Capital Input Contribution of Information Technology

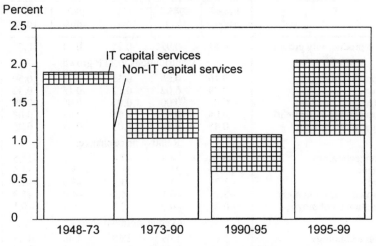

Note: Input contributions are the average annual (percentage) growth rates, weighted by the income shares.

Figure 9: Capital Input Contribution of Information Technology by Type

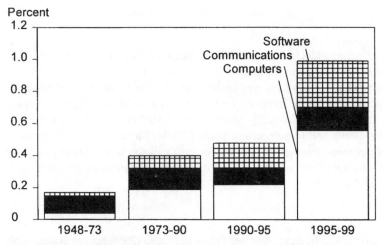

Note: Input contributions are the average annual (percentage) growth rates, weighted by the income shares.

Table 7: Sources of Total Factor Productivity Growth

	1948– 1999	1948– 1973	1973– 1990	1990– 1995	1995– 1999
Total factor productivity growth	0.61	0.92	0.25	0.24	0.75
	Contributions to TFP growth				
Information technology	0.16	0.06	0.19	0.25	0.50
Computers	0.09	0.02	0.12	0.15	0.32
Software	0.02	0.00	0.02	0.05	0.09
Communications equipment	0.05	0.03	0.06	0.05	0.08
Noninformation technology	0.45	0.86	0.06	−0.01	0.25
	Relative price changes				
Information technology	−6.16	−4.3	−7.4	−7.2	−11.5
Computers	−23.01	−23.5	−21.1	−18.0	−34.5
Software	−3.29	−3.0	−3.2	−3.9	−4.8
Communications equipment	−3.71	−3.1	−4.2	−4.0	−5.3
Noninformation technology	−0.41	−0.9	0.0	0.1	−0.1
	Average nominal shares				
Information technology	2.07	1.09	2.60	3.46	4.26
Computers	0.40	0.10	0.61	0.81	0.94
Software	0.51	0.08	0.60	1.30	1.84
Communications equipment	1.16	0.91	1.39	1.34	1.48
Noninformation technology	97.20	98.46	96.55	95.35	94.35

Note: Average annual rates of growth. Prices are relative to the price of gross domestic income. Contributions are relative price changes, weighted by average nominal output shares.

the price of semiconductors. For the semiconductor industry the expression is dominated by the decline in the price of semiconductors.[26]

Jorgenson et al. (1987) have employed Domar's (1961) model to trace aggregate productivity growth to its sources at the level of individual industries (Jorgenson et al. 1987: 63–66, 301–322). More recently, Harberger (1998), Gullickson and Harper (1999), and Jorgenson and Stiroh (2000a, 2000b) have used the model for similar purposes. Productivity growth for each industry is weighted by the ratio of the gross output of the industry to GDP to estimate the industry contribution to aggregate TFP growth.

---

[26]   Dulberger (1993), Triplett (1996), and Oliner and Sichel (2000) present models of the relationships between computer and semiconductor industries. These are special cases of the Domar (1961) aggregation scheme.

Figure 10: Contributions of Information Technology to Total Factor Productivity Growth

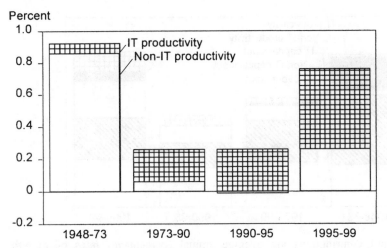

Note: Contributions are average annual (percentage) relative price changes, weighted by average nominal output shares from Table 7.

If semiconductor output were only used to produce computers, then its contribution to computer-industry productivity growth, weighted by computer-industry output, would precisely cancel its independent contribution to aggregate TFP growth. This is the ratio of the value of semiconductor output to GDP, multiplied by the rate of semiconductor price decline. In fact, semiconductors are used to produce telecommunications equipment and many other products. However, the value of semiconductor output is dominated by inputs into IT production.

The Domar aggregation formula can be approximated by expressing the declines in prices of computers, communications equipment, and software relative to the price of gross domestic income, an aggregate of the prices of capital and labor services. The rates of relative IT price decline are weighted by ratios of the outputs of IT products to the GDP. Table 7 reports details of this TFP decomposition for 1948–1999; the IT and non-IT contributions are presented in Figure 10. The IT products contribute 0.50 percentage points to TFP growth for 1995–1999, compared to 0.25 percentage points for 1990–1995. This reflects the accelerating decline in relative price changes resulting from shortening the product cycle for semiconductors.

Figure 11: Sources of Gross Domestic Product Growth

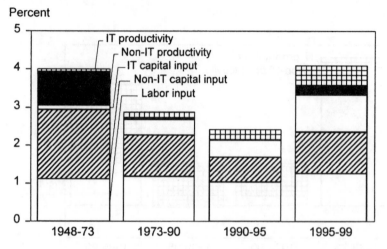

Percent

Note: Input contributions are average annual (percentage) rates of growth, weighted by average nominal income shares from Table 6. Productivity contributions are from Table 7.

f.   Output Growth

This subsection presents the sources of GDP growth for the entire period 1948 to 1999. Capital services contribute 1.70 percentage points, labor services 1.14 percentage points, and TFP growth only 0.61 percentage points. Input growth is the source of nearly 82.3 percent of U.S. growth over the past half century, while TFP has accounted for 17.7 percent. Figure 11 shows the relatively modest contributions of TFP in all subperiods.

More than three-quarters of the contribution of capital reflects the accumulation of capital stock, while improvement in the quality of capital accounts for about one-quarter. Similarly, increased labor hours account for 80 percent of labor's contribution; the remainder is due to improvements in labor quality. Substitutions among capital and labor inputs in response to price changes are essential components of the sources of economic growth.

A look at the U.S. economy before and after 1973 reveals familiar features of the historical record. After strong output and TFP growth in the 1950's, 1960's, and early 1970's, the U.S. economy slowed markedly through 1990, with output growth falling from 3.99 percent to 2.86 percent and TFP growth declining from 0.92 percent to 0.25 percent. The growth in capital inputs also slowed from

Figure 12: Sources of Average Labor Productivity Growth

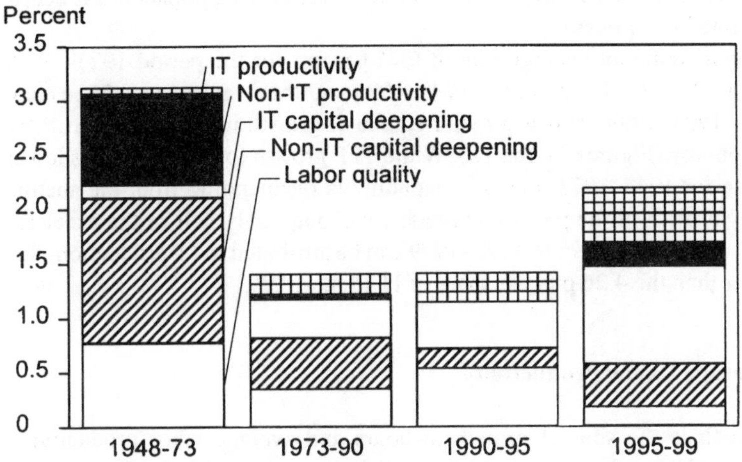

Percent

Note: Contributions are from Table 8.

4.64 percent for 1948–1973 to 3.57 percent for 1973–1990. This contributed to sluggish ALP growth – 2.82 percent for 1948–1973 and 1.26 percent for 1973–1990.

Relative to the early 1990's, output growth increased by 1.72 percent in 1995–1999. The contribution of IT production almost doubled, relative to 1990–1995, but still accounted for only 28.9 percent of the increased growth of output. Although the contribution of IT has increased steadily throughout the period 1948–1999, there has been a sharp response to the acceleration in the IT price decline in 1995. Nonetheless, more than 70 percent of the increased output growth can be attributed to non-IT products.

Between 1990–1995 and 1995–1999 the contribution of capital input jumped by 0.97 percentage points, the contribution of labor input rose by only 0.24 percent, and TFP accelerated by 0.51 percent. Growth in ALP rose by 0.92 percentage points as more rapid capital deepening and growth in TFP offset slower improvement in labor quality. Growth in hours worked accelerated as unemployment fell to a 30-year low. Labor markets have tightened considerably, even as labor-force participation rates increased.[27]

The contribution of capital input reflects the investment boom of the late 1990's as businesses, households, and governments poured resources into plant and equipment, especially computers, software, and communications equipment. The contribution of capital, predominantly IT, is considerably more important than

---

[27] Katz and Krueger (1999) analyze the recent performance of the U.S. labor market.

the contribution of labor. The contribution of IT capital services has grown steadily throughout the period 1948–1999, but Figure 9 reflects the impact of the accelerating decline in IT prices.

After maintaining an average rate of 0.25 percent for the period 1973–1999, TFP growth fell to 0.24 percent for 1990–1995 and then vaulted to 0.75 percent per year for 1995–1999. This is a major source of growth in output and ALP for the U.S. economy (Figures 11 and 12). While TFP growth for 1995–1999 is lower than the rate for 1948–1973, the U.S. economy is recuperating from the anemic productivity growth of the past two decades. Although only half of the acceleration in TFP from 1990–1995 to 1995–1999 can be attributed to IT production, this is far greater than the 4.26 percent share of IT in the GDP.

g.   Average Labor Productivity

Output growth is the sum of growth in hours and average labor productivity. Table 8 shows the breakdown between growth in hours and ALP for the same periods as in Table 6. For the period 1948–1999, ALP growth predominated in output growth, increasing just over 2 percent per year for 1948–1999, while hours increased about 1.4 percent per year. As shown in equation (3), ALP growth depends on capital deepening, a labor-quality effect, and TFP growth.

Table 8: Sources of Average Labor Productivity Growth

	1948– 1999	1948– 1973	1973– 1990	1990– 1995	1995– 1999
Gross domestic product	3.46	3.99	2.86	2.36	4.08
Hours worked	1.37	1.16	1.59	1.17	1.98
Average labor productivity	2.09	2.82	1.26	1.19	2.11
Contribution of capital deepening	1.13	1.45	0.79	0.64	1.24
Information technology	0.30	0.15	0.35	0.43	0.89
Noninformation technology	0.83	1.30	0.44	0.21	0.35
Contribution of labor quality	0.34	0.46	0.22	0.32	0.12
Total factor productivity	0.61	0.92	0.25	0.24	0.75
Information technology	0.16	0.06	0.19	0.25	0.50
Noninformation technology	0.45	0.86	0.06	-0.01	0.25
Addendum					
Labor input	1.95	1.95	1.97	1.70	2.18
Labor quality	0.58	0.79	0.38	0.53	0.20
Capital input	4.12	4.64	3.57	2.75	4.96
Capital stock	3.37	4.21	2.74	1.82	2.73
Capital quality	0.75	0.43	0.83	0.93	2.23

Notes: Average annual percentage rates of growth. Contributions are defined in equation (3) of the text.

Figure 12 reveals the well-known productivity slowdown of the 1970's and 1980's, emphasizing the acceleration in labor productivity growth in the late 1990's. The slowdown through 1990 reflects reduced capital deepening, declining labor-quality growth, and decelerating growth in TFP. The growth of ALP slipped further during the early 1990's with a slump in capital deepening only partly offset by a revival in labor-quality growth and an up-tick in TFP growth. A slowdown in hours combined with slowing ALP growth during 1990–1995 produced a further slide in the growth of output. In previous cyclical recoveries during the postwar period, output growth accelerated during the recovery, powered by more rapid growth of hours and ALP.

Accelerating output growth during 1995–1999 reflects growth in labor hours and ALP almost equally.[28] Comparing 1990–1995 to 1995–1999, the rate of output growth jumped by 1.72 percentage points – due to an increase in hours worked of 0.81 percentage points and another increase in ALP growth of 0.92 percentage points. Figure 12 shows the acceleration in ALP growth is due to capital deepening as well as faster TFP growth. Capital deepening contributed 0.60 percentage points, offsetting a negative contribution of labor quality of 0.20 percentage points. The acceleration in TFP added 0.51 percentage points.

h.   Research Opportunities

The use of computers, software, and communications equipment must be carefully distinguished from the production of IT.[29] Massive increases in computing power, like those experienced by the U.S. economy, have two effects on growth. First, as IT producers become more efficient, more IT equipment and software is produced from the same inputs. This raises productivity in IT-producing industries and contributes to TFP growth for the economy as a whole. Labor productivity also grows at both industry and aggregate levels.

Second, investment in information technology leads to growth of productive capacity in IT-using industries. Since labor is working with more and better equipment, this increases ALP through capital deepening. If the contributions to aggregate output are captured by capital deepening, aggregate TFP growth is unaffected (Baily and Gordon 1988). Increasing deployment of IT affects TFP growth only if there are spillovers from IT-producing industries to IT-using industries.

---

[28]   Stiroh (2000) shows that ALP growth is concentrated in IT-producing and IT-using industries.

[29]   Economics and Statistics Administration (2000: 23 [Table 3.1]) lists IT-producing industries.

Top priority must be given to identifying the impact of investment in IT at the industry level. Stiroh (1998) has shown that this is concentrated in a small number of IT-using industries, while Stiroh (2000) shows that aggregate ALP growth can be attributed to productivity growth in IT-producing and IT-using industries. The next priority is to trace the increase in aggregate TFP growth to its sources in individual industries. Jorgenson and Stiroh (2000a, 2000b) present the appropriate methodology and preliminary results.

4.   Economics on Internet Time

The steadily rising importance of information technology has created new research opportunities in all areas of economics. Economic historians, led by Chandler (2000) and David (2000),[30] have placed the information age in historical context. The Solow (1987) Paradox, that we see computers everywhere but in the productivity statistics,[31] has provided a point of departure. Since computers have now left an indelible imprint on the productivity statistics, the remaining issue is: Does the breathtaking speed of technological change in semiconductors differentiate this resurgence from previous periods of rapid growth?

Capital and labor markets have been severely impacted by information technology. Enormous uncertainty surrounds the relationship between equity valuations and future growth prospects of the American economy.[32] One theory attributes rising valuations of equities since the growth acceleration began in 1995 to the accumulation of intangible assets, such as intellectual property and organizational capital. An alternative theory treats the high valuations of technology stocks as a bubble that burst during the year 2000.

The behavior of labor markets also poses important puzzles. Widening wage differentials between workers with more and less education has been attributed to computerization of the workplace. A possible explanation could be that high-skilled workers are complementary to IT, while low-skilled workers are substitutable. An alternative explanation is that technical change associated with IT is skill biased and increases the wages of high-skilled workers relative to low-skilled workers.[33]

---

[30]   See also David (1990) and Gordon (2000).

[31]   Griliches (1994), Brynjolfsson and Yang (1996), and Triplett (1999) discuss the Solow Paradox.

[32]   Campbell and Shiller (1998) and Shiller (2000) discuss equity valuations and growth prospects. Kiley (1999), Brynjolfsson and Hitt (2000), and Hall (2000) present models of investment with internal costs of adjustment.

[33]   Acemoglu (2000) and Katz (2000) survey the literature on labor markets and technological change.

Finally, information technology is altering product markets and business organizations, as attested by the large and growing business literature,[34] but a fully satisfactory model of the semiconductor industry remains to be developed.[35] Such a model would derive the demand for semiconductors from investment in information technology in response to rapidly falling IT prices. An important objective is to determine the product cycle for successive generations of new semiconductors endogenously.

The semiconductor industry and the information technology industries are global in their scope with an elaborate international division of labor.[36] This poses important questions about the American growth resurgence. Where is the evidence of a new economy in other leading industrialized countries? An important explanation is the absence of constant-quality price indexes for semiconductors and information technology in national accounting systems outside the U.S.[37] Another conundrum is that several important participants – Korea, Malaysia, Singapore, and Taiwan – are "newly industrializing" economies. What does this portend for developing countries like China and India?

As policy makers attempt to fill the widening gaps between the information required for sound policy and the available data, the traditional division of labor between statistical agencies and policy-making bodies is breaking down. In the meantime, monetary policy makers must set policies without accurate measures of price change. Similarly, fiscal policy makers confront ongoing revisions of growth projections that drastically affect the outlook for future tax revenues and government spending.

The stagflation of the 1970's greatly undermined the Keynesian Revolution, leading to a New Classical Counterrevolution led by Lucas (1981) that has transformed macroeconomics. The unanticipated American growth revival of the 1990's has similar potential for altering economic perspectives. In fact, this is already fore-shadowed in a steady stream of excellent books on the economics of information technology.[38] We are the fortunate beneficiaries of a new agenda for economic research that could refresh our thinking and revitalize our discipline.

---

[34]   See, for example, Grove (1996) on the market for computers and semiconductors and Christensen (1997) on the market for storage devices.

[35]   Irwin and Klenow (1994), Flamm (1996: 305–424), and Helpman and Trajtenberg (1998: 111–119) present models of the semiconductor industry.

[36]   The role of information technology in U.S. economic growth is discussed by the Economics and Statistics Administration (2000); comparisons among OECD countries are given by the Organization for Economic Cooperation and Development (2000).

[37]   The measurement gap between the United States and other OECD countries was first identified by Wykoff (1995). Schreyer (2000) has taken the initial steps to fill this gap.

[38]   See, for example, Shapiro and Varian (1999), Brynjolfsson and Kahin (2000), and Choi and Whinston (2000).

References

Acemoglu, D. (2000). Technical Change, Inequality, and the Labor Market. NBER Working Paper 7800. National Bureau of Economic Research, Cambridge, MA.

Baily, M.N., and R.J. Gordon (1988). The Productivity Slowdown, Measurement Issues, and the Explosion of Computer Power. *Brookings Papers on Economic Activity* (2): 347–420.

Berndt, E.R. (1991). *The Practice of Econometrics: Classic and Contemporary*. Reading, MA: Addison-Wesley.

BLS (U.S. Bureau of Labor Statistics) (1983). *Trends in Multifactor Productivity, 1948–1981*. Washington, DC: U.S. Government Printing Office.

Bosworth, B.P., and J.E. Triplett (2000). What's New About the New Economy? IT, Growth and Productivity. International Productivity Monitor (2): 19–30.

Brynjolfsson, E., and L.M. Hitt (2000). Beyond Computation: Information Technology, Organizational Transformation and Business Performance. *Journal of Economic Perspectives* 14(4): 23–48.

Brynjolfsson, E., and B. Kahin (2000). *Understanding the Digital Economy*. Cambridge, MA: MIT Press.

Brynjolfsson, E., and S. Yang (1996). Information Technology and Productivity: A Review of the Literature. *Advances in Computers* 43(1): 179–214.

Campbell, J.Y., and R.J. Shiller (1998). Valuation Ratios and the Long-Run Stock Market Outlook. *Journal of Portfolio Management* 24(2): 11–26.

Chandler, A.D., Jr. (2000). The Information Age in Historical Perspective. In A.D. Chandler and J.W. Cortada (eds.), *A Nation Transformed by Information: How Information Has Shaped the United States from Colonial Times to the Present*. New York: Oxford University Press.

Choi, S.-Y., and A.B. Whinston (2000). *The Internet Economy: Technology and Practice*. Austin, TX: SmartEcon Publishing.

Chow, G.C. (1967). Technological Change and the Demand for Computers. *American Economic Review* 57(5): 1117–1130.

Christensen, C.M. (1997). *The Innovator's Dilemma*. Boston: Harvard Business School Press.

Cole, R., Y.C. Chen, J.A. Barquin-Stolleman, E.R. Dulberger, N. Helvacian, and J.H. Hodge (1986). Quality-Adjusted Price Indexes for Computer Processors and Selected Peripheral Equipment. *Survey of Current Business* 66(1): 41–50.

Congressional Budget Office (2000). *The Budget and Economic Outlook: An Update*. Washington, DC: U.S. Government Printing Office.

Council of Economic Advisers (2000). Annual Report. In *Economic Report of the President*. Washington, DC: U.S. Government Printing Office.

David, P.A. (1990). The Dynamo and the Computer: An Historical Perspective on the Productivity Paradox. *American Economic Review* 80(2): 355–361.

David, P.A. (2000). Understanding Digital Technology's Evolution and the Path of Measured Productivity Growth: Present and Future in the Mirror of the Past. In E. Brynjolfsson and B. Kahin (eds.), *Understanding the Digital Economy*. Cambridge, MA: MIT Press.

Denison, E.F. (1957). Theoretical Aspects of Quality Change, Capital Consumption, and Net Capital Formation. In Conference on Research in Income and Wealth (ed.), *Problems of Capital Formation*. Princeton, NJ: Princeton University Press.

Denison, E. (1989). *Estimates of Productivity Change by Industry*. Washington, DC: Brookings Institution Press.

Denison, E. (1993). Robert J. Gordon's Concept of Capital. *Review of Income and Wealth* 39(1): 89–102.

Diewert, W.E. (1976). Exact and Superlative Index Numbers. *Journal of Econometrics* 4(2): 115–146.

Diewert, W.E., and D.A. Lawrence (2000). Progress in Measuring the Price and Quantity of Capital. In L.J. Lau (ed.), *Econometrics and the Cost of Capital*. Cambridge, MA: MIT Press.

Domar, E. (1961). On the Measurement of Technological Change. *Economic Journal* 71(December): 709–729.

Dulberger, E.R. (1989). The Application of a Hedonic Model to a Quality-Adjusted Price Index for Computer Processors. In D.W. Jorgenson and R. Landau (eds.), *Technologic and Capital Formation*. Cambridge, MA: MIT Press.

Dulberger, E.R. (1993). Sources of Decline in Computer Processors: Selected Electronic Components. In F.F. Murray, M.E. Manser, and A.H. Young (eds.), *Price Measurements and Their Uses*. Chicago: University of Chicago Press.

Economics and Statistics Administration (2000). *Digital Economy 2000*. Washington, DC: U.S. Department of Commerce.

Fisher, I. (1922). *The Making of Index Numbers*. Boston: Houghton-Mifflin.

Flamm, K. (1989). Technological Advance and Costs: Computers versus Communications. In R.C. Crandall and K. Flamm (eds.), *Changing the Rules: Technological Change, International Competition, and Regulation in Communications*. Washington, DC: Brookings Institution Press.

Flamm, K. (1996). *Mismanaged Trade? Strategic Policy and the Semiconductor Industry*. Washington, DC: Brookings Institution Press.

Fraumeni, B.M. (1997). The Measurement of Depreciation in the U.S. National Income and Product Accounts. *Survey of Current Business* 77(7): 7–23.

Gollop, F.M. (2000). The Cost of Capital and the Measurement of Productivity. In L.J. Lau (ed.), *Econometrics and the Cost of Capital*. Cambridge, MA: MIT Press.

Gordon, R.J. (1989). The Postwar Evolution of Computer Prices. In D.W. Jorgenson and R. Landau (eds.), *Technology and Capital Formation*. Cambridge, MA: MIT Press.

Gordon, R.J. (1990). *The Measurement of Durable Goods Prices*. Chicago: University of Chicago Press.

Gordon, R.J. (1998). Foundations of the Goldilocks Economy: Supply Shocks and the Time-Varying NAIRU. *Brookings Papers on Economic Activity* (2): 297–333.

Gordon, R.J. (2000). Does the "New Economy" Measure Up to the Great Inventions of the Past? *Journal of Economic Perspectives* 14(4): 49–74.

Greenspan, A. (2000). Challenges for Monetary Policy-Makers. Board of Governors of the Federal Reserve System. Washington, DC, October 19.

Greenwood, J., Z. Hercowitz, and P. Krusell (1997). Long-Run Implications of Investment-Specific Technological Change. *American Economic Review* 87(3): 342–362.

Greenwood, J., Z. Hercowitz, and P. Krusell (2000). The Role of Investment-Specific Technological Change in the Business Cycle. *European Economic Review* 44(1): 91–115.

Griliches, Z. (1994). Productivity, R&D, and the Data Constraint. *American Economic Review* 94(2): 1–23.

Grimm, B.T. (1997). Quality Adjusted Price Indexes for Digital Telephone Switches. Bureau of Economic Analysis. Washington, DC, May 20.

Grimm, B.T. (1998). Price Indexes for Selected Semiconductors: 1974–1996. *Survey of Current Business* 78(2): 8–24.

Grove, A.S. (1996). *Only the Paranoid Survive: How to Exploit the Crisis Points that Challenge Every Company.* New York: Doubleday.

Gullickson, W., and M.J. Harper (1999). Possible Measurement Bias in Aggregate Productivity Growth. *Monthly Labor Review* 122(2): 47–67.

Hall, R.E. (2000). e-Capital: The Link between the Stock Market and the Labor Market in the 1990's. *Brookings Papers on Economic Activity* (2): 3–118.

Harberger, A.C. (1998). A Vision of the Growth Process. *American Economic Review* 88(1): 1–32.

Hayashi, F. (2000). The Cost of Capital, Q, and the Theory of Investment Demand. In L.J. Lau (ed.), *Econometrics and the Cost of Capital.* Cambridge, MA: MIT Press.

Hecht, J. (1999). *City of Light.* New York: Oxford University Press.

Helpman, E., and M. Trajtenberg (1998). Diffusion of General Purpose Technologies. In E. Helpman (ed.), *General Purpose Technologies and Economic Growth.* Cambridge, MA: MIT Press.

Hercowitz, Z. (1998). The "Embodiment" Controversy: A Review Essay. *Journal of Monetary Economics* 41(1): 217–224.

Herman, S.W. (2000). Fixed Assets and Consumer Durable Goods for 1925–1999. *Survey of Current Business* 80(9): 19–30.

Ho, M.S., and D.W. Jorgenson (2000). The Quality of the U.S. Workforce, 1948–1999. Department of Economics, Harvard University, Cambridge, MA.

Hulten, C.R. (2001). Total Factor Productivity: A Short Biography. In C.R. Hulten, E.R. Dean, and M.J. Harper (eds.), *New Developments in Productivity Analysis.* Chicago: University of Chicago Press.

International Technology Road Map for Semiconductors (2000). *2000 Update.* Austin, TX: Sematech Corporation.

Irwin, D.A., and P.J. Klenow (1994). Learning-by-Doing Spillovers in the Semiconductor Industry. *Journal of Political Economy* 102(6): 1200–1227.

Jorgenson, D.W. (1996). *Postwar U.S. Economic Growth*. Cambridge, MA: MIT Press.

Jorgenson, D.W. (1997). *Capital Theory and Investment Behavior*. Cambridge, MA: MIT Press.

Jorgenson, D.W. (2000). *Econometrics and Producer Behavior*. Cambridge, MA: MIT Press.

Jorgenson, D.W., and Z. Griliches (1996). The Explanation of Productivity Change. In D.W. Jorgenson (ed.), *Postwar U.S. Economic Growth*. Cambridge, MA: MIT Press.

Jorgenson, D.W., and K.J. Stiroh (1995). Computers and Growth. *Economics of Innovation and New Technology* 3(3–4): 295–316.

Jorgenson, D.W., and K.J. Stiroh (1999). Information Technology and Growth. *American Economic Review* 89(2): 109–115.

Jorgenson, D.W., and K.J. Stiroh (2000a). U.S. Economic Growth and the Industry Level. *American Economic Review* 90(2): 161–167.

Jorgenson, D.W., and K.J. Stiroh (2000b). Raising the Speed Limit: U.S. Economic Growth in the Information Age. *Brookings Papers on Economic Activity* (1): 125–211.

Jorgenson, D.W., and K.-Y. Yun (1991). *Tax Reform and the Cost of Capital*. New York: Oxford University Press.

Jorgenson, D.W., and K.-Y. Yun (2001). *Lifting the Burden: Tax Reform, the Cost of Capital, and U.S. Economic Growth*. Cambridge, MA: MIT Press.

Jorgenson, D.W., F.M. Gollop, and B.M. Fraumeni (1987). *Productivity and U.S. Economic Growth*. Cambridge, MA: Harvard University Press.

Katz, L.F. (2000). Technological Change, Computerization, and the Wage Structure. In E. Brynjolfsson and B. Kathin (eds.), *Understanding the Digital Economy*. Cambridge, MA: MIT Press.

Katz, L.F., and A. Krueger (1999). The High-Pressure U.S. Labor Market of the 1990's. *Brookings Papers on Economic Activity* (1): 1–87.

Kiley, M.T. (1999). Computers and Growth with Costs of Adjustment: Will the Future Look Like the Past? Board of Governors of the Federal Reserve System, Washington, DC, July.

Konus, A.A., and S.S. Byushgens (1926). On the Problem of the Purchasing Power of Money. *Economic Bulletin of the Conjuncture Institute*, Supplement (1926): 151–172.

Landefeld, J.S., and R.P. Parker (1997). BEA's Chain Indexes, Time Series, and Measures of Long-Term Growth. *Survey of Current Business* 77(5): 58–68.

Lau, L.J. (ed.) (2000). *Econometrics and the Cost of Capital*. Cambridge, MA: MIT Press.

Lucas, R.E., Jr. (1967). Adjustment Costs and the Theory of Supply. *Journal of Political Economy* 75(4, Part 1): 321–334.

Lucas, R.E., Jr. (1981). *Studies in Business-Cycle Theory*. Cambridge, MA: MIT Press.

Moore, G.E. (1965). Cramming More Components onto Integrated Circuits. *Electronics* 38(8): 114–117.

Moore, G.E. (1996). Intel – Memories and the Microprocessor. *Daedalus* 125(2): 55–80.

Moore, G.E. (1997). An Update on Moore's Law. Santa Clara, CA: Intel Corporation, September 30.

Moulton, B.R. (2000). Improved Estimates of the National Income and Product Accounts for 1929–1999: Results of the Comprehensive Revision. *Survey of Current Business* 80(4): 11–17, 36–145.

OECD (Organization for Economic Cooperation and Development) (2000). *A New Economy?* Paris: OECD.

Oliner, S.D., and D.E. Sichel (1994). Computers and Output Growth Revisited: How Big Is the Puzzle? *Brookings Papers on Economic Activity* (2): 273–317.

Oliner, S.D., and D.E. Sichel (2000). The Resurgence of Growth in the Late 1990's: Is Information Technology the Story? *Journal of Economic Perspectives* 14(4): 3–22.

Parker, R.P., and B.T. Grimm (2000). Recognition of Business and Government Expenditures on Software as Investment: Methodology and Quantitative Impacts, 1959–1998. Bureau of Economic Analysis, Washington, DC, November 14.

Petzold, C. (1999). *Code: The Hidden Language of Computer and Software*. Redmond, WA: Microsoft Press.

Rashad, R. (2000). The Future – It Isn't What It Used to Be. Seattle, WA: Microsoft Research, May 3.

Ruttan, V.W. (2001). The Computer and Semiconductor Industries. In V.W. Ruttan, *Technology, Growth, and Development*: An Induced Innovation Perspective. New York: Oxford University Press.

Schreyer, P. (2000). The Contribution of Information and Communication Technology to Output Growth: A Study of the G7 Countries. Working Papers 8(66). OECD, Paris.

Shapiro, C., and H.R. Varian (1999). *Information Rules*. Boston: Harvard Business School Press.

Shiller, R. (2000). *Irrational Exuberance*. Princeton, NJ: Princeton University Press.

Solow, R.M. (1957). Technical Change and the Aggregate Production Function. *Review of Economics and Statistics* 39(3): 312–320.

Solow, R.M. (1960). Investment and Technical Progress. In J.A. Kenneth, S. Karlin, and P. Suppes (eds.), *Mathematical Methods in the Social Sciences, 1959*. Stanford, CA: Stanford University Press.

Solow, R.M. (1987). We'd Better Watch Out. *New York Review of Books*, July 12.

Stiroh, K.J. (1998). Computers, Productivity, and Input Substitution. *Economic Inquiry* 36(2): 175–191.

Stiroh, K.J. (2000). Information Technology and the U.S. Productivity Revival: What Does the Industry Data Say? Staff Reports 115. Federal Reserve Bank of New York, New York.

Tobin, J. (1969). A General Equilibrium Approach to Monetary Theory. *Journal of Money, Credit and Banking* 1(1): 15–29.

Triplett, J.E. (1986). The Economic Interpretation of Hedonic Methods. *Survey of Current Business* 66(1): 36–40.

Triplett, J.E. (1989). Price and Technological Change in a Capital Good: Survey of Research on Computers. In D.W. Jorgenson and R. Landau (eds.), *Technology and Capital Formation*. Cambridge, MA: MIT Press.

Triplett, J.E. (1996). High-Tech Industry Productivity and Hedonic Price Indices. In OECD (ed.), *Industry Productivity: International Comparison and Measurement Issues*. Paris: OECD.

Triplett, J.E. (1999). The Solow Productivity Paradox: What Do Computers Do to Productivity? *Canadian Journal of Economics* 32(2): 309–334.

Whelan, K. (1999). Computers, Obsolescence, and Productivity. Board of Governors of the Federal Reserve System, Washington, DC.

Wolfe, T. (2000). Two Men Who Went West. In T. Wolfe (ed.), *Hooking Up*. New York: Farrar, Straus, and Giroux.

Wykoff, A.W. (1995). The Impact of Computer Prices on International Comparisons of Productivity. *Economics of Innovation and New Technology* 3(3–4): 277–293.

Young, A. (1989). BEA's Measurement of Computer Output. *Survey of Current Business* 69(7): 108–115.

Catherine L. Mann

The New Economy: End of the Welfare State?

1. Introduction

The new economy transforms relationships between consumers and firms by changing the boundaries of products and marketplaces, by innovating new ways to transact in goods and services, and by enabling whole new activities that depend on the network of information and information technologies that bind the world ever closer together. Together these changes highlight the economics of networks and of information, both of which create tensions between the global commercial reach of firms and customers and the local jurisdiction and authority of law and policymakers.

Policymakers view this dynamism with differing degrees of urgency and dismay – urgency, because of the potential for large productivity gains that will yield higher standards of living, and dismay, because the transformative forces that generate these new economy gains may, at the same time, undermine policymakers' ability to do the job of government.

Just as the new economy is changing the commercial landscape, so too is it affecting the "business" and "relationships" of governments and policymakers. What is the "business" of government? Procurement, raising and redistributing taxes, and providing public services are some. What about the "relationships" of government? Among other relationships, government is sometimes the advocate for citizens whose voices may be ignored by firms (as in minority interests) and sometimes is the advocate for society's future (as in pollution legislation). The dynamism of the new economy significantly affects the business of government, and the forces of the new economy bring new challenges and dimensions into government relationships with its citizens.

A particular set of fiscal tools and economic outcomes seem to characterize the business and relationships between government, firms, and citizens in the welfare state. That is, in the archetypal welfare state, high tax revenues fund generous public services, and policymakers use rules to govern and moderate the lives and environment of their citizens.

This essay will sketch out the forces of the new economy on two dimensions of government business and government relationship: (1) tax and expenditure systems, and (2) the issue of privacy and use of personal information. New economy forces are deeply affecting these issues and they are ones where the characteristics of the welfare state are most prominent. Can the archetypal welfare state survive the new economy?

For tax and expenditure systems, I conclude that transaction-based tax regimes will be stressed by the forces of the new economy and will need to evolve in response to the more complex and global nature of production. But governments still will be able to raise revenues to finance public expenditures, and will continue to be able to differentiate themselves by level of taxation and extent of expenditure: homogenization of tax rates or of public services is not inevitable. On the other hand, the extent to which public expenditures focus on moderating outcomes versus supporting transformation will likely have to change in order for the productivity gains of the more dynamic new economy to be enjoyed.

With regard to privacy and the use of personal information, I conclude that there are several possible sources of market imperfection, which allow for welfare-enhancing policymaker intervention to ensure proper functioning of the marketplace for information and privacy. However, the type of intervention is extremely important. In a technologically dynamic market, intervention must preserve the private sector's incentive to innovate. Thus, whereas government should be an advocate for voices ignored by the market, enforcing where necessary, a rules-based approach that yields a homogeneous outcome is less efficacious.

Therefore, the new economy does not portend the end of the ability of the state to play a significant role in enhancing the well-being of its citizens. But, it does mean that the government must change the way it sets policies on behalf of its citizens in order to change the way that citizens respond to both policies and the marketplace. Some might see in these changes the end of the welfare state as they know it.

2.   The New Economy: ICT Investment, New Markets, and Transformation

Information and networking technologies, and increasingly the information itself, are key drivers of the new economy. But, it is the response of the market participants to transform their activities that generates the gains, not the technologies alone. That is, information technologies (computers, hardware, and software) have been used to process numbers, create databases, and enhance corporate operations for quite some time (at least in the United States). And, firms have collected and processed information about prices, preferences, inventories, and inputs to improve internal operations and sales. But most of these technologies and information have been kept internal to a firm. The revolution of the new economy builds on and extends information technologies to give global reach, interoperability, and accessibility to the firms, consumers, and government (see Shapiro and Varian 1999).

a.   New Markets and New "Bundles" of Product, Geography, Time, and Information

The structure and capabilities of the Internet and information and communications technologies reduce frictions in the marketplace in the three dimensions of time, geography, and information. Production is more globalized, products are tailored to the specific needs of the user, and are delivered much more quickly. Consider Dell.com on-line site to configure and purchase a computer with the exact features you want, all delivered next day to your home. Or, consider interactive customer service in the native language of the caller, available 24 hours a day, and responding to specific questions associated with a particular order. The *Financial Times* packages its materials in several different ways, updates it continuously for different time zones, links to stories in other sources, and transmits through several distribution channels to satisfy the information needs of specific recipients. Internet access means that artisans in remote villages in Vietnam can sell into the global market. Business-to-business exchanges and auctions widen the range of participants, improve price revelation, and allow more timely purchase and delivery of parts and services.

The global new economy marketplace increasingly creates product "bundles," whereby a so-called "final good (or service)" is now being bundled into and priced uniquely for time, location, shopping and delivery method. Airlines have used this strategy for pricing seats for some time, as have package delivery services, such as FedEx. The Internet and ICTs allow such bundling to become much more prevalent, which at the same time creates more market niches for firms to occupy. For example, some Bloomberg clients pay for real-time stock prices; others get that information for free, but 20 minutes delayed; while a third group pays for a time series of the historical data. The customer needs are different, so Bloomberg bundles its information in different ways, creating more value to both the firm and the customer. Or, some people buy shirts from LandsEnd.com on-line and some from Nordstrom in the shopping center, not because the shirts are different, but because preferences for touching, customer assistance, convenience, and other factors, such as shopping-as-entertainment, matter. The shirt is just one part of the product bundle that is being purchased. Even for intermediate good producers, such as industrial supplies, the Internet and ICTs enhance this ability to bundle and use time, geography, and information more effectively.

What with bundling of tangibles and intangibles and strategic alliances around the globe, it is increasingly difficult to determine exactly where (in a geographical sense) or when (in terms of the stage of production and bundling) value is created. Product bundles can be offered through firms that can locate anywhere, whose locations can change quickly, and whose ultimate residence may be hard to track down. Even tangible merchandise, purchased at a point in time and at a particular location may only be identified by the delivery destination of record, not the ultimate user. With a bundle characterized by a digitized and downloaded transaction, neither the origin point nor the ultimate user may be determinable (e.g., digital music). And, some transactions will take place intermittently, through an intermediary, and involve the "rental" of intellectual property (e.g., use of software via application service providers). These issues have important implications for tax systems where jurisdictions often are bounded by political or geographic borders, rather than by commercial or economic relationships.

The enhanced role for information in the new economy also creates new policy challenges. With the Internet, information increasingly resides between the originator and the user, is used interactively (consider the examples of "cookies" or of application service providers), and is aggregated into databases. Both user and originator are key to having this wealth of information and using it to transform economic activity to generate greater welfare. But the user of the information (a firm) may have greater economic power in the relationship than the creator of the information (an individual). Moreover, the collection of information that is the database has the economic characteristic of a "public good." As is well known from economic theory, public goods may open the door for explicit public policy intervention so as to properly price or internalize the difference between the social and the private value of the activity.

b.   Economic Gains Come from Transforming Activities, Not Just ICTs

The lower frictions to using time and geography join with the information and network characteristics of the Internet marketplace to allow more ways for business to create value. Firms can focus on which part of the value-added chain that they do best and outsource other parts to subsidiaries or strategic allies anywhere on the globe. Moreover, more stages of production can be digitized (blueprints and software production, for example) where "assembly" and the delivery of value is via the network itself. From aircraft to architectural designs, more production is being done on the Internet by international teams. Without these transformations of the scope, pace, and location of economic activity, less benefit will come from the Internet.

Consider Table 1 which shows a decomposition of labor productivity growth over the 1990s for the United States and for Australia.

Table 1: Labor Productivity Growth and Its Components, 1991–1995 Compared to 1996–1999[a]

	Australia		United States	
	1991–1995	1996–1999	1991–1995	1996–1999
Labor productivity growth	2.1	4.1	1.5	2.6
Contribution from:				
Information technology	0.9	1.3	0.5	1.0
Other capital	0.1	0.6	0.1	0.4
Multifactor productivity growth (e.g., transformation)	0.8	2.2	0.5	1.2

[a] Contribution from labor quality for the United States is not reported, for Australia not available.

Source: Gruen (2001: 68 [Table 1]).

In both economies, labor productivity growth nearly doubled between the first and second half of the 1990s. In both economies, ICT investment is a large part of the story, with about one-third of labor productivity growth in the second half of the 1990s coming from investment in ICTs. That investment story is often what other policymakers see and want to emulate, but it represents only the beginning of the productivity story.

The more important driver of the gains of the new economy is how individuals, firms, markets, and governments using that technology transform what they do in that dynamic environment. In both economies, half of the increase in labor productivity comes from increased multifactor productivity. Multifactor productivity (MFP) measures how the economy uses its existing resources to produce more. An increase in MFP reflects the outcome of doing things differently in an economy, in order to get more output out of the same or fewer inputs (capital, equipment, labor). In other words, MFP is a proxy for restructuring and transformation. Going forward, it is the step-up in multifactor productivity that will enrich the economy and raise living standards, not just capital deepening represented by ICT investment in hardware and software.

Dynamic transformation in the new economy along with the importance of investment in ICT capital suggests the need for flexibility in business entry and exit, changes in job tenure and nature, and constant skill upgrading. These issues have important implications for the scope and method of government expenditures and rules for unemployment and pension benefits, on the one-hand, and education and training on the other.

3.   The Welfare State: Expenditures and Rules to Moderate Outcomes

There is a huge literature on what the welfare state is, a literature which cannot adequately be reviewed here, and which, in any case, is not monolithic in its characterization of what the welfare state *is*. However, in considering this literature in light of the essential ingredients of the new economy, two questions emerge:

- Transformation is integral to the economic gains of the new economy. How do tax and expenditure systems of the archetypal welfare state interact with the challenge of economic transformation?
- Information is an essential component of the new economy, yet it presents the policy challenge of market imperfections. How does the archetypal welfare states deal with market imperfections?

As a general characterization, the policies of the welfare state focus on ensuring stability for workers and the economy, rather than on encouraging the transformation of business and activities. To this end are regulations on hiring and firing, as well as on business entry and exit. Skill training for existing jobs may be excellent, but the incentive for taking-up new skills for new businesses is limited by the fact that new businesses are only slowly being created. The replacement wage under the unemployment regime is high, enabling extended periods of unemployment. Public sector employment is generally large, and may be used as a counter-cyclical tool. Pension systems are generous, and the incentives to work once the pensionable age is reached are minimal. Access to education and health care comes through universal provisioning by the government. Collectively, these public sector policies are expensive, requiring substantial tax revenues to support them. Moreover, the tax system plays a key role in the redistribution of income. So, the regulatory regime, the expenditure regime, and the tax regime all play roles in achieving the objective of the welfare state of a high degree of income equality and social cohesion. Individuals in the welfare state vote their preferences for both the tools and the outcomes as part of the political process.

With regard to problems of market imperfection, the archetypal welfare state intervenes through rules and regulations, rather than emphasizing market-based incentives to close the gap between private and social measures of cost (or benefit). The belief is that, if the objective is clear, rules and regulations to target the objective will reach it with greater certainty than leaving the outcome to chance or the interpretation of the marketplace. Moreover, market-based incentives may be applied differently across classes of workers and firms, which may contravene the overall objective of social equality. Once again, individuals in the welfare state vote their preferences for both the tools and outcomes as part of the political process.

Against this extremely simple backdrop description of the welfare state, the next two sections of the paper consider how the new economy forces affect policymakers in the two areas highlighted here: fiscal systems and treatment of personal information. The market-incentive system, as exemplified by United States policies, and the archetypal welfare state, as exemplified by European Union policies, are reviewed and compared in these two areas.[1]

4.   Evolution of Tax and Expenditure Systems in the New Economy

Global reach, value creation through information, product "bundling" and production alliances – key attributes of the new economy – put pressure on existing tax and expenditure systems. Policymakers can ignore or try to offset these pressures. But, a more proactive approach, which is the one being taken by the private sector in transforming its own business activities, is to consider how fiscal systems might need to evolve.[2]

Global reach implies a great overlap of national jurisdictions. International coordination of tax policies, though not necessarily homogenization of tax rates, will likely be necessary in the future. Policymakers need to consider carefully how best to target the tax (and other parts of the fiscal) system to meet revenue needs, citizens' needs, and any social objectives of the redistribution of income. In the end, the forces of the new economy may imply a fiscal system more focused on individual income taxation than on taxation of transactions or the corporation.

Value creation is increasingly complex. Are the product "bundles" goods or services, or both, or neither? Do sales generate business income or do leases generate royalties? Both indirect and direct tax systems that depend on knowing and distinguishing the "what, who, where, and how" of transactions will fit poorly the emerging reality of economic activity.

Greater mobility of firms and activities may make transactions more difficult to trace (or make the cost of doing so unrealistic or the erosion of privacy concomitant thereto unacceptable). This puts a greater premium on increasing the incentives for voluntary compliance and reducing the incentives for forum shopping both within and across jurisdictions.

---

[1]   The United States and European Union were chosen to clarify the economic issues through use of specific example. It is not the objective of this paper to be the definitive description of either U.S. or EU policies.

[2]   This section draws on Chapter 6 of Mann et al. (2000) and on Mann (2000).

On the plus side, the innovations of the Internet have great potential for reducing the cost of tax administration and for increasing the ability of the government to serve its constituents. Moreover, since the new economy promises higher productivity growth, tax revenues could rise without increased tax rates. In the end, the same level of social expenditures could be financed with lower tax burdens on account of the greater efficiency of fiscal administration and higher potential growth.

Yet, the current response by policymakers is to hold on to the status quo. Why? Many tax systems depend on indirect taxes, such as sales taxes, value-added taxes (VAT) or goods and services taxes (GST) to raise a substantial share of government revenues.[3] Thus, policymakers are concerned about the potential erosion of their tax revenue right now.[4] Firms and individuals want to know how much they need to pay and to whom. So, most analyses of new economy and tax tend to focus on the specifics of how to implement existing tax systems in a changing environment.

a.   What and How to Tax? The United States and European Union Compared

Various domestic and international groups have been discussing how to apply tax law to Internet and e-commerce transactions.[5] The most challenging areas are sales and value-added taxes, particularly when tax treatment of goods and services differs, when digitized transactions and activities cloud the determination of permanent establishment, and when the "character" of income earned (e.g., business

---

3   In the OECD, all the countries except the United States have or will soon have a VAT/ GST system. In the countries of the European Union (EU), VAT revenues account for about 30 percent of total tax revenues. In the US states, sales and goods taxes account for about 12 percent of total revenues, but range to much higher percentages in some states.

4   Efforts to measure the potential loss in tax revenues are difficult because of dynamic response. For the United States, Goolsbee and Zittrain (1999) calculate a loss over the next few years of less than 2 percent of sales tax revenues. For the full range of countries around the world, Teltscher (2000) also finds a loss of tax revenues of less than 1 percent overall, although the figure is higher for some countries.

5   Among international organizations, the OECD membership, in conjunction with non-member governments and private sector groups representing business and tax accountants, has since 1997 been analyzing how electronic commerce might impact international and domestic taxes. The outcome of that effort was the "Tax Framework Conditions," which reaffirms five key principles that guide governments generally in the application of taxes within the overall regime: neutrality, efficiency, certainty and simplicity, effectiveness and fairness, and flexibility. See http://www.oecd.org//daf/fa/e_ com/e_com.htm#top_e_commerce.

profits vs. royalty income) is unclear. Yet the challenge is not only the treatment of domestic transactions. What happens when transactions cross international borders and the tax treatment is different?[6]

Both the United States and the European Union have been struggling with how to apply sales taxes and value-added taxes to e-commerce transactions, both within and across borders.[7] Neither body fully recognizes that decisions taken in the domestic arena have implications for the cross-border application of these types of taxes. Inconsistent tax treatment of transactions between the United States and the European Union, and within each country as well, has already surfaced.

In the United States, when the Congress passed the Internet Tax Freedom Act in 1998 (which kept domestic Internet transactions free from any "new" taxes for three years but did not revoke existing sales taxes or use taxes), it mandated review of the implications of electronic commerce for domestic sales taxes. A majority of members of the Gilmore Commission proposed that digital products downloaded over the Internet (including software, books, or music) should not be taxed. In the interests of tax neutrality, their tangible equivalents should also be tax exempt. This represented a "harmonizing down" approach, which could generate pressures for lower sales tax rates overall in order to make more consistent the treatment of purchases over the Internet and through other means for products not explicitly exempted.

The Commission's proposal has implications for taxing authority and tax jurisdiction. Indeed, one objective of the Commission's proposal was to encourage states and localities to simplify their own structures and reduce the myriad state and local taxes (some 30,000), which are both administratively cumbersome and encourage tax-strategizing behavior.[8] Implications at the international level were

---

[6] See *The OECD Model Tax Convention*, which is a blueprint that many countries have used as a framework for bilateral tax treaties. It apportions tax responsibility and revenue so as to avoid double taxation of income earned through foreign investment. An overview is available at http://www.oecd.org//daf/fa/treaties/treaty.htm. See also: http://www.oecd.org//daf/fa/material/mat_07.htm#material_Model for the most recent information on the articles of the model convention.

[7] The VAT is a tax on supplies of goods and services applied at all stages of the production process. It is charged by the supplier and then credited by the users of the inputs in the course of doing business. Each transaction leaves an invoice path, so the VAT system essentially relies on "double-entry" bookkeeping by VAT-registered businesses on both sides of a transaction. The final consumer is not a VAT-registered entity, so ultimately pays the tax. The US sales tax system is different in that final users (usually retail) pay the tax, principally only on tangible property (with exceptions) and usually not on services. Business inputs generally are exempt from the tax.

[8] The National Governors Association is examining how to simplify their sales taxes and use taxes so as to apply computer technologies to tax administration. See Streamlined Sales Tax project http://www.nga.org/nga/newsRoom/1,1169,C_PRESS_RE-LEASE^D_1067,00.html, December 22, 2000.

not addressed, since the Commission did not have the mandate to address cross-border issues.

In contrast to the United States, the EU tax authorities are trying to draw a bright line between goods and services purchased over the Internet, and to a greater extent than the United States already have captured these transactions in their tax orbit. All electronic transmissions (those under the general term "soft goods," such as software, books, or architectural drawings) have been classified as services which, therefore, should be taxed at the appropriate VAT rate.[9] Whereas the EU ruling would seem to simplify and increase certainty in the tax environments, there are many different rules governing applicable location and rates for taxing services so the simplicity is part illusion. Moreover as the creation of product bundles becomes more complex, the bright line fades.[10]

Unlike the United States, which has not addressed the cross-border issue, the European Union has proposed that businesses both within and outside the European Union apply, collect, and remit VAT taxes on products (including software, books, and music) purchased or downloaded from the Internet by non VAT-registered entities.[11] The European Union has suggested that non-EU firms should establish their tax identity within an EU locality in order to determine which rate of tax to charge when selling such products business-to-business.[12] In essence, using the argument of tax neutrality, the European Union is "harmonizing up" by applying service-VAT rates to sales of all digital products and is proposing that non-EU firms become EU firms to establish a tax presence even if they do not need to establish such a presence for any other economic reason. This extra-territorial application of tax authority is a key jurisdictional challenge posed by digital transactions in the new economy.[13]

All told, the higher information content of bundles created in the global Internet marketplace will highlight disparities in tax systems and jurisdictions. The rates to apply to transactions, the jurisdiction to collect the tax, the party to remit

---

[9]   For an overview of the treatment of e-commerce transactions see http://europa.eu.int/scadplus/leg/en/lvb/l31041.htm.

[10]   For a different view, see Bach et al. (2000).

[11]   See "Europe Plans to Collect Tax on Some Internet Transactions" by Edmund L. Andrews, *New York Times*, March 2, 2000; http://www.nyt.com/library/tech/00/03/biztech/articles/02tax.html. The amount to date of "lost" tax revenue from such cross-border sales appears by all accounts to be miniscule. Of greater import, it appears, is the argued disadvantage of bricks-and-mortar stores vis-à-vis on-line merchants who have not had to collect VAT.

[12]   Document of the EU Commission regarding electronic commerce and indirect taxation: http://www.europa.eu.int/scadplus/leg/en/lvb/l31041.htm.

[13]   There are challenges to direct taxation as well. For a further discussion of these issues, which further supports the main points of the text, see Mann et al. (2000).

the tax, and the allocation of income to different governments will be increasingly difficult. Tax systems have been static, founded on rules formed incrementally by case law or infrequent multilateral negotiations. Continuing with this approach will yield an increasingly rules-driven and fragmented system that invites evasion and forum shopping, is costly to administer and is distortionary, and does not support the maximum benefits that can be achieved with the new economy. Policymakers should look to the future not hang on to the tax regimes of the past. So, what kind of domestic tax system and international tax agreement would raise revenues in an efficient, effective, and equitable manner?

b.   Tax to Better Match Jurisdiction of Tax and Expenditures

Among the ways to raise tax revenues, taxing labor's remuneration has probably been the least affected by the transformation of products, production processes, or marketplaces by the new economy. Labor, by and large, remains within the same political jurisdiction as the tax authority.[14] This matters because matching the jurisdiction of the tax regime to that of the provision of government services better allows the preferences of voters to be reflected in both tax rate and level of social expenditures. Moreover, in the knowledge-intensive new economy, the source of value-added is increasingly labor-based, rather than based on commodity resources or manufacturing processes. Taxing labor's wages avoids the issues of keeping track of location and number of transactions in the production chain or classifying the outcome of what the worker did in terms of good, service, or neither. All told, taxing worker income sidesteps the problems of the complexity of the product "bundle."

There also are potential savings in tax administration. First, there are fewer workers in the world than transactions, particularly when the current method of taxation is VAT. Firms pay close attention to how much they pay their workers and where their workers are located. Using methods that include reporting, auditing, or declaration, tax authorities can work with firms to ensure compliance. Moreover, tax authorities can work with firms that engage in cross-border transactions and production alliances to ensure the proper accounting for incomes earned. True, a firm must be willing to comply with an extraterritorial request for information about its workers' compensation. But, this is less onerous than actually collecting and remitting tax revenues. Private firms should not be the taxing authority, but they should cooperate with it.[15]

---

[14]   This is not to say that labor cannot move. But, it is relatively less mobile than firms, particularly at the margin. And, many highly skilled migrants will work for firms that are contained in the tax orbit of some jurisdiction.

[15]   Flows of information about wages and compensation between firms and the tax authority do raise privacy concerns.

The questions of fairness and compliance inevitably arise when labor income is taxed relatively more than consumption or capital income. Tax evasion is why many countries chose the VAT, GST, or tariff systems to begin with. These are not new issues, but the reduced ability to tax value added, transactions, or corporations raises the stakes for finding appropriate approaches to these issues, and charting a course toward changing tax regimes to reflect the new realities.

Under a new tax regime, the level of social expenditures can remain secure. But what about the choice of social expenditures? The essence of the new economy is the transformation of economic activities to achieve higher productivity growth: innovation, business entry and exit, workers moving between firms and staying in the labor force on their own terms because their skills are needed. What kind of social expenditures and regulation can enhance this transformation?

Voluminous analysis suggests that achieving an environment supportive of transformation is not obvious or easy.[16] The key points to be made in this essay are
- high levels of social spending are still possible, but the tax regime needs to evolve to support this;
- transformation of activities is key to the gains of the new economy, so social spending and regulation must encourage change in the environment of workers and firms, not try to inhibit or moderate change.

5.   Imperfections in the Market for Information

Networked information technologies and, increasingly, the information itself are driving the benefits of the Internet marketplace. For example, when all members of a global supply chain can follow the whole process on-line, operating efficiency increases, throughput quickens, and all members of the supply chain benefit from reduced inventory costs and increased quality. With more customer information, firms can meet detailed product preferences saving time and targeting demand more effectively, thus reducing the cost and annoyance of misdirected marketing. The marketplace, as well, functions more efficiently and effectively: when information from both buyers and sellers appears on a business-to-business auction site or exchange, better pricing of products (for example, office supplies), superior usage of equipment (for example, in trucking), and quicker elimination of excess (say of past-season fashion clothing) all are now possible. The opportunities of global electronic commerce created by information technologies increase the

---

[16]   See the extensive studies in OECD (1995, 1998, 2001).

value of information and the ease of obtaining valuable content. But, with this much information, the potential for misuse also arises.[17]

There is a tension between collectors of information, the relatively few firms that collect and aggregate information, and providers of information, the very many individual business or consumer users whose behavior and characteristics may or may not be collected with their acquiescence. Aggregators[18] highly value information because they can disect, combine, and either use or sell the information to others to produce better-tailored products and more efficient processes. These firms want to collect information from everyone and may ignore individual users who want fewer personal or unique business data collected. Under these circumstances, concerned users face an undesirable choice: use the Internet, but be fearful that the information collected may be used inappropriately; or do not use the Internet, and lose the benefits of this new medium for information and business activity.

a.   Comparing the "Market" vs. the "Mandate" Approach to Resolving the Imperfection

What is the role for policy intervention to balance these sides – the demands by individuals to control and protect their personal information against the promises of those who want it to create new products and services? Broadly, there are two approaches. Policymakers can *mandate* a specific standard that all firms must follow in collecting and using data. For example, the EU "privacy directive," characterized in general terms, mandates a specific standard for the treatment of most personal data of EU residents.[19] Or, policymakers can promote incentives so that the market innovates and improves the range of choices on whether and how data are collected, compiled, and cross-referenced. The U.S. approach, characterized broadly, in which legislation addresses only financial, medical, and children's information, and where private entities determine and adhere to self-regulatory guidelines, is an example of a more market-oriented approach.

Is there a winner (in an economic sense) between the mandate and the market approach to balancing the benefits of information use with the concerns over the use of data? The economic theory of the second best suggests that the market so-

---

[17]   For more discussion of the nature of information as a "public good" in the Internet marketplace, see Mann et al. (2000: 37–41).

[18]   Aggregators include firms that collect data for their own line of business. They may also sell the data to other aggregators whose principal objective is to analyze click-stream data.

[19]   Correctly termed, European Directive on Protection of Personal Data, July 25, 1995.

lution and the mandate solution cannot be ranked. In neither case will the needs of all individuals be met, nor can we be sure that society's well-being is maximized.

On the one hand, because there are many users and few aggregators, the market approach is likely to yield an incomplete set of "information-use" policies. So the privacy preferences of each unique user may not be met. What are the consequences? Consider a business example. Suppose a firm worries so much about revealing strategic business information by participating in a B2B marketplace that it refuses to participate. Not only is this firm worse off, the benefits of having such an exchange are reduced by having fewer participants. More generally, the value of the Internet derives from its participants, and increases exponentially with the number of users. So if a fear of participating reduces participation, this exponentially reduces the benefits of the Internet to both individuals and to society.

On the other hand, the mandate solution is a "one-size-fits-all" policy which assumes that each person or business has the same preference over use of information as is spelled out in the mandate. Because people and businesses are not all alike in their attitudes toward privacy, some specific preferences may not be met. In this case, those left out would probably disclose more information to get more tailored products and services. With a mandate policy, some buyers and sellers will not bother to log on. As in the case above, the value of the Internet is reduced exponentially because the number of participants falls.

Which policy approach results in the greater number of unhappy users? This is unknown, which is why the alternative policies cannot be ranked in terms of their impact on efficiency or society's well-being.

What is the difference between the two approaches? Under the market approach, firms continue to face incentives to try to satisfy specific and heterogeneous privacy demands, particularly if those demands are effectively communicated to the information aggregators and are backed by enforcement – points where government intervention could be valuable. The incentives come from the very network benefits (translated into potential profits) that are lost if the privacy options are insufficient and users defect. By contrast, under the mandate approach, the private sector has fewer incentives to innovate to resolve market imperfections, since there are common rules for all to follow, and the enforcement issue remains.

b.   What about the Safe Harbor Approach?

Beyond the theory of these alternatives and how they might work within the domestic marketplace is the important issue of the overlap of government jurisdictions. What happens when the economic marketplace encompasses users and aggregators in both jurisdictions? One example of a bridge between the two different approaches to privacy protection is the March 14, 2000, "safe-harbor" agreement between the United States and European Union.[20] Under the agreement, American firms receiving personal data from the European Union can subscribe to guidelines promulgated by self-regulatory organizations such as the Better Business Bureau's BBB*OnLine*, thereby making a commitment to follow the EU rules for data on EU individuals. The firms could be subject to legal action by the U.S. Federal Trade Commission if they do not abide by their commitment.

Does "safe harbor" represent an interoperable approach?[21] It would appear to ensure continuity of U.S.-EU cross-border data flows, but this is actually a different problem than that of the adequate provision of privacy alternatives. Moreover, countries not party to the safe-harbor agreement wonder what will happen to their firms. Must they follow the EU "privacy directive"? Can they enter the U.S. safe harbor by following the U.S. Department of Commerce guidelines? Do they need to carve out their own agreement – if so with whom? Without a common understanding about how to treat information, the possibility remains that cross-border data flows could be fragmented, routed around some countries and through other countries, with the potential for great loss to efficiency and global network benefits. More important than data-flows, the safe-harbor arrangement between the United States and the European Union does not yield new privacy options for users, which is the true crux of the matter.

In such a technologically dynamic environment, retaining the incentive for private sector innovation is crucial. The market-oriented approach and technological entrepreneurship offer the greatest potential to come up with innovative solutions to meet the great variety of privacy demands. Innovations such as Anonymizer and Pretty Good Privacy (PGP) come from individual firms. The Platform for Privacy Preferences (P3P) is the outcome of an industry-group discussion and could become a standard feature on Internet browsers.

Will the combination of market incentives and technological prowess be sufficient to generate a full set of privacy solutions to meet all needs? Policymakers in the United States (where the market-oriented policy approach is strongest) must push harder to get firms to respond to market demands for privacy alternatives. One way is to threaten with restrictive legislation if consumer demands for privacy options are ignored and opportunities to improve information-use policies squandered. For example, the plethora of privacy legislation put forward before the U.S. Congress in 2001 threatened the market-oriented approach, although did not yield mandated standards. A more active statement by policymakers is needed and clearer threats outlined if the private sector is to respond appropriately.

---

[20] See www.doc.com/safeharbor for the U.S. presentation of the agreement.

[21] For additional discussion of Safe Harbor, see Farrell (forthcoming).

6.   Final Observations: Evolving Concept of What the Welfare State Is

The benefits from the new economy can be gained only through transforming the activities of individuals, business, and governments. A key component of those gains is a closer alignment of the interests of the consumer and the producer, which implies information-intensity and greater heterogeneity in product "bundles." Policymakers need to allow for these transformations, for the intensive use of information, and for heterogeneity in output.

However, these aspects of the new economy can cause problems for the archetypal welfare state. First, transformation of activities will, at least for some time, engender volatility in employment and businesses, and differential returns to skills, among other things. To the extent that the archetypal welfare state smoothes out these changes, either the transformation may not occur or the cost of smoothing them out could be quite high in terms of income support. Second, information is a key ingredient to the transformation and the creation of heterogeneous product bundles. To the extent that the archetypal welfare state mandates a uniform approach to the use of information, taking the view that it knows best what its constituents want, the heterogeneity in interests will not emerge to inform the marketplace.

How might the old welfare state evolve into the new welfare state for the new economy? To reduce the costs of transformation, the key is labor force policies and business market policies. The new welfare state for the new economy will focus even more on policies that allow workers and firms to take advantage of opportunities coming from change, rather than focusing on moderating outcomes and avoiding change. A high level of government spending commitment to these objectives can be met through an evolving tax environment that will ultimately focus more on taxing income and less on taxing transactions.

To reduce the potential for misuse of information while also allowing the value of heterogeneity to emerge, the new welfare state should focus on preserving the private sector's incentives to innovate. At the same time, the government can play a role in informing citizens about their choices, and enforce the private sector's commitments when necessary. Individuals need to know more about what the value of their information is and how it can be used. Firms need to be held responsible for information use, and enforcement of mis-action must be swift. Because only the primate sector can evolve new strategies for both using and protecting information – preserving the incentives to innovate is paramount.

The new welfare state will be characterized more by incentives and responsibilities. The public sector needs to promote incentives so that the private sector – defined either as an individual or as a business – works to transform the economy, to close the market imperfections in information, and to manage the problems of cross-border jurisdictional overlap in tax regimes. The private sector – as individuals and firms – must be willing to take advantage of training, education, and business assistance so that it can adjust, must be willing to work with the public sector to pay for such activities, and must come up with strategies that meet the demands for a fuller range of information-use options. This is not the end of the welfare state, it is a welfare state for a dynamic environment that focuses on enabling transition to achieve superior productivity and growth, rather than one that focuses on moderating outcomes and attenuating possibilities. It is much better to ensure that a sailor has a good yacht and good training to sail the sea during exciting weather rather than to relegate him/her to a stagnant pond.

References

Bach, S., M. Hubbert, and W. Müller (2000). Taxation of E-Commerce: Persistent Problems and Recent Development. *Vierteljahrshefte zur Wirtschaftsforschung* (4): 657–678.

Farrell, H. (forthcoming). Negotiating Privacy across Arenas – The EU-US "Safe Harbor" Discussions. In A. Héritier (ed.), *Common Goods: Reinventing European and International Governance.* Lanham, Maryland: Rowman and Littlefield.

Goolsbee, A., and J. Zittrain (1999). Evaluating the Costs and Benefits of Taxing Internet Commerce. *National Tax Journal* 52(3): 413–428.

Gruen, D. (2001). Australias' Strong Productivity Growth: Will It Be Sustained? Reserve Bank of Australia Bulletin, February.

Mann, C.L. (2000). Transatlantic Issues in Electronic Commerce. Working Paper 00–7. Institute for International Economics, Washington, D.C. Available at www.iie.com. Also translated in Italian in *Il WTO dopo Seattle: Scenari a confronto,* edited by I. Falautano and P. Guerrieri and published as IAI Quaderni No. 12, October 2000, Rome.

Mann, C.L., S.E. Eckert, and S. Cleeland Knight (2000). *Global Electronic Commerce: A Policy Primer.* Washington, D.C.: Institute for International Economics.

OECD (1995). *Jobs Study.* Paris: OECD.

OECD (1998). *Fostering Entrepreneurship.* Paris: OECD.

OECD (2001). *The New Economy: Beyond the Hype.* Paris: OECD.

Shapiro, C., and H.R. Varian (1999). *Information Rules: A Strategic Guide to the Network Economy.* Boston: Harvard Business School Press.

Teltscher, S. (2000). Revenue Implications of Electronic Commerce: Issues of Interest to Developing Countries. Mimeo. UNCTAD, April 2000.

Comment on Catherine L. Mann

Rüdiger Soltwedel

In her paper, Catherine Mann looks at the tax and expenditure systems for financing public goods (with a specific view at the welfare state) and at market imperfections with respect to information privacy both of which are under the gun in the new economy.

The starting point of the paper is that, in the new economy, intangible assets and products as well as digitized services can be provided by remote suppliers; due to the bundling of tangibles and intangibles and strategic alliances around the globe it will be increasingly difficult to determine exactly where (in a geographical sense) and when (in terms of the stage of production and bundling) value is created. This entails important implications for the "what, who, where and how" in a transaction-based tax system (Mann, this volume, p. 87). Her suggestion is that the tax system should be changed to rely more on direct taxation and, in doing so, should give more emphasis on taxing labor income. The (European) archetypal welfare state would have to give way to an institutional environment that is more conducive to the adjustment to changes "that allow workers and firms to take advantage of opportunities coming from change, rather than focusing on moderating outcomes and avoiding change." (Mann, this volume, p. 96).

Furthermore, the paper looks at the challenges that result from the specificities of the good "information" and the imperfections in the market for information with regard to privacy and the use of personal information. The flip side of the huge opportunities of global electronic commerce is the potential misuse of individual information, i.e., the inappropriate use of private information that may result in a suboptimal exploitation of network economies and, hence, a slowing down in the pace of innovation. In order to restrict inappropriate use of personal information but, at the same time, keep the innovative momentum of the system, Catherine Mann prefers a concept of rather general framework guidelines set by the government within which firms compete in offering the customers a range of choices for protecting their privacy to a concept where policymakers define specific (mandatory) standards. In my comment, I will not go into the information-privacy issue since I have strong sympathy with her market-driven approach.

In claiming "that transaction-based tax regimes ... will need to evolve in response to the more complex and global nature of production" (Mann, this volume, p. 82), Catherine Mann certainly makes a valid point, all the more so as virtually all international commerce involving business-to-business (B2B) transactions – the vast majority of all international trade – will be affected (McLure 2000: 10).[1] The IC-driven new general purpose technology will broaden and deepen the networking in international business activities and will give the international division of labor an additional boost. The behavior of internationally active firms exerts substantial pressure on governments: Since long, these firms have been exploiting tax burden differentials by appropriately setting transfer prices for transactions within their realm of activity. In particular, they often strategically shape the pattern of expenditure: the incidence of high expenditure of those firms correlates positively with tax rates. Moreover, if subsidiaries are subject to high corporate taxes, the mother companies tend to take recourse to bank loans instead of using equity to reduce the tax burden (Jacobs and Spengel: 1996). This sort of strategic behavior with the aim of tax minimization will be further strengthened by the new economy because value creation is becoming "increasingly complex" and a "greater mobility of firms and activities may make transactions more difficult to trace" (Mann, this volume, p. 87).

It may be argued that the level of taxation alone is not decisive for firms' decisions where to locate. Rather, this level in relation to those benefits provided to firms in the form of public services is the relevant criterion. Nations, or rather: governments compete for internationally mobile factors also on the basis of their performance capabilities, e.g., infrastructure, legal protections, and social climate. A high level of taxation turns out to be a disadvantage when the private gains from these services are too low. In other words, benefit taxation may sustain potentially quite substantial differentials in tax rates without discouraging foreign investment or inducing a flight of domestic sources of internationally mobile investment funds. However, free riding on benefits may become easier in the Internet age, making this benefit taxation argument less relevant over time.

The international integration (or name it globalization) of markets fosters institutional and locational competition. The increasing competitive pressure entails the beneficial function of controlling government behavior not to excessively provide public goods but to provide (only) those public goods that really have benefits for the citizens and firms and to provide these efficiently. Thus, globalization and the new economy raise the pressure for policymakers to do their job right. Tax competition in such a situation means that government should rethink the balance

---

[1]   This aspect certainly is more important than the loss in tax revenue that may result from on-line shopping of consumers (business-to-consumers; B2C). Projections of the future evolution of e-commerce vary broadly in magnitude and reflect a clear withering of e-commerce euphoria over time, but what seems to hold is the assessment that the share of B2B is by far higher than the one of B2C: "The largest share of e-commerce takes place between businesses (at present, they account for 70 to 85 per cent of all electronic sales) and B2B e-commerce is expected to experience more rapid progression than B2C over the next few years" (Coppel 2000: 7).

in providing the appropriate amount and structure of public goods, should rethink the role of government at large. Redefining the role and the size of government could entail a reduction in expenditure and, hence, financing requirements, and thus allow for a reduction in the tax burden.

In her suggestion of changing the traditional tax and expenditure systems, Catherine Mann envisages a more important role for taxing the most immobile factor of production, i.e. labor. Her recommendation is to shift the tax system from the emphasis on indirect taxation towards direct taxation: "Taxing labor's wages avoids the issues of keeping track of location and number of transactions in the production chain or classifying the outcome of what the worker did in terms of good, service, or neither. All told, taxing worker income sidesteps the problems of the complexity of the product 'bundle'" (Mann, this volume, p. 91). Whether these assertions hold for Germany is, however, an open question.

Germany – apart from having too high a government involvement in, and interference with, the economy and therefore too high an overall tax burden – used to have a particular emphasis on direct taxation, namely income and profit taxation. From the outset, the orientation on income has caused the pursuit of a systemically poorly conceived concept. Subsequently, there was hardly any system orientation left, having been replaced by the pursuit of "particularity" and of "pragmatism." The tax code had degenerated into the favorite toy for pursuing the most diverse economic and socio-political aims, resulting in a chaotic jumble of regulations. The tax code had become incomprehensible to the average citizen (and often to firms as well, in particular to SMEs who have to pay the highest compliance costs). Selective amendments through which the system was adapted to changing conditions in the world economy as well as to German unification have complicated the system even more. In view of these weaknesses and their consequences in the locational competition for investment, the need for a thoroughgoing tax reform had become most urgent especially in the area of direct taxation. Academics in Germany have largely suggested a paradigm shift toward taxing expenditures with the objective of a low overall tax burden, a broader tax base and low rates. In the political arena, there was a response to the need for a reform, but it fell short of the more far-reaching objective of the academic critics.

Furthermore, it is open to doubt whether labor compensation really is the ample inelastic source for future tax revenue, at least in Germany. To a large extent, the welfare state is already financed by reducing the take-home-pay of workers, mainly by the employee and employer contributions to social security and unemployment insurance. We ought not forget that there has been an intense discussion about the disincentive effects of the German tax and transfer system, about emigration of capital and labor. The degree to which labor is mobile seems to have increased over the last two decades or so. There has been a lot of anecdotal evidence about the exodus of the elite, i.e., the declining attractiveness of Germany for the ranks with the highest qualifications. And there is more evidence of the out-migration into the black economy.[2] If Catherine Mann's suggestion were to be implemented at face value, this out-migration might be given an additional impetus. Her suggestions would obstruct the zeal in reforming the welfare state towards making the recipients of welfare benefits accept more readily work and/or increase their work efforts.

There can be no doubt that the new economy will have profound impacts upon the tax and expenditure system and will make it more difficult for governments to collect taxes. Catherine Mann's concern to deal with the challenges of the new technology and its impacts upon doing business is highly relevant. Her suggestions to tax labor more heavily, though, leave many questions open. That there is a lot of food for thought but not yet a ready-to-use recipe in the academic debate has been shown by Stehn (2002). But, as the evolution of the new economy has just started and will take time, there is no need to hurry with decision making. In any event, we may read the message of Catherine Mann's paper in a similar vein as the advice by Hal Varian (that he made with respect to adapting sales and use taxes): "Instead of adding another patch of poorly designed and inefficient system, it would make more sense to use the current attention being paid to sales taxes as an opportunity to make some fundamental changes" (2000: 9).

There is, however, one particular issue in Catherine Mann's suggestions that is highly relevant for Germany, and perhaps Europe as a whole: The archetypal welfare state needs fundamental reform to give incentives for adjustments to change instead of securing the financial means to resist change: "Transformation of activities is key to the gains of the new economy, so social spending and regulation must encourage change in the environment of workers and firms, not try to inhibit or moderate change" (Mann, this volume, p. 92). This is a long-standing discussion in Germany, with abounding academic advice[3] and little acceptance by the beneficiaries of the welfare state, or even the electorate at large, and, hence, hardly a powerful political force to implement fundamental reforms. Perhaps more of a crisis is needed in public finance to raise the costs of inertia and make the need for change more obvious.

---

[2]   Most probably, it is the high level of (direct plus indirect) taxes as such that is conducive to moonlighting; however, while a high level of indirect taxation may have a stronger effect on the decision whether to consume or to save (and, certainly, on "do-it-yourself"), a high level of direct taxation is important for the question whether or not to work in the official economy.

[3]   See the annual reports of the Council of Economic Experts in Germany or Soltwedel (1997) for a comprehensive overview of a systemic reform.

References

Coppel, J. (2000). E-commerce: Impacts and Policy Challenges. OECD Economics Department Working Papers 252. Paris.

Jacobs, O.H., and C. Spengel (1996). Aspekte einer Reform der Unternehmensbesteuerung in Europa. In H. Siebert (Ed.), *Steuerpolitik und Standortqualität. Expertisen zum Standort Deutschland.* Tübingen: Mohr Siebeck.

McLure, C. (2000). Alternatives to the Concept of Permanent Establishment. *CESifo Forum* (3): 10 – 16.

Soltwedel, R. (1997). Dynamik der Märkte – Solidität des Sozialen. Leitlinien für eine Reform der Institutionen. Kiel Diskussionsbeiträge 297/298. Institut für Weltwirtschaft, Kiel.

Stehn, J. (2002). Leviathan in Cyberspace: How to Tax E-Commerce. Kiel Discussion Papers 384. Institute for World Economics, Kiel.

Varian, H. (2000). Taxation of Electronic Commerce – A U.S. View. *CESifo Forum* (3): 3 – 9.

II.
Microeconomics
in the New Economy

Norbert Berthold and Rainer Fehn

Labor Market Policy in the New Economy

1. Introduction

When will the new economy arrive in Germany and boost productivity and employment as it has done in the United States over the last decade? This has certainly been one of the more frequently asked questions in Germany recently, a question which is vexing policymakers and economists alike, in particular as Germany is once again at the bottom of growth rates even among Euro-area countries. However, the recent downturn in the U.S. economy has raised doubt about whether the German labor market will ever benefit to a comparable extent as the U.S. labor market from a badly needed positive new economy effect. This skepticism is justified even though the recent slowdown in growth in the United States might turn out to be short-lived and mainly of cyclical nature, thus possibly not reflecting deeply rooted structural weaknesses and imbalances (Bosworth 2001). The key problem in Germany and also in the other large continental European countries like France, Italy, and Spain appears to be structural rigidities and an institutional framework which is not well suited to cope with the completely new economic environment which is nowadays often dubbed the new economy. As long as major structural changes toward a more flexible and employment-oriented institutional setup are not initiated, it seems unlikely that the old world will fully benefit from an invigorating new economy effect, thus falling again substantially behind compared to the United States. Naturally, given its title, this paper deals mainly with the labor market aspects of the new economy and with its consequences for labor market policy.

The dismal situation in labor markets in Germany and several other large continental European countries is by no means a new phenomenon, though. Rather, unemployment has ratcheted upwards since the mid-1970s and most of the existing unemployment is of a structural nature (Siebert 1997). Thus, merely expanding aggregate goods demand is not a promising route for improving labor market performance. Much has been written about continental European unemployment

Remark: We thank the participants in the Paderborn conference and especially Michael Burda, Holger Fricke, Michael Neumann, Oliver Stettes, and Sascha von Berchem for helpful comments without implicating them.

and about the enormous political difficulties in implementing the structural reforms which are a prerequisite for achieving lasting progress on the labor market front (Saint-Paul 1998; Berthold and Fehn 1996a). Such necessary reforms affect a wide range of policy areas, such as labor, goods and capital markets, and the social security and tax systems.

It is usually argued that entrenched insiders in the labor market lose from such structural reforms and that they therefore fiercely resist actually implementing them. However, while intuitively plausible, this type of reasoning has lost some of its appeal due to recent economic developments. The choice for insiders is not between maintaining the status quo or losing in the short to medium run due to structural reforms. Rather, the 1990s have witnessed drastic changes in the international economic environment, so-called globalization along with the arrival of the new economy, which evidently makes maintaining the status quo an unstable and unfeasible policy option. Although it is still a bit early for a definitive judgment, the new economy seems to have spawned something like a new Kondratieff cycle, so that countries which are not able to adjust their institutional settings adequately will invariably fall behind. The dichotomy in economic developments in the 1990s between especially the United States and possibly also some European countries such as the United Kingdom, Ireland, Switzerland, and the Netherlands on the one hand, and the laggard continental European countries Germany, France, Italy, and Spain on the other hand justifies such an assessment.

The arrival of the new economy seems to have at least interrupted the long-term process of convergence in per capita income among the highly developed OECD countries. The United States has spurted ahead again in terms of GNP growth although it already had the highest per capita income of the large OECD countries at the beginning of the 1990s. Similarly, while employment stagnated or even fell in a country like Germany, the United States managed to achieve large-scale employment growth in the 1990s, mainly in the service sector, in the information technology (IT) industry, the biotech sector, and in knowledge-based industries in general. Much of this employment growth has come about via the creation of new firms. Contrary to a widespread prejudice in continental Europe, many of the newly created jobs are well paid, involving people who have the skills needed in these fledgling economic sectors or in old economy firms which make use of the new technologies (Acemoglu 1999). High up on the list of requirements for such people are proficiency with computers, and verbal, cognitive, and communicative skills, along with a great versatility in performing different tasks and in working in teams (OECD 1999a). To be sure, the United States has also created a large number of low-skilled jobs, the so-called "hamburger flipping jobs," which are often hardly sufficient to support a family. Hence, income differentiation has widened considerably although the United States is trying to keep the working poor problem in check with the Earned Income Tax Credit System, which supplements low market incomes via the tax system. The historically almost unique boom in the 1990s has certainly helped to mitigate the working poor problem in the United States.

Continental Europe and especially Germany need both, more skilled employment and more job opportunities for unskilled workers. It is impossible or prohibitively expensive to qualify everybody with the skills needed by the new technological production methods. Nonetheless, labor market policy has to play a key role in raising the number of people with the skills needed by firms nowadays. In order to discuss the kind of labor market policies needed by the new economy, this paper is organized as follows. Chapter 2 describes how the new economy affects the labor market. Chapter 3 lays out the implications that the new economy has for labor market policy. Chapter 4 provides conclusions.

2.   How Does the New Economy Affect the Labor Market?

There is no precise definition of what the new economy really is, and it is also unclear whether the new economy measures up to the second industrial revolution of 1860–1900, which made a golden age of productivity growth possible and which was based on a number of great inventions ranging from electricity, motor and air transport, motion pictures, radio, chemical products, medicine, etc. (Gordon 2000; Nordhaus 2001; Jorgenson and Stiroh 2000). However, technological progress in information and communications technology, data processing, the almost complete computerization of working life, the widespread use of the Internet, and the growing importance of human capital appear to constitute integral parts of the new economy. The new economy, furthermore, seems to be characterized by greater network and economies of scale effects, thus potentially raising labor productivity. Economies of scale effects are due to very high fixed costs of developing new products along with extremely low variable costs of producing additional units and positive network externalities. This assessment is especially valid with respect to information products (Issing 2000; Siebert 2000; Baily and Lawrence 2001).

The new economy effect was the most pronounced in the United States during the 1990s, where the speed limit for growth and the critical threshold for the unemployment rate before inflationary forces are unleashed seem to have changed for the better due basically to a nonnegligible positive supply shock which apparently reduced the NAIRU from 6 percent to around 4 percent in the course of the last decade (Bosworth and Triplett 2000). No clear-cut new economy effect has yet been detected for any European country, although they differ widely in adopting new technologies, with especially the southern European countries and, as a matter of fact, Germany also lagging behind (Daveri 2000). Hence, most Scandinavian countries, along with the United Kingdom, the Netherlands, Switzerland, and Ireland seem to have a greater potential for a positive new economy effect from this perspective. Considering that the IT technologies which foster the new economy are equally available among OECD countries, there can be little doubt that the stark differences in their widespread adoption must be largely related to institutional differences which facilitate or obstruct the development of a new economy. The new economy in the United States has to a great extent come about via the creation of new firms and innovative products. Hence, entrepreneurial spirit and incentives must be sufficiently developed, along with an institutional setting which does not unnecessarily obstruct risky investments in any way, such as via red tape, via high firing costs, or via underdeveloped venture capital markets.

The economic environment has changed drastically in the course of the last two decades. While the postwar decades were characterized by a period of fairly stable economic and employment growth, things have become much more unstable since the mid-1970s to early 1980s. Political decisions to tear down trade barriers and to open up capital accounts for international capital flows, along with revolutionary technological developments, have triggered an unprecedented process of globalization which has made the world almost like a village. With the possible exception of Africa, countries are linked via a dense web of trade relations and capital flows which makes them mutually interdependent.[1] It seems pretty clear in hindsight that those countries benefited most from the globalization process which were the quickest and the most determined in opening up their borders for trade and somewhat less clear for capital flows, such as many Southeast Asian countries. However, globalization also has a downside, e.g., it has created a more volatile economic environment with greater and more frequent shocks (Bertola and Ichino 1995; Ljungqvist and Sargent 1998). Furthermore, contagion effects in the course of financial crises have become more likely, as has been demonstrated, e.g., by the Asian crisis. Not all economies are equally well prepared to cope with the resulting diminished stability of labor demand.

Not only the stability of labor demand has fallen, but the structure of labor demand has also changed. Labor demand is shrinking in the highly developed OECD countries in the industrial sector, while it is expanding in the service sector, in the information technology sector, in the biotech sector, and more generally in knowledge-based industries (SVR 2000). Furthermore, the regional concentration of labor demand within countries is growing due possibly to the increasing importance of local technological spillovers and positive agglomeration and network effects. German reunification is a special case of regionally concentrated labor demand due to a political shock. Finally, the development of labor demand with respect to

---

[1]   Such economic mutual interdependence breeds peaceful behavior, as could be witnessed during the crisis between the United States and China during the recent Hainan incident.

skills differs greatly in the highly developed OECD countries. Whereas labor demand for skilled workers is growing overall, labor demand for unskilled workers is falling, thus worsening their income and employment opportunities. The changing nature of the skills which are required by firms makes high adaptability, along with life-long learning, of the workforce more important. This requirement of workers is reinforced by shorter product life and production cycles.

While these changes in the structure of labor demand are almost undisputed and are clearly reflected in unemployment statistics across OECD countries, it is still an open question whether globalization or skill-biased technological progress is the main driving force for these developments. Technological progress has certainly become more rapid and is biased in favor of skilled workers but technological progress and globalization are simply too closely interrelated in order to clearly draw the line. Advancements in communication technology and reductions in transportation costs were probably a prerequisite for the globalization of economic transactions, and this globalization in turn enhanced the speed of skill-biased technological progress. In any case, it is usually argued that due to both processes it has become harder for unskilled workers to find decently paid jobs in the highly developed OECD countries. Opening up the EU to the East is likely to further accentuate all of these developments in Western Europe, in particular the regional concentration of labor demand and the imbalance between labor demand for and labor supply of unskilled workers.

However, it is not as clear as is often assumed that the bottom end of the income distribution will lose due to the new economy, which is largely based on innovative IT products. Information becomes more easily available due to IT, thus increasing competition between knowledge producers and enlarging their markets. Some of the knowledge producers will win, others will lose, while nonknowledge producers at the bottom end could even gain in the end in absolute terms if they are not easily replaced by IT-based production. This is the case because they are primarily consumers of IT-based knowledge, which should become cheaper relative to other goods. Demand for non-IT-based services will most likely persist. It does not therefore make sense even from this equity perspective to artificially try to qualify everybody to become an IT-knowledge producer; besides it is questionable whether such a far-fetched attempt would be feasible (Saint-Paul 2001).

It is by no means only formal qualifications which matter more now than in the past for being hired and for moving up on the career ladder. So-called soft skills are clearly gaining ground (Lindbeck and Snower 1997, 1998, 2000; Snower 1997). The IT revolution and the omnipresence of computers in firms have fundamentally transformed the production process in favor of flexibility, teamwork, and multitasking. Specialization of employees on certain well-defined tasks as in the Tayloristic or Fordistic mode of production is increasingly obsolete. Rather, employees are now expected to perform multiple tasks and to use their proficiency in one task to increase their productivity in other tasks. There is considerable empirical evidence that the post-Fordistic or holistic organization of firms and the widespread "job rotation" it engenders is now becoming predominant, thus changing substantially the skill requirements of firms. Physical strength and the flawless execution of repetitive actions is nowadays much less important to firms than creativity, the ability to work with computers, to manage a wide range of different tasks, to solve problems independently, to work in a team (which requires communicative skills and social competence). Language skills and international mobility have also become more important due to the globalization process. Persons with the same formal qualifications might differ a lot in these various respects, so that they are also valued very differently by firms. Concerning economic policy, the big question is of course, what is the best, i.e., the most cost-efficient way of equipping people with the various skills required by firms so that they will not end up in the low-skill, bad-job trap.

Supervision of workers by firms has become more difficult, thus raising motivation and efficiency wage problems. As the importance of investments in human capital and of quasi rents has grown, it is essential nowadays for firms to have workers who are themselves highly motivated to excel and to contribute to the overall success of their firms. Hence, the classical dichotomy between managers or entrepreneurs, who make the decisions, and workers, who diligently execute these decisions with as little room for discretionary maneuvering as possible, is becoming increasingly blurred. Any modern firm which wants to benefit from the full potential of its skilled workforce needs to get its employees involved in decentralized decision making, thus providing them with a strong incentive to make their team, their profit center and in the end their firm successful (OECD 1999a; Bickenbach and Soltwedel 1998). This allows the badly needed quicker reactions to the nowadays rapidly changing market conditions and also allows production which fits the more heterogeneous demands of customers better. Ensuring homogeneous products of high quality via centralized supervision has become less important due to the almost complete automatization and computerization of nonetheless relatively flexible production lines (Black and Lynch 2000).

While in the past firms constituted an island of central planning in a wide sea of market forces according to R. Coase, such market forces are nowadays gaining substantial ground even within firms which are now flatter and less hierarchically structured. Decentralized, relatively small, and customer-oriented teams with a changing composition of people form profit centers and these profit centers compete with each other for scarce resources. Hence, the task of top management is increasingly becoming restricted to making strategic decisions and to implementing the appropriate organizational structure in their firms, while daily decisions are delegated to local profit centers and teams. The big leaps in productivity in the 1990s in the United States do not at least seem to be based on people working much harder than before, but rather on technological developments and on new institutional frameworks which enable people to work differently. Market forces are driving firms toward greater sharing of authority, risk, and rewards (Freeman 2000).

Interestingly, these changes in the organization of production seem to have also altered the comparative advantage of women compared to men as regards household activities and working on formal jobs. Women are more likely to possess the skills which are now increasingly demanded by firms, compared to say physical strength which used to be more important in the past. As early as when they were hunters, men became more specialized in activities making use of their greater physical strength, while household activities of women inevitably involved more multitasking. Furthermore, teaching children how to communicate and educating children has accustomed women to solving complex incentive problems and has possibly equipped them on average with greater social competence. Hence, the rapidly increasing integration of women into formal jobs in many OECD countries is not only the result of greater labor supply by women, but probably also stems from greater demand by firms for the specific skills of women. Countries, such as Germany, which lag quite a bit behind in this respect, not least due to an institutional framework which makes it difficult to combine having a family with working on a formal job, are therefore likely to forgo substantial growth opportunities.

It has in any case become more important for countries to have a workforce at their disposal which is skilled in a broad sense, versatile, adaptable and mobile. Much more than in the past, workers themselves need to become small entrepreneurs in order to be successful. The formerly relatively clear-cut distinction between labor and leisure, between office and home, is becoming increasingly blurred by the new economy, thus transforming society in a quite fundamental way and requiring new institutional arrangements. This increases especially the importance of life-long learning, but also the opportunity set for combining family and work which is particularly beneficial to women.

The changes brought about by the arrival of the new economy concerning in particular the labor market create both an enlarged opportunity set for countries and a higher adjustment burden. Countries which are characterized by a rigid or ill-designed institutional framework for labor, goods and capital markets, and have social security and tax systems which grossly reduce work incentives and stifle entrepreneurial activity, not only forgo the potential benefits of the new economy, e.g., for employment and per capita GNP growth, but may actually face deteriorating employment performance. Hence, the capacity to adjust such an ill-designed institutional framework is crucial for tapping the potential benefits of the new economy. Especially flexible relative prices, such as flexible real wage costs for firms and flexible wage structures with respect to regions, sectors, and qualifications, are becoming crucial. If relative prices are rigid and if workers are furthermore not able to adjust fast enough by being mobile and by enhancing their human capital, growing unemployment is kind of an inevitable result. In particular the large continental European countries seem to have trodden down this path into limbo during the 1990s, while the United States appears to have entered into a virtuous circle which has only very recently come to a possibly temporary halt. Given the fact that rising unemployment produces an unsustainable situation sooner or later, the question inevitably arises which kind of policy changes in particular concerning the labor market could help the lackluster continental European countries to escape the current vicious circle in favor of a virtuous circle.

3.   Implications of the New Economy for Labor Market Policy

Labor market policy must primarily be aimed at two key objectives in the age of the new economy. First, the institutional framework in the labor market must be designed to at least come close to fully exploiting the potential for productivity and employment growth which is created by the new economy. This affects in particular the degree of centralization of wage bargaining, decision making within firms, and firing costs. Second, it is sometimes argued that the new economy, along with the heralded IT revolution, could trigger a digital divide and an apartheid economy between those who are successful in the new economy and are sufficiently proficient at using IT and those who are not up to mastering its challenges (Freeman 2000). Labor market policy should aim at preventing such a damaging development. However, providing people with the respective skills and qualifications via active labor market policies is at most a second-best policy instrument. The foundations for being successful in the new economy are laid much earlier, namely, when children are attending the education system and when being educated by one's parents. Improving and adapting the different branches of the education system to meet the various challenges created by the new economy must therefore be high up on the political agenda for upgrading the workforce via the buildup of appropriate human capital. The education system is not the focus of this paper though, and we will only briefly touch upon this topic in the concluding remarks.

a.   Risk and Reward Sharing between Workers and Firms

The new economy and also more competitive and globalized capital markets induce firms to specialize more on their core competencies (Lindbeck and Snower

1997, 1998, 2000; Snower 1997). This greater specialization across firms stands in marked contrast to the shrinking degree of specialization of workers within firms. Hence, while it was still common two decades ago that firms diversified and workers specialized, almost the reverse is true nowadays. Multitasking and the breakdown of occupational barriers brought about by the new economy and the accompanying organizational revolution amount to the reversal of a trend in which productivity improvements are achieved via the increased specialization of workers within firms. The beginning of this trend toward greater specialization within firms dates back as far as the first industrial revolution and was already described extensively by Adam Smith in his seminal writings. However, this fundamental change in the organizational structure of firms has far-reaching consequences for the appropriateness of different wage-bargaining systems. In a nutshell, centralized systems of wage bargaining, which cede relatively little room to firms for maneuvering with respect to wages in order to mitigate incentive and efficiency wage problems, are becoming more and more inefficient. They prevent firms from offering their employees adequate incentives to perform the appropriate mix of tasks, thus reducing their profit opportunities and investment incentives. Allowing much greater wage drift is not a solution, as this undermines the system and is therefore not acceptable to central wage setters.

Centralized wage bargaining has long been praised by many economists as a system which allows the internalization of various externalities, in particular, with respect to inflationary pressures and unemployment insurance (Calmfors and Driffill 1988). It is the core principle of any system of centralized wage bargaining that the same wage should be paid for the same job irrespective of the individual economic situation of the firm in which the job is performed. This hallmark of centralized wage bargaining "equal pay for equal work" depends crucially on workers with similar profiles having similar productivities even if they perform different tasks. There even exist two efficiency arguments in its favor. It supposedly helps profitable firms to grow faster and destroys firms whose efficiency is below average more quickly, thus possibly promoting structural change when workers are highly mobile. Furthermore, the possibilities for inefficient rent sharing on the firm level due to insiders holding up firms are reduced by centralized wage bargaining systems.

Several countries nonetheless decentralized their systems of wage bargaining during the 1980s and 1990s (Freeman and Gibbons 1993; Katz 1993; Berthold and Fehn 1996b). While some might view this institutional evolution across countries toward more decentralized wage bargaining as a coordination or policy failure which lowers social welfare, the new economy with its organizational revolution and the accompanying move from Fordism to post-Fordism provides a powerful economic rationale for this international pattern of institutional change. Central wage setters have little choice but to set wages schematically and to fix one wage or a narrow range of wages for every broadly defined group of tasks. However, the new economy and multitasking make this practice inherently inefficient, since the productivity of a particular worker depends even less than previously not only on his formal qualifications for this one task but also on the other tasks which he is performing and, in addition, to a great extent on his soft skills. Workers, even if they have similar formal profiles, are unlikely to perform the same set of complementary tasks at different holistic firms. Overall productivity of such seemingly similar workers, along with their incentive problems, must be expected to differ across firms in a post-Fordist environment (Ramaswamy and Rowthorn 1993; Lindbeck and Snower 1997). Since people within any particular education, occupation, and job tenure group are likely to vary considerably in terms of their social competence, cognitive skills, judgment, and ability to perform multiple tasks, wage dispersion even among people with similar formal qualifications needs to increase in order to keep pace with the new economy and the accompanying IT and organizational revolution.

To give a simple example, if wages are set on the central level according to the productivity of versatile workers who can make great use of task complementarities, workers who are not able to do so are likely to end up being unemployed. Hence, centralized wage bargaining systems impose a growing efficiency cost on OECD countries by artificially compressing the wage distribution (Davis and Henrekson 2000). Allowing greater wage drift is not a sustainable solution because this would slowly undermine the operability of the central wage bargaining system. The new economy and skill-biased technological progress improve the outside option of workers with the skills demanded by firms, thus reducing their incentive to stay within a union or to join a union in the first place. The result is the observable decline in union membership across OECD countries, which is the basis for any centralized wage bargaining system, and in the end a greater wage differentiation (Acemoglu et al. 2001).

Labor is becoming more heterogeneous because of the new economy and is, even less than in the past, a single-purpose factor which is easily comparable across firms with respect to formal qualifications. The organizational revolution is furthermore likely to trigger a sharp increase in the number of occupational clusters relative to the traditional number of occupational categories. This makes it even more difficult than in the past for centralized wage bargaining parties to establish broad occupational categories within which wage uniformity could be imposed without great efficiency losses. In addition, the dissolution of functional departments in favor of small customer-oriented teams and in favor of profit centers which produce highly differentiated products is also increasing the heterogeneity of task clusters across firms, thus further complicating life for central wage bargaining parties.

It is hardly conceivable that the principle of "equal pay for equal work," which is the foundation of any centralized wage bargaining system, could be amended by redefining work along holistic lines. The dramatic rise in the heterogeneity of workers' skills which matter, of tasks, and of task complementarities even within a particular industry would require that central wage bargaining parties dispose over vast amounts of information which is furthermore very quickly obsolete. This up-to-date information conglomerate is just as unlikely to be available to central wage bargaining parties as full information about production technologies, customer demands, etc., was to traditional communist central planners. Labor markets are becoming more like product markets with respect to heterogeneity, thus raising the efficiency losses associated with centralized wage bargaining toward the level associated with those of centralized price fixing. In short, asymmetric information problems between firms and workers on the one hand and centralized wage bargaining parties on the other hand have risen, thereby reducing the optimal degree of centralization of wage bargaining.

It seems to be a reasonable conjecture that the international trend over the last two decades toward more decentralized wage bargaining, e.g., in the United States, the United Kingdom, Australia, New Zealand, the Scandinavian countries, and Italy, is at least partly related to this set of reasons, because the described efficiency costs in the end amount to forgone opportunities for GNP and employment growth (Lindbeck and Snower 1997). This assessment fits with the observation that new economy firms usually do not join centralized wage bargaining arrangements and often even offer remuneration packages to their employees which contain profit sharing components and/or stock options of their firms in order to mitigate the growing incentive and efficiency wage problems. Such remuneration packages have great advantages for new economy firms: First, wage pressure is reduced and payroll costs become more flexible. Second, they foster more decentralized decision making and make it easier to split firms up into profit centers. Hence, from this perspective the new economy promotes the creation of a share economy, thus blurring the historic division between capital and labor (Freeman 2000).

Germany lags behind in the international trend toward more decentralized wage bargaining, which boils down to some kind of profit sharing even without explicitly linking wages to profits of their firms. This is the case because wages negotiated at the firm level depend greatly on the profitability of the specific firm. It is well known that a sizable number of firms in east Germany do not pay according to industry-wide wage agreements even though they belong to the employers' association, but this kind of behavior is clearly illegal. Nonetheless, in the end the gulf between official centralized wage agreements and economic reality in east Germany might help to break up the bargaining cartel which was imposed on east Germany by west Germany after reunification.

If unions, employers federations, and the government would like to avoid an uncontrolled collapse of the current institutional setting, it is advisable to preemptively make centralized wage agreements more flexible and to cede greater decision-making power to firms (Berthold and Fehn 1996b). Most important, wage negotiations and agreements at the firm level should be legalized without reservation if a qualified majority of the firm's workers agrees to differ from the central wage agreement. In cases where wage negotiations at the firm level failed, the central wage agreement would continue to serve as the fall back position. If this is not feasible, there are some alternatives which are more in line with the current system. First, central wage agreements can only fix a corridor for wage changes within the industry, with the specific wage rate to be determined at the firm level. Second, central wage agreements can contain a provision that part of the fixed wage change is allowed to be replaced by a profit sharing component by mutual consent at the firm level. Third, central wage agreements can contain special wage clauses for disadvantaged groups of the labor market like the long-term unemployed or elderly workers. Fourth, the legal possibility for the government to declare a wage agreement as generally binding for all firms of an industry, even those which do not belong to the employers' association, should be abolished. In sum, all institutional arrangements and legal barriers in Germany which obstruct the path toward greater wage flexibility and wage differentiation according to local conditions should be scrutinized very closely as to whether they are really economically beneficial under the conditions of the new economy.

b.   Employee Participation in Decision Making

It is to be expected that employees who are to share a greater part of the idiosyncratic risk of firms via decentralized wage bargaining and profit sharing want to have a greater voice in their firm's decision making process, too. This also makes economic sense, as authority, risk, and reward sharing should go hand in hand (Freeman and Gibbons 1993; Freeman 2000).The question arises, though, whether firms also benefit from greater participation of workers in decision-making processes and whether they are therefore voluntarily willing to involve workers to a greater extent in decision making. From an economic policy point of view, it is worth determining whether some kind of legal intervention is needed, possibly along the lines of the German codetermination law and its planned extensions (Berthold and Stettes 2001).

Codetermination by workers is justified from an economic perspective if such a transfer of control, information, and decision rights enhances the efficiency of working relations. Labor contracts are a typical case of an incomplete contract which allows, in principle, ex post opportunistic behavior by both parties, firms and workers, possibly giving rise to holdup problems (Caballero and Hammour 1998). Codetermination rights can at least potentially foster a cooperative working relationship, thus enhancing the incentive of workers to put maximum effort and creativity into their job. This is especially likely if extended codetermination rights are part of an encompassing bargaining package between firms and their workers. They can furthermore possibly reduce problems of asymmetric information on the part of management if workers are, as is often argued, more likely to share their superior information with management in an institutional framework with codetermination. Such cooperative behavior produces a quasi-rent which differs across firms. As opportunistic behavior is more easily observable for collective bodies than for individuals, control costs of incomplete contracts can also fall. Hence, codetermination rights can at least theoretically lower transaction and information costs, thus enhancing economic efficiency. If these advantages outweigh the possible benefits of ex post opportunistic behavior, both sides, firms and workers, will then voluntarily enter into such an institutional arrangement. Relatively flexible work contracts with an institutional framework for ex post bargaining are especially preferable for both parties if continuous investments in the human capital of employees are necessary in order to adjust to quickly changing economic conditions. Workers are then more willing to invest in firm-specific human capital, which could otherwise potentially fall victim to holdup behavior by firms.

However, extending the participation rights of workers in firm's decision making is likely to have a hump-shaped type of effect on the profitability of the firm and on general economic efficiency. Figure 1 roughly describes the relevant situation before the onset of the new economy, such as in the late 1970s and early 1980s. The index of participation rights, x, of workers are given on the horizontal axis, while the associated revenues are given on the vertical axis. Revenues to the economy as a whole are denoted by $R(x)$ (upper curve), revenues to firms by $[1- t(x)]R(x)$ (lower curve), and revenues to workers by $t(x)R(x)$ (difference between upper and lower curve). If x is equal to one, workers completely call the shots in firms without interference by management or providers of capital, reflecting the model of the Yugoslav firm. As is well known, such a setup is highly inefficient, though. If x is, in contrast, equal to zero, workers have no say whatsoever in the decision making of firms. Such a situation is reminiscent of firms in the 19th and early 20th century with a highly Tayloristic organization. It is safe to assume that output is larger than in the case of worker-dominated firms, as the latter type of firms does not in general meet the market test anywhere in liberal societies.[2] Yet, such a completely hierarchical top-down organizational structure was also no longer optimal for firms as of at least about two decades ago, before the arrival of the new economy, and much less so for workers and for the economy as a whole. According to Figure 1, even then firms preferred to involve workers to some extent in decision making, with their optimal solution being x_0^f. However, workers of

---

[2]   A notable exception might be the Kibbutz system in Israel. However, this system was created under very special circumstances after the Holocaust and the foundation of Israel and seems to be in decline nowadays, too.

course wanted to obtain much larger decision-making rights, as is reflected in their optimal solution x^l. For the economy as a whole, the intermediate solution x^* would have been optimal. Bargaining between workers and firms at the firm level will yield an intermediate solution between the two optima, which could have in principle come close to the aggregate optimum in x^*, depending on relative bargaining power. For any level of participation rights beyond x^d firms would prefer to actually go back to the Tayloristic mode of production.

The question arises therefore, why should it be necessary to decree codetermination rights by law if they are indeed advantageous to both, firms and workers. After all, conditions determining which kind of codetermination arrangement is useful will probably vary from firm to firm and it must be assumed that local negotiating partners know those conditions better than a centralized legislative body, which cannot make distinctions according to local conditions. Some kind of market failure is a necessary condition to justify such legal intervention. Assuming realistically that the political decision-making process also works far from perfectly well, a much stronger assumption is in fact needed to justify legal intervention,

Figure 1: Employee Participation in Decision Making and Value of Firms

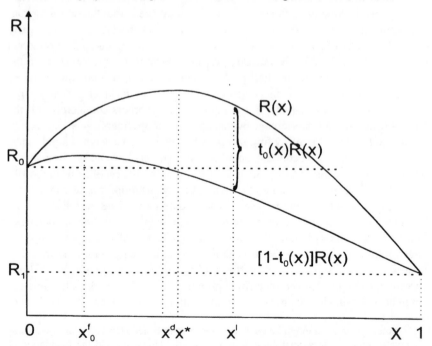

Source: Berthold and Stettes (2001).

namely, that even an imperfect political solution dominates the less than optimal market solution.

There exist at least three arguments why a legislative solution might be useful. First, each individual worker at the firm level has an incentive to behave as a free rider in firm-level negotiations, i.e., not to exercise voice himself but rather to count on his fellow workers to do so. Such behavior is likely to improve his standing with management and his chances for promotions. Codetermination rights, in contrast to wage payments, have the character of a collective good for each individual worker. Hence, it is in this respect more difficult for workers to organize at the firm level than it is for management, which yields an asymmetry in bargaining power. The free-bargaining solution concerning codetermination rights might therefore systematically deviate downwards from the social optimum, leaving, in principle, some room for improvement via government interference.

Second, ceding codetermination rights to workers voluntarily might give rise to an adverse selection problem for each individual firm doing so. When workers are about to be laid off, such codetermination rights usually involve some say in protecting any quasi-rents which have been created, thus increasing de facto firing costs for such firms and the effective degree of employment protection of workers in such firms. Yet, workers are likely to possess superior information concerning their own abilities compared to firms prior to hiring. Hence, workers, who know that they are of relatively poor quality, will systematically prefer to apply for jobs at firms with codetermination rights, as this increases somewhat their protection against being dismissed ex post. In contrast, good workers will then prefer to be hired by firms without voluntary codetermination rights, as the average productivity of workers in the firm will affect the wage of each individual worker. A general legislative solution can obviously mitigate or possibly even solve this adverse selection problem.

Third, especially small and medium-size firms and firms which have only recently been founded tend to have a reputation problem in the labor market. Markets, i.e., not only the labor market but also the product and the capital market, will hardly react if they do not abide by any voluntary agreement with their workers concerning codetermination rights. This reduces the ex ante credibility of such an agreement for workers in these firms. The credibility of such voluntary agreements is only high ex ante if ex post opportunistic behavior of firms is severely punished by markets, possibly in the form of good workers no longer applying or the products of such firms being avoided by customers. Yet, such mechanisms are only likely to function with large and well-known firms which receive a great deal of attention from the media. With a legal solution, such reputation problems are not an issue, as it is then relatively easy for workers to enforce compliance by firms via suing them in labor courts.

Hence, there exist nonnegligible arguments in favor of some kind of a legal solution. To be sure, a legal solution also has substantial drawbacks. Ceding codetermination rights to workers should ideally be part of an encompassing package deal between workers and firms also involving such issues as wages, profit sharing components, or work organization. Other typical parts of such a package deal between workers and firms would concern the financing of investments in the human capital of the firm's workforce, streamlining work organization according to efficiency criteria and working time arrangements. Transferring greater codetermination rights to its workers would constitute a possible "quid pro quo" in such a package deal. Obviously, such a "do ut des" approach no longer works if codetermination rights are simply decreed by law. This strengthens asymmetrically the bargaining position of workers and is unlikely to make them more willing to compromise on other issues. It must be feared that workers will abuse such legal codetermination rights to simply extract a greater share of the rents which are created by the activities of the firm without actually increasing the total size of the pie (Caballero and Hammour 1997).

There is in fact some empirical evidence for firms listed on the stock market which supports this pessimistic view. Gorton and Schmid 2000 show with an extensive empirical study that the German codetermination law, which transfers control rights from capital owners to workers, not only makes the voting rights attached to shares less valuable, but that it also reduces the return on assets, the market-to-book ratio, and the return on equity. According to their empirical results and contrary to general wisdom in Germany, the German system of legally instituted codetermination rights makes employees influence firms' decisions in such a way that the restructuring efforts of shareholders in response to economic shocks are resisted and delayed, thus increasing the systematic risk to which firms are exposed. German firms have apparently reacted to these extended codetermination rights of workers by raising their leverage. Greater debt financing reduces the size of free cash flows in firms and thus also the potential for appropriation activities of workers because this would quickly endanger the existence of the firm and thus also the jobs of its workers. Hence, legislation on codetermination has a similar effect on the optimal capital structure of firms as the threat of impending unionization in the United States.

The often propagated efficiency-enhancing effects of German legislation on codetermination must also be doubted due to the fact that this institutional setup has not been adopted by other countries and that Anglo-Saxon firms in particular tend to be reluctant to invest in Germany due to codetermination. If the German approach were really so successful, lawmakers in other countries, along with foreign firms, should have realized its beneficial effects by now. In conjunction with the aforementioned information problems of any centralized legislative body concerning the particular needs of individual firms with respect to participation of workers in decision making, it appears preferable to set up only a general framework from which workers and firms can deviate at the firm level by mutual consent. This legal institutional framework would, just as in the case of wage bargaining, only serve as a fallback position if consent by workers and firms could not be reached voluntarily at the firm level.

The usefulness of the current German legalistic approach must especially be doubted when also taking new economy effects into account. In changing the organization of firms from Fordism to post-Fordism, firms' benefits from involving their workers in the decision-making process increase substantially, thus making the rising section of their return curve in Figure 1 steeper and moving the optimum from the point of view of firms to the right and closer to the aggregate optimum. The incentive for such firms to have workers with all their accumulated knowledge participate more and in a cooperative way in actual decision making in firms rises. Hence, the archaic conflict of interest between capital and labor is reduced, and nowadays both sides often have similar or even parallel interests, thus reducing the need for legislative interference in order to keep their relationship peaceful and fruitful. This is reflected in the fact that even in the United States, one-third of workers in firms with more than 50 employees report that they serve on employee involvement committees. These workers make more suggestions for improvement than other employees and are more committed to their firms, thus enhancing productivity (Freeman 2000).

In sum, legal codetermination rights are neither a blessing nor a curse as such. An assessment rather depends on the specific legislation and the economic environment under which it is passed. It appears, however, that contrary to current efforts by lawmakers in Germany not more but rather less legal interference in the issue of codetermination by workers is called for by the new economy. Participation rights of workers should nowadays as much as possible become part of an encompassing bargaining package at the firm level, between management or entrepreneurs and workers, concerning the sharing of authority, risk, and reward, thus also involving a number of other key issues. Several of the planned changes in the German law regulating codetermination rights of workers make little economic sense. This is the case as concerns, e.g., the quota for women in works councils or the extended rights for participation in decision making of works councils in qualification measures, team-working, combining family and work, and safeguarding employment and protecting the environment. The same negative assessment holds for allowing works councils to extend their activities even to those parts of the workforce which do not want to be represented by works councils, for increasing the number of people who are members of the works councils in firms with more than 100 employees, and for forcing firms with only 200 instead of 300 employees to have one employee as a full-time member without normal work obligations in the works council (Schnabel 2001; Berthold and Stettes 2001).

It is less than obvious that these changes are justified by efficiency arguments. The decision making of firms will often be further slowed down which is the opposite of what is necessary in the age of the new economy. Opportunistic behavior by insiders is encouraged, as they obtain a number of soft criteria for interfering with decisions by management which increase their appropriation potential. Arguing, as the German government does, that democracy costs money and that the costs are covered by positive productivity effects is therefore not at all satisfactory. It neglects in particular that the increase in costs hits mostly relatively small firms, which, however, benefit least from legal codetermination, because they usually entertain a cooperative relationship with their workforce anyway even without any legal codetermination rights for their workers. Competitive pressure on labor and goods markets forces them to do so without any prodding by the government. The envisioned changes in the German law regulating codetermination must therefore be regarded as being mainly part of a gift exchange between unions and the SPD/Green government, with the government rewarding the unions for complacency in other areas such as the tax reform which was passed in the year 2000 and which was relatively favorable to (big) business.

c.   Employment Protection Legislation

Another important and controversial labor market institution which differs greatly across OECD countries is employment protection legislation (EPL) with its implied firing costs. EPL is in general considerably more restrictive in continental European countries than in Anglo-Saxon countries (Blanchard and Wolfers 1999; OECD 1999b). In particular the United States, with its "employment at will" principle, is usually ranked very low with respect to firing costs. Within continental Europe, firing costs tend to be higher in southern European countries than in northern European countries. Northern European countries usually protect workers against negative shocks via relatively generous unemployment insurance and welfare assistance (Buti et al. 1998). Firing costs increased substantially in some continental European countries like Germany and France in the late 1960s and early 1970s and have stayed roughly at this higher level since then (Caballero and Hammour 1997). However, one of the first measures of the new SPD/Green government in Germany was to extend the scope of EPL to apply to small firms with only five or more employees.

It is not obvious how EPL affects labor market performance, because there are opposing effects at work. There exist several arguments as to why some EPL might be superior to the free market solution with no EPL, not only for reasons of equity but also for reasons of efficiency (Bentilola and Bertola 1990). First, EPL in the form of severance payments forces firms to internalize some of the costs which they impose on workers who are dismissed and on society at large. Second, EPL smoothes employment over the business cycle, because firms will then be more reluctant to fire workers in recessions, as this would make them incur firing costs which they might avoid by simply hoarding workers over the downturn. Third, EPL protects workers against arbitrary dismissals by firms, thus possibly creating a more trustful working relationship between firms and workers and making workers more willing to invest in firm-specific human capital.

These arguments in favor of some EPL notwithstanding, there are also a number of counterarguments which caution against raising EPL too much. First, EPL increases total labor costs, thus reducing labor demand at given wage costs. It is sometimes argued that EPL is viewed as insurance against adverse shocks by workers and that wages will therefore fall in reaction to higher EPL, as workers are willing to pay an insurance premium. However, this argument is not convincing in the context of EPL, which is imposed by the government and not the result of negotiations between workers and their respective firm. In the latter case, a package deal might be struck between workers and firms involving lower wages in return for higher employment protection ceded by firms, e.g., in the form of severance payments. Workers have no reason to make such wage concessions if the government raises their bargaining power unilaterally via imposing higher EPL on firms. On the contrary, it must be expected that their wage demands will become more aggressive once they are hired and enjoy protection via EPL, because their potential to appropriate firms after having been hired is raised (Caballero and Hammour 1997). Insiders will not be dismissed by firms as long as wages do not exceed their marginal productivity plus firing costs (Lindbeck and Snower 1988). The negative effect on labor market performance is greater, the larger the long-run elasticity of substitution between capital and labor is. Recent empirical evidence pointing to a long-run elasticity of substitution between capital and labor which exceeds the threshold value of one suggests that the long-run negative effects of expanding EPL are considerably larger than hitherto assumed (Berthold et al. 2000).

Second, these considerations also shed some doubt on the assertion that EPL helps to create firm-specific human capital. Due to borrowing restrictions of workers, such firm-specific human capital must be financed mostly by firms as long as the government does not step in fully (Acemoglu 1996). However, high EPL then works in the opposite direction, because firms have a lower incentive to invest in the firm-specific human capital of their workers. High EPL enables workers to appropriate ex post a large part of the quasi-rents which are created by investing in firm-specific human capital, thus reducing the incentive of firms to act as financiers in this respect.

Third, EPL makes firms more reluctant to hire workers at given wage costs. Labor market flows in and out of unemployment are unambiguously reduced by EPL (OECD 1999b). While there is no clear-cut effect on total unemployment resulting from lower labor market flows, the reduced hiring rate due to EPL makes unemployment more persistent and raises long-term unemployment, which is especially problematic not only from an economic but also from a political point of view. Hence, it is more difficult for dismissed workers in countries with high EPL to obtain a regular job again than for dismissed workers in a laissez-faire country such as the United States. EPL therefore increases the segmentation of the labor market into insiders and outsiders (Lindbeck and Snower 1988; Kugler and Saint-Paul 2000).

In addition to these general arguments against EPL, which apply irrespective of economic conditions, the above-described transition to the new economy makes it likely that countries with relatively low EPL fare better nowadays with respect to labor market performance. EPL is especially bad for employment when big structural breaks occur such as is the case with the new economy, because firms are then very reluctant to hire new workers, while EPL cannot prevent dismissals in firms or sectors which are going down the drain anyway. Furthermore, economic conditions have become more volatile over the last 15 years due to globalization and the transition to the new economy, with shocks occurring more frequently and with shocks also being greater in size. However, such a development toward a less stable economic environment is not innocuous with respect to the effects of EPL on labor market performance. The negative effect of EPL on labor demand is greater in a volatile than in a tranquil economic environment and is especially harmful to firms which are largely financed via debt rather than via equity, because labor becomes a quasi-fixed production factor with which firms cannot quickly adjust to changing economic conditions. Thus, quasi-equilibrium unemployment is raised if unions do not exercise sufficient wage restraint in return (Bertola and Ichino 1995; Fehn 2001).

There are two additional arguments why EPL might be especially problematic in the context of the new economy. It can be shown that firms in high-EPL countries are induced to specialize on relatively secure goods at later stages in their product life cycles in order to avoid paying firing costs (Saint-Paul 1996). New and innovative goods with a high failure risk but which are essential for the transition to the new economy are first developed and produced in low-EPL countries, such as the United States, and only move later on to high-EPL countries, such as Germany, which then tend to refine their production via process innovations. Furthermore, large-scale creation of new firms has been a hallmark of the new economy in the United States. However, newly founded firms often face financial restrictions, and a high rate of new firms per period depends on a well-functioning venture capital market in order to circumvent such financial restrictions as much as possible. Venture capitalists in the form of business angels also often help their portfolio firms to survive the especially risky start-up period by counseling and advising them. Empirical studies show, though, that the growth of the venture capital market, which clearly helps a country to be a successful player in the new economy, depends greatly on labor market flexibility, so that countries with a rigid labor market due to high EPL have a lower chance from this perspective to benefit from a positive new economy effect than countries with low EPL and a more flexible labor market (Jeng and Wells 2000; Fehn 2001).

Considering though that there are countervailing effects of EPL on labor market performance, the direction and size of the net impact is after all an empirical question. There exist by now numerous cross-country studies concerning the effect of labor market institutions on unemployment (Nickell 1997; Blanchard and Wolfers 1999; Morgan and Mourougane 2000; OECD 1999b provides an overview of empirical studies). EPL is often found to have an insignificant effect on the unemployment rate, and if the effect is significant, it usually raises the unemployment rate but with a small impact coefficient. Most of these studies suffer from three important shortcomings, though. First, the time period which is investigated often only extends up to the early 1990s, so that most of the 1990s when the transition to new economy got under way is left out. If the new economy matters, this tends to bias the results in favor of EPL. Second, these empirical studies usually only consider the effect on the standardized unemployment rate and not on employment, where the negative effect can be expected to be more pronounced. Third, they either include only institutional variables concerning the labor market or supplement them merely with goods market variables. Capital market variables are, as a rule, completely left out. This might be an important shortcoming, because it is reasonable to assume that a well-functioning capital market, especially with respect to venture capital, has become more important for labor market performance with the new economy. If all three of these shortcomings are amended with the time period under consideration, extending from 1986 to 1999, and with labor, goods, and capital market variables included as explanatory variables, EPL does indeed turn out to have a significant and negative effects on labor market performance across OECD countries, raising the standardized unemployment rate and lowering employment. As expected, the negative effect of EPL on employment is more pronounced than the positive impact on unemployment (Belke and Fehn 2000).[3]

In sum, one can be pretty sure that lowering EPL would help to fight unemployment and to raise employment in the age of the new economy. Conversely, the policy of the current German government with respect to EPL must be regarded as flawed if lowering unemployment is indeed one of the key policy objectives. Extending EPL also to small firms and restricting the possibilities for fixed-term labor contracts does not match the requirements of the new economy. If outright re-

---

[3]   Feld and Santoni (2001) show empirically that EPL also reduced economic growth rates in the EU countries.

ductions of EPL are politically not feasible due to resistance by insiders, it should at least be much more clearly stated in the law when dismissals by firms are legal, so that labor courts have less discretion in their rulings on disputes between firms and laid-off workers. The current insecure legal situation and the tendency of labor courts to interpret unclear cases in favor of workers do not help to raise hiring rates in Germany. Lower firing costs would also fit well with the above-described desideratum of more decentralized wage bargaining. It would help to prevent locally negotiated wages to be excessively affected by insider-outsider and rent-seeking considerations.

d.   Innovative and Tailor-Made Active Labor Market Policies

It is an important policy question which contribution active labor market policy (ALMP) can make to fighting persistent unemployment in the age of the new economy. ALMP in combination with institutional reforms of the welfare state must primarily aim at preventing long-term unemployment. The longer a person is unemployed, the more this person gets out of touch with the real labor market with respect to qualifications and work routines, and there is a rising risk that this person will never be employed on a regular job again. This assessment holds especially under the conditions of the new economy, where qualification requirements of firms are rapidly changing and where the continuous ability to apply ever-more sophisticated IT products in one's job is essential. Hence, a vicious circle of rising (long-term) unemployment and rising taxes and social security contributions to finance this unemployment must be prevented from occurring. Reforms of ALMP and the welfare state must therefore be designed in such a way that they not only help the unemployed and especially the long-term unemployed to find a regular job again but that persons concerned also always have a strong financial incentive to accept regular jobs even if they are only part-time or require initially relatively few qualifications.

In order to be sustainable, ALMP must pave the way for the unemployed back into regular jobs and not simply hide unemployment. This is in principle possible because ALMP can lower the quasi-equilibrium unemployment rate via a number of channels under the assumption that even laissez-faire labor markets do not work perfectly well and even more so in real-world labor markets, which especially in Continental Europe are characterized by numerous rigidities (Calmfors 1994; Jackman 1994; Katz 1994; Berthold and Fehn 1997). First, ALMP can improve the efficiency of the matching process by providing information to both sides of the labor market about the other side of the market and via counseling activities. Second, ALMP can serve as a work test, as it is possible and common even in welfare states to cut transfer and insurance payments to those of the unemployed who refuse to participate in ALMP schemes offered to them. This is politically much more difficult without such offers even after very long unemployment spells. Third, it can, theoretically, raise competitive pressure on insiders by keeping effective labor supply high, e.g., if it prevents the unemployed from getting out of touch with the real labor market. Fourth, if it is less attractive to participate in ALMP schemes than to be unemployed, perhaps because the time advantage and the possibility to work tax free on the black market is lost; then the fallback position of insiders in wage negotiations falls, thus reducing wage pressure and raising employment. Fifth, ALMP can at least theoretically improve the matching process by qualifying the unemployed according to the needs expressed by firms. This is probably the most important channel in the context of the new economy because the new economy changes and increases the qualifications which firms demand of workers, in particular, with respect to the aforementioned soft skills. Providing the unemployed with the respective skills via ALMP might therefore constitute a possible route out of mass unemployment, as labor supply then better matches the labor demand of firms. However, it is important to keep in mind in this respect that it is not the case that firms simply switch from one set of skill requirements to another, possibly higher but still well-defined set of skill requirements. Rather, firms in the new economy are very heterogeneous in their expectations, and their skill requirements change quickly, thus demanding great versatility of workers. This immediately reduces the probability that a centralized ALMP which organizes qualification programs off the job can make a significant positive contribution to equipping adults with the relevant skills and to lowering (long-term) unemployment. It suggests that it must be a key objective of ALMP to get the unemployed and especially the long-term unemployed back into regular working life as quickly as possible and to have them continuously acquire the relevant skills on the job.

Due to the increasing importance of ALMP as an instrument especially in Germany after reunification, efforts have been stepped up recently to evaluate whether or not ALMP can be judged as successful or not.[4] While there was quite a bit of optimism among economists at the beginning of the 1990s about the efficacy of ALMP in fighting unemployment, the results of these evaluations in Germany and a few years earlier in Sweden, which is the hub of ALMP among OECD countries, can only be called disappointing.[5] This is the case in spite of all the aforementioned theoretically possible positive effects of ALMP on labor market performance. Current ALMP both in Germany and Sweden largely serves to hide unemployment and helps very little in reintegrating the unemployed and especially the

---

[4]   See especially Heckman et al. (1999).

[5]   See, for Sweden, Calmfors (1995), Calmfors and Skedinger (1995), Robinson (1995) and Forslund and Krueger (1997). See, for Germany, Fitzenberger and Prey (1997), Kraus et al. (2000), Lechner (1998, 1999) and Steiner and Hagen (2000). Martin (2000) gives an overview over the effects of ALMP in OECD countries.

long-term unemployed back into the regular labor market. Current ALMP has strong wage-raising effects; an expansion of ALMP increases wage pressure by more than an equivalent expansion in regular employment, probably because the government thereby tends to become the "employer of last resort," thus blurring responsibility for employment performance which should rest primarily with unions and employer associations and not with the government. Empirical investigations which use employment growth in the private sector or the sum of official unemployment and people participating in ALMP as target variables usually find that if ALMP has a significant positive effect at all, it is very small. Providing information to both sides of the labor market and counseling the unemployed appear to be the most efficient components of ALMP. Another useful component seems to have been the installation of temp agencies which hire workers and lend them to private firms on a temporary basis. A relatively large percentage of the employees working for such temp agencies have thereby found the way back into the regular labor market (Almus et al. 1998; Lechner et al. 2000). In sum, given these empirical results of ALMP at least in the form currently pursued in countries such as Germany and Sweden, it is overall by no means a panacea in fighting unemployment.

These sobering empirical results raise the question about the weaknesses of currently pursued ALMP. Arguing that it is better to finance employment instead of unemployment is from an economic point of view not sufficient to massively expand expenditures on ALMP, as has especially been the case in east Germany. ALMP must effectively raise competitive pressure for insiders by outsiders of the labor market. It appears to be one of the key weaknesses of current ALMP that this objective is not at all achieved and that it often tries to qualify the unemployed off the job, therefore not being successful in qualifying them according to the needs of firms. Substitution and displacement effects of ALMP on regular employment further reduce its efficacy. It is very difficult to design ALMP off the job in such a way that it conveys useful skills to participants without displacing or substituting regular employment. Participants of ALMP in Germany not only receive their unemployment benefits or welfare assistance payments but are also paid up to 90 percent of official wages in regular jobs. Since many workers on regular jobs, especially in east Germany, do not receive these official and centrally negotiated wages, there is in effect close to no difference between the income of participants in ALMP and of many regular workers. Finally, ALMP is as a norm quite a bit more expensive than simply granting benefits to the unemployed, so that the wedge between real gross labor costs to firms and real net consumption wages of regular workers is magnified by ALMP. All this inevitably results in rising wage pressure and reduces regular employment (Berthold and Fehn 1997; Calmfors and Lang 1995).

It must also be taken into account that participants of ALMP often thereby renew their claims to unemployment benefits, thus extending de facto actual benefit duration. However, numerous empirical studies have shown that a long benefit duration is very harmful for labor market performance, raising in particular the rate of long-term unemployment (Burda 1997; Scarpetta 1996; Nickell 1997; Nickell and Layard 1999). The institutional setup is especially counterproductive in Germany, where the local municipalities have a strong incentive to place recipients of welfare assistance in some ALMP scheme regardless whether or not this actually increases their chance of being reintegrated into the regular labor market. This is the case because welfare assistance is paid for by local municipalities, whereas unemployment benefits and the ensuing unemployment assistance is financed by contributions of firms and workers as well as by the federal government. Hence, there is a kind of carrousel effect with strong incentives for externalizing burdens instead of trying to find real solutions.

In order to avoid negative side effects of ALMP and to maximize the probability that it actually raises regular employment, it must heed a number of principles. It must concentrate on where it is most efficient, i.e., on providing information and on counseling the unemployed, thus raising the efficiency of the matching process. In order to prevent wage pressure on the regular labor market from rising, wages obtained when participating in ALMP should still lie considerably below those wages which are de facto paid for regular employment; and ALMP should concentrate on helping disadvantaged groups on the labor market such as the long-term unemployed. Participation in ALMP should not lead to claims to unemployment benefits, thus avoiding any carrousel effects and there should be strict time limits on participation in ALMP. Those unemployed who refuse to participate in ALMP should not receive insurance and transfer payments anymore. As much as possible, ALMP should help to get the unemployed back into regular firms so that they can acquire the relevant skills on the job. Finally, as qualification requirements differ considerably between firms and regions, ALMP should be organized on the decentralized local level where information about local conditions is best available.

For the German case, the following kind of rough package approach could make sense (Berthold et al. 2001). The first step for activating the unemployed and for financing work instead of unemployment must be a significant cut in the duration of unemployment benefits, e.g., down to the U.S. duration of six months. After these six months, welfare assistance steps in. Unemployment assistance should be abolished. This stick approach is sweetened by a number of carrots, i.e., financial incentives for the unemployed to actively search for jobs. If they find a job, their regular income should no longer lead to an essentially one-to-one reduction in welfare assistance payments. It would make more sense to only impose an effective tax rate of say 50 percent instead of 100 percent for a limited period of time and then to slowly increase the cut in welfare assistance payments to 100 percent. This would abolish the currently existing unemployment trap especially for the less-qualified unemployed.

If they have still not found a job after say another six months, the unemployed get monthly vouchers in addition, like in the "benefit transfer program" (Snower 1994; Orszag and Snower 2000). The value of these vouchers increases with each additional month spent in unemployment, with a maximum after about two years in unemployment. The unemployed can offer these vouchers to any firm which is willing to hire them and only the firm can cash in these vouchers at the labor office of the local municipality. Hence, they act as a kind of wage subsidy and should therefore also be granted for a limited time period only and should also be phased out gradually once the unemployed person has obtained a job. Firms should receive more money from the labor office for a given voucher if they can prove that they did not only hire the unemployed but that they trained them and updated their skills. The qualification part of the voucher system is especially important due to the new economy with its rapidly changing skill requirements.

Local municipalities would be in charge of running these systems and should get substantial leeway in deciding the size of welfare benefits of, in particular, those unemployed who are able to work. Cutting their claims somewhat while leaving those of unemployed persons who are essentially unable to work, e.g., due to disabilities or little children, would further enhance the search activities of those of the unemployed who are able to work and would help to achieve greater wage differentiation and to install a low-wage sector. Local municipalities should also have some room for deciding the details of the financial rewards, e.g., how quickly supplementary welfare assistance and these vouchers are phased out after employment is obtained. Any further activities concerning ALMP, like qualification and community work programs, should also be organized on the local level so that there is a good chance that the unemployed will really get qualifications according to local market needs and so that, in particular, the effect of ALMP as a willingness-to-work test is maximized.

However, there should be no illusions. Even the best qualification programs, be they on the job or off the job, cannot provide all the unemployed with the kind of encompassing skills which tend to be demanded by firms nowadays. It is therefore essential that a low-wage sector be installed so that the number of workers who are currently locked out of the regular labor market will be substantially reduced. The above-described package should help in doing so, but of course unions and employer associations must make their contribution by opening up their wage agreements and by granting much greater decision-making power to the firm level.

4.   Conclusions

Only an encompassing set of institutional improvements in labor markets and a determined reorientation of labor market policy in favor of activation and against alimentation of the unemployed can help to make Continental European labor markets successfully meet the challenges posed by the onset of the new economy. The above-described package should help Germany in particular to abandon its current position as being among the most sclerotic West European countries, thus spurring economic and employment growth. However, complacency and political inertia are very high in Germany, making determined institutional reforms, which would hurt a large part of the electorate in the short run, not particularly likely. It seems, in fact, that resistance to appropriate supply-side policies on the labor market is so high in Germany that the walls of the labor market fortress will, if at all, only crumble in times of a deep crisis.

However, reforming labor market institutions and labor market policy in the outlined direction is only part of the economic policy package which is actually needed to tap the possible benefits of the new economy. Competitive goods and capital markets, especially a well-developed venture capital market, are also essential components, just as well as a tax and social security system which do not stifle but rather spur entrepreneurial incentives (Boeri et al. 2000; Burda 2000; Fehn 2001). Another key policy area has also just been mentioned briefly so far, this is the education system. It is essential to prepare people for the challenges posed by the new economy when they are young because any repair activities involving adults such as ALMP are bound to exhibit a rather small efficiency. Lifelong learning has become more important and can be improved in Germany, but the basic skills, such as reading, writing, and the versatility to cope with different tasks, along with mathematical and communicative skills, have to be acquired when people are young. Germans have boasted for a long time that their education system is supposedly one of the best among OECD countries. However, it is almost uncontroversial by now that there is plenty of room to improve the German university system. More surprisingly, the long-heralded German system of high-school education has also come under fire recently because of the results of international tests. Only the apprenticeship system of vocational training still seems to be an asset by international comparison.

Institutional reforms of the education system must therefore be high up on the economic policy agenda for making Germany meet the challenges posed by the new economy. More competition and more decentralized decision making with regard to schools and universities along with at least some form of tuition and an expanded system of scholarships should be integral parts of such a reform package. One of the targets should be to combine an earlier start in working life with an expanded system of lifelong learning. It is interesting to note in this respect that the reforms of the German high-school system in the 1970s, which favored greater specialization of students, probably went into the wrong direction considering that general skills and not early specialization is called for now by the new economy. The United States with its strong emphasis on a broad liberal arts education in good colleges seems to be better prepared for the new economy also from this perspective. Taking, furthermore, into account what kind of "reforms" have recently been undertaken on the German labor market, a key lesson seems to be that reforms should not be undertaken for their own sake but that they must rather go in the right direction to really constitute an improvement.

References

Acemoglu, D. (1996). Credit Constraints, Investment Externalities and Growth. In A. Booth and D. Snower (eds.), *Acquiring Skills.* Cambridge, Mass.: Cambridge University Press.

Acemoglu, D. (1999). Changes in Unemployment and Wage Inequality: An Alternative Theory and Some Evidence. *American Economic Review* 89(5): 1259–1278.

Acemoglu, D., P. Aghion, and G. Violante (2001). Deunionization, Technical Change and Inequality. CEPR Discussion Paper 2764. Centre of Economic Policy Research, London.

Almus, M., et al. (1998). Die gemeinnützige Arbeitnehmerüberlassung in Rheinland-Pfalz – eine ökonometrische Analyse des Wiedereingliederungserfolgs. ZEW Discussion Paper 36. Zentrum für Europäische Wirtschaftsforschung, Mannheim.

Baily, M., and R. Lawrence (2001). Do We Have a New E-Economy? NBER Working Paper 8243. National Bureau of Economic Research, Cambridge, Mass.

Belke, A., and R. Fehn (2000). Institutions and Structural Unemployment: Do Capital-Market Imperfections Matter? Working Paper 00.8. Center for European Studies, Program for the Study of Germany and Europe, Harvard University, Cambridge, Mass.

Bentilola, S., and G. Bertola (1990). Firing Costs and Labour Demand: How Bad Is Eurosclerosis? *Review of Economic Studies* 57(3): 381–402.

Berthold, N., and R. Fehn (1996a). The Positive Economics of Unemployment and Labor Market Flexibility. *Kyklos* 49(4): 583–613.

Berthold, N., and R. Fehn (1996b). Evolution von Lohnverhandlungssystemen – Macht oder ökonomisches Gesetz? In W. Zohlnhöfer (ed.), *Die Tarifautonomie auf dem Prüfstand.* Schriften des Vereins für Socialpolitik, N.F. Vol. 244. Berlin: Duncker und Humblot.

Berthold, N., and R. Fehn (1997). Aktive Arbeitsmarktpolitik – wirksames Instrument der Beschäftigungspolitik oder politische Beruhigungspille? *Ordo* 48: 411–435.

Berthold, N., and O. Stettes (2001). Die betriebliche Mitbestimmung in Deutschland: Gratwanderung zwischen Markt- und Staatsversagen. *WiSt* 30(10): 506–512.

Berthold, N., R. Fehn, and E. Thode (2000). Falling Labor Share and Rising Unemployment: Long-Run Consequences of Institutional Shocks? Working Paper 00.2. Center for European Studies, Program for the Study of Germany and Europe, Harvard University, Cambridge, Mass.

Berthold, N., R. Fehn, and S. v. Berchem (2001). *Innovative Beschäftigungspolitik – Wege aus der Strukturkrise*. Bad Homburg: Herbert-Quandt-Stiftung.

Bertola, G., and A. Ichino (1995). Wage Inequality and Unemployment: United States versus Europe. *NBER Macroeconomics Annual*: 13–54.

Bickenbach, F., and R. Soltwedel (1998). Produktionssystem, Arbeitsorganisation und Anreizstrukturen: Der Paradigmenwechsel in der Unternehmensorganisation und seine Konsequenzen für die Arbeitsmarktverfassung. *Schriften zu Ordnungsfragen der Wirtschaft* 57: 491–533.

Black, S., and L. Lynch (2000). What's Driving the New Economy: The Benefits of Workplace Innovation. NBER Working Paper 7479. National Bureau of Economic Research, Cambridge, Mass.

Blanchard, O., and J. Wolfers (1999). The Role of Shocks and Institutions in the Rise of European Unemployment: The Aggregate Evidence. NBER Working Paper 7282. National Bureau of Economic Research, Cambridge, Mass.

Boeri, T., G. Nicoletti, and S. Scarpetta (2000). Regulation and Labour Market Performance. CEPR Discussion Paper 2420. Centre of Economic Policy Research, London.

Bosworth, B. (2001). The Outlook for the U.S. Economy: Soft or Hard Landing? *CESifo Forum* 2(1): 14–20.

Bosworth, B., and J. Triplett (2000). What's New About the New Economy? IT, Economic Growth and Productivity. Discussion Paper in Economics. Brookings Institution, Washington, D.C., October.

Burda, M. (1997). Unemployment Compensation: Theory and Practice. In H. Giersch (ed.), *Reforming the Welfare State*. Berlin: Springer.

Burda, M. (2000). Product Market Regulation and Labor Market Outcomes: How Can Deregulation Create Jobs. *IFO-Studien* 46(1): 55–72.

Buti, M., L.R. Pench, and P. Sestito (1998). European Unemployment: Contending Theories and Institutional Complexities. Policy Papers 98/1. European University Institute Florence. San Domenico di Fiesole.

Caballero, R., and M. Hammour (1997). Jobless Growth: Appropriability, Factor Substitution, and Unemployment. NBER Working Paper 6221. National Bureau of Economic Research, Cambridge, Mass.

Caballero, R., and M. Hammour (1998). The Macroeconomics of Specificity. *Journal of Political Economy* 106(4): 724–767.

Calmfors, L. (1994). Active Labour Market Policy and Unemployment: A Framework for the Analysis of Crucial Design Features. Seminar Paper 563. Institute for International Economic Studies, Stockholm.

Calmfors, L. (1995). What Can We Expect from Active Labor Market Policy? *Beihefte der Konjunkturpolitik* 43: 11–30.

Calmfors, L., and J. Driffill (1988). Bargaining Structure, Corporatism and Macroeconomic Performance. *Economic Policy* 6(1): 13–61.

Calmfors, L., and H. Lang (1995). Macroeconomic Effects of Active Labour Market Programmes in a Union Wage-Setting Model. *Economic Journal* 105(May): 601–619.

Calmfors, L., and P. Skedinger (1995). Does Active Labour Market Policy Increase Employment? Theoretical Considerations and Some Empirical Evidence from Sweden. Seminar Paper 590. Institute for International Economic Studies, Stockholm.

Daveri, F. (2000). Is Growth an Information Technology Story in Europe too? Working Paper. Universita di Parma and IGIER, September 12.

Davis, S., and M. Henrekson (2000). Wage-Setting Institutions as Industrial Policy. NBER Working Paper 7502. National Bureau of Economic Research, Cambridge, Mass.

Fehn, R. (2001). Schöpferische Zerstörung und struktureller Wandel: Wie beeinflussen Kapitalbildung und Kapitalmarktunvollkommenheiten die Beschäftigungsentwicklung. Habilitation Thesis, University of Würzburg.

Feld, L., and A. Santoni (2001). Arbeitsmarktregulierung und Wirtschaftswachstum: Empirische Ergebnisse für 12 EU-Länder von 1971 bis 1993. Mimeo. University of St. Gallen.

Fitzenberger, B., and H. Prey (1997). Assessing the Impact of Training on Employment – The Case of East Germany. *Ifo-Studien* 43(1): 69–114.

Forslund, A., and A. Krueger (1997). An Evaluation of Swedish Active Labour Policy: New and Received Wisdom. In R. Freeman, R. Topel, and B. Swedenborg (eds.), *The Welfare State in Transition – Reforming the Swedish Model*. Chicago: University of Chicago Press.

Freeman, R.B. (2000). Shared Capitalism or Apartheid Economy? *CentrePiece – The Magazine for Economic Performance*. Spring 2000, Vol. 5 (1). See also http://www.CENTREPIECE-MAGAZINE.COM/Spring00/CAPITALISM.htm

Freeman, R.B., and R. Gibbons (1993). Getting Together and Breaking Apart: The Decline of Centralized Bargaining. NBER Working Paper 4464. National Bureau of Economic Research, Cambridge, Mass.

Gordon, R. (2000). Does the "New Economy" Measure up to the Great Inventions of the Past? NBER Working Paper 7833. National Bureau of Economic Research, Cambride, Mass.

Gorton, G., and F. Schmid (2000). Class Struggle Inside the Firm: A Study of German Codetermination. NBER Working Paper 7945. National Bureau of Economic Research, Cambridge, Mass.

Heckman, J., R. LaLonde, and J. Smith (1999). The Economics and Econometrics of Active Labour Market Programs. In O. Ashenfelter and D. Card (eds.), *Handbook of Labor Economics*. Vol. 3A. Amsterdam: Elsevier.

Issing, O. (2000). How to Promote Growth in the Euro Area: The Contribution of Monetary Policy. *International Finance* 3(3): 309–327.

Jackman, R.A. (1994). What Can Active Labour Market Policy Do? *Swedish Economic Policy Review* 1(1): 221–257.

Jeng, L.A., and P.C. Wells (2000). The Determinants of Venture Capital Funding: Evidence across Countries. *Journal of Corporate Finance* 6(3): 241–289.

Jorgenson, D., and K. Stiroh (2000). Raising the Speed Limit: U.S. Economic Growth in the Information Age. *Brookings Papers on Economic Activity* (1): 125–211.

Katz, H.C. (1993). The Decentralization of Collective Bargaining: A Literature Review and Comparative Analysis. *Industrial and Labor Relations Review* 47(1): 3–22.

Katz, L. (1994). Active Labor Market Policies to Expand Employment and Opportunity. In Federal Reserve Bank of Kansas City (ed.), Reducing Unemployment: *Current Issues and Policy Options*. Jackson Hole, Wyoming.

Kraus, F., P. Puhani, and V. Steiner (2000). Do Public Work Programs Work? Some Unpleasant Results form the East German Experience. In S. Polachek (ed.), *Research in Labour Economics* 19. JAI Press: Amsterdam.

Kugler, A., and G. Saint-Paul (2000). Hiring and Firing Costs, Adverse Selection and the Persistence of Unemployment. CEPR Discussion Paper 2410. Centre of Economic Policy Research, London.

Lechner, M. (1998). *Training the East German Labour Force – Microeconometric Evaluations of Continuous Vocational Training after Unification*. Heidelberg: Physica.

Lechner, M. (1999). Earnings and Employment Effects of Continuous Off-the-Job Training in East Germany after Unification. *Journal of Business and Economic Statistics* 17(1): 74–90.

Lechner, M., et al. (2000). The Impact of Non-Profit Temping Agencies on Individual Labour Market Success in the West German State of Rhineland-Palatinate. ZEW Discussion Paper 00-02. Zentrum für Europäische Wirtschaftsforschung, Mannheim.

Lindbeck, A., and D.J. Snower (1988). *The Insider-Outsider Theory of Employment and Unemployment*. Cambridge, Mass.: MIT Press.

Lindbeck, A., and D.J. Snower (1997). Centralized Bargaining, Multi-Tasking and Work Incentives. CEPR Discussion Paper 1563. Centre of Economic Policy Research, London.

Lindbeck, A., and D.J. Snower (1998). The Division of Labour Within Firms. CEPR Discussion Paper 1825. Centre of Economic Policy Research, London.

Lindbeck, A., and D.J. Snower (2000). The Division of Labor and the Market for Organizations. CESifo Working Paper 267. Center for Economic Studies, Munich.

Ljungqvist, L., and T. Sargent (1998). The European Unemployment Dilemma. *Journal of Political Economy* 106(3): 514–550.

Martin, J. (2000). What Works Among Active Labour Market Policies: Evidence from OECD Countries' Experiences. *OECD Economic Studies* 30(1): 79–113.

Morgan, J., and A. Mourougane (2000). Structural Unemployment and Labour Market Institutions in Europe. Paper Presented at the ECB Labour Market Workshop in December. Frankfurt am Main.

Nickell, S. (1997). Unemployment and Labour Market Rigidities: Europe versus North America. *Journal of Economic Perspectives* 11(3): 55–74.

Nickell, S., and R. Layard (1999). Labor Market Institutions and Economic Performance. In O. Ashenfelter and D. Card (eds.), *Handbook of Labor Economics*. Vol. 3C. Amsterdam: Elsevier.

Nordhaus, W. (2001). Productivity Growth and the New Economy. NBER Working Paper 8096. National Bureau of Economic Research, Cambridge, Mass.

OECD (1999a). *Employment Outlook.* Chapter 4: New Enterprise Work Practices and Their Labour Market Implications. Paris: OECD.

OECD (1999b). *Employment Outlook.* Chapter 2: Employment Protection and Labour Market Performance. Paris: OECD.

Orszag, M., and D.J. Snower (2000). The Effectiveness of Employment Vouchers: A Simple Approach. *German Economic Review* 1(4): 385–419.

Ramaswamy, R., and R. Rowthorn (1993). Centralized Bargaining, Efficiency Wages and Flexibility. IMF Working Paper 25. International Monetary Fund, Washington, D.C.

Robinson, P. (1995). The Decline of the Swedish Model and the Limits to Active Labour Market Policy. Discussion Paper 259. Centre for Economic Performance, London School of Economics, London.

Saint-Paul, G. (1996). Employment Protection, International Specialization, and Innovation. CEPR Discussion Paper 1338. Centre of Economic Policy Research, London.

Saint-Paul, G. (1998). The Political Consequences of Unemployment. *Swedish Economic Policy Review* 5(2): 259–296.

Saint-Paul, G. (2001). Information Technology and the Knowledge Elites. CEPR Discussion Paper 2761. Centre of Economic Policy Research, London.

Scarpetta, S. (1996). Assessing the Role of Labour Market Policies and Insitutional Settings on Unemployment: A Cross-Country Study. *OECD Economic Studies* (26): 43–98.

Schnabel, C. (2001). Höhere Kosten, unsichere Erträge: Zur Reform des Betriebsverfassungsgesetzes. *WiSt* 30(3): 121.

Siebert, H. (1997). Labor Market Rigidities – At the Root of Unemployment in Europe. *Journal of Economic Perspectives* 11(3): 37–54.

Siebert, H. (2000). The New Economy – What Is Really New? Kiel Working Paper 1000. Kiel Institute for World Economics, Kiel.

Snower, D.J. (1994). The Simple Economics of Benefit Transfers. CEPR Discussion Paper 1086. Centre of Economic Policy Research, London.

Snower, D.J. (1997). The Organizational Revolution and Its Implications for Job Creation. Discussion Paper in Economics 97-17. Birkbeck College, University of London, London.

Steiner, V., and T. Hagen (2000). *Von der Finanzierung der Arbeitslosigkeit zur Förderung der Arbeit, Analysen und Handlungsempfehlungen zur Arbeitsmarktpolitik.* ZEW-Wirtschaftsanalysen 51. Baden-Baden: Nomos.

SVR (2000). *Chancen auf einen höheren Wachstumspfad.* Jahresgutachten des Sachverständigenrates zur Begutachtung der gesamtwirtschaftlichen Entwicklung. Stuttgart: Metzler-Poeschel.

Comment on Norbert Berthold and Rainer Fehn

Michael C. Burda

There can be no doubt that the technological revolution that we now glibly call the "new economy" has implications for the labor market. In their paper, Berthold and Fehn express a deep concern that these consequences are primarily negative for Continental Europe, and for Germany in particular. Their thesis – which I share to a large extent – is that labor market institutions may pose a significant hindrance to dealing with the changes that the new economy will bring. By looking to the leading country in this development, the United States, one can indeed learn a great about the forces which European and other labor markets, with their attendant institutional rigidities and regulations, will soon face. Many of the details, however, are necessarily speculative and therefore subject to a very large errors. A good example is the unexpected meltdown of the new economy which has occurred since the conference was held, and my final comments will be addressed to this equally interesting aspect of the subject.

For me at least, any discussion of a phenomenon of this magnitude must differentiate sharply between positive and normative dimensions. A positive analysis would ask what the new economy – which I define to include the Internet, wireless telecommunications, broadband data transmission technologies, and the spectacular advances observed in personal computers – means for labor markets and labor market outcomes. This is already a tall order: it means first understanding precisely what the shocks entail, which sectors they will impinge upon, how labor demand will change, how labor supply will respond, and how institutions will affect the functioning of labor markets. Obviously, policy recommendations must be driven by a clear picture of what is really happening in the United States rather than generic prescriptions for more labor market flexibility. While the authors were long on discussing how bad the representative European (in particular, German) economy works and how it should be reformed, they were short on facts relevant to the new economy per se in Germany, or anywhere for that matter. In my comments, I will offer some facts which support their thesis. In addition, I will add a few thoughts of my own.

1.   What Does the New Economy Mean for Labor Markets? Facts from the United States

What does the new economy really mean for labor markets? While the new economy – which for me is rather an issue of technology and furthermore one of only the past decade – involves primarily shifts in both sectoral and occupational demand for labor, the evidence suggests that occupational shifts will be just as important as sectoral ones. Not only will some professions dry up and disappear, but we will also witness big swings in sectoral employment within broader classifications. These changes must be viewed in the context of the long-standing trend of a growing service economy with both producer- and consumer-related elements. In the United States, it is important to note that producer services have assumed the greater role since the late 1980s. Recent growth in employment was singularly dominated by *business services* in the years 1995–2000 (40 percent of all employment growth in the period). As the authors themselves would agree, it is a (disingenuous?) misrepresentation by critiques of liberal labor market policies to assert that U.S. job growth is nothing but a swelling army of burger flippers and security guards (Table 1). Employment growth in higher-paid producer service sectors outpaced that in retail and personal services.

Taking the analysis one step further, the hefty expansion of business services is an *intermediate good* phenomenon. Thus, one obvious influence of the new economy is that it reshuffles firm structures, as the enhanced ability to communicate and to manage has allowed a sizable increase in the outsourcing of firm activities. Many of these activities were never part of the firm's core competency. Examples are legal advising, accounting and control, business consulting, catering, building and grounds maintenance, etc. It is not simply that firms are flattening their organizational structure; rather, they are simply divorcing themselves from the production of *intermediate* inputs that they produced earlier as a foregone conclusion. The logical conclusion is that these shifts must have led to an increase in the demand for occupations which manage, advise, and transfer technical competency. The new economy, together with advances in communications and data processing, has accelerated this trend. The striking increase in the demand for managerial occupations in the United States can be found in Table 2; for international evidence, see Burda and Dluhosch (1999).

Finally, the new economy has induced sharp swings in labor demand *within* broad sectors at the narrow level of classification. Some of the fastest growing and fastest shrinking three- and four-digit sectors in the U.S. economy in the hot years 1995–2000 are in the same one- or two-digit class. For example, in computer/peripherals/software retailing (5054), employment grew by 55.5 percent, and in radio/television retailing (5731) by 35.6 percent, while employment in housing ap-

Table 1: An Overview of Sectoral Employment Growth in the U.S. Economy, 1995–2000 (percent)

Industry	Cumulative employment change 1995–2000	Employment change 1999–2000	Contribution to change in aggregate U.S. employment 1995–2000
Total	12.6	2.3	100.0
Total private	13.8	2.3	91.0
Mining	−8.5	−2.6	−0.3
Construction	27.3	5.8	9.1
Manufacturing	−0.6	−0.7	−0.8
Durable goods	3.8	0.0	2.8
Nondurable goods	−6.1	−1.4	−3.3
Transportation	15.7	3.1	4.2
Communications	16.4	3.9	1.5
Electric, gas, and sanitary services	−7.8	−1.4	−0.5
Wholesale trade	13.7	2.8	5.9
Retail trade	11.3	1.9	21.8
Finance	12.5	1.0	2.8
Insurance	7.6	0.8	1.2
Real estate	12.5	2.6	1.2
Services (U.S. definition) of which:	22.8	3.7	50.9
Hotels and other lodging places	12.4	1.7	1.3
Personal services	6.2	2.8	0.5
Business services	45.0	5.8	20.0
Amusement/recreation services	20.5	5.9	1.9
Health services	9.6	1.4	6.0
Legal services	8.7	1.9	0.6
Educational services	24.7	3.5	3.4
Social services	27.8	5.3	4.4
Engineering/management	33.5	6.1	6.2

Source: Bureau of Labor Statistics. *Employment and Earnings.* May issues, 1995–2000.

pliance retailing (572) declined by 12.1 percent over the same period, and in sewing needlework and piecegoods retailing (5949) by 27.6 percent. While any individual sector in the table rarely contributes more than 1 percent to the employment expansion, the summation of these developments over all sectors documents significant within-sector change.

It should be evident how these shifts are linked to changing technologies in the new economy and given my limited time, I will not pursue this line here. The positive question for me is: what can one learn from the U.S. experience for Europe and Germany in particular? To begin with, I have to complain that German statistical sources are embarrassingly meager in this area, considering the usual punctilious detail which otherwise characterizes German data. There is a real information

Table 2: An Overview of Employment Growth in the U.S. Economy by Occupation, 1995–2000 (percent)

Occupational category	Cumulative employment change 1995–2000	Employment change 1999–2000	Contribution to change in aggregate U.S. employment 1995–2000
Total	8.5	1.7	100.0
Executive, administrative, and managerial	18.8	2.3	29.9
Professional speciality	14.2	0.6	24.5
Technicians and related support	13.0	6.3	4.8
Sales occupations	8.0	0.0	11.4
Administrative support, including clerical	3.2	2.3	5.5
Service occupations	9.3	3.7	15.1
Precision production, craft, and repair	8.3	–0.4	10.5
Operators, fabricators, and laborers	0.4	1.1	0.6
Farming, forestry, and fishing	–6.9	3.3	–2.2

Source: Bureau of Labor Statistics. *Employment and Earnings.* May issues.

deficit in Germany, and the blame lies with the *Bundesanstalt für Arbeit* in Nürnberg as well as with the immediate consumers of its data, which include the Federal Statistical Agency and the Council of Economic Advisers. Until more political pressure is applied, we will know precious little about how the new economy affects German labor markets.

From a theoretical perspective, it is possible to conclude that *mobility* is the central factor conditioning the ultimate effect of the new economy and is therefore its central challenge. Market-driven incentives to change firms, jobs, occupations, industries, and place of residence will increase as the relative scarcity of new economy versus old economy workers becomes acute. Those who move first will get the largest rents. They will tend to be younger, better educated, without a family or a partner. Those who take advantage of the scarcity differential will profit. Those who do not – the less mobile, the attached, those with families – may find themselves unemployed, and thus forced to make the less palatable choice between a new job and sector and long-term unemployment. As human capital deteriorates in unemployment, so will the choice set available to the unemployed.

While hindrances to mobility can also be "natural" (age, sex, family status, innate skills), one is clearly more interested in man-made barriers (severance regulations, unemployment benefits, distorted investments in specific versus general human capital, etc.). The authors certainly are right to suspect that labor market institutions that provide unconditional income support will inhibit mobility, which is always costly. It will be necessary to implement new policies which explicitly subsidize more general and transferable skills. As the authors argue, new policies will be necessary to develop an adaptable workforce; as the population of Germany and Europe ages, this must go beyond maintaining good primary schools and the apprenticeship system: the university system will have to be radically reformed and lifelong learning will have to be subsidized. Much of this could be paid for by simply abolishing or scaling back ineffective active labor market policies, as argued by Schmidt and Zimmermann (2001). The authors are correct in pointing out that the suppression of the temporary work agencies in Germany is a hindrance to information exchange and transfer, as well as a benchmark for the mediocre performance of the Bundesanstalt für Arbeit.

2.   What Policy Reforms Are Called For?

Incentives must be set right if mobility is to occur, but the adoption of the new economy may also depend on distaste for mobility, which certainly varies across countries and may be lower in Continental Europe than in the United States. The appropriate policy depends on the underlying welfare function and the subjective preference ordering. It contains a value judgment which I, as an American in a den of Europeans, do not have the authority to make. It also depends on the correct identification of the underlying market failure, which the authors have not really bothered to do.

Put more directly, I cannot believe that Germany's labor market rigidities are simply the result of a giant accident or that they arose out of a vacuum. This is where I most missed some contribution from the authors. Moreover, market failures can be corrected, even by market forces. For example, the argument that unions provide "wage insurance" by smoothing pay over states of the world has been accepted as an alternative or even complementary goal of union behavior (Agell and Lommerud 1992; Burda 1995); yet with advancing sophistication of financial technologies, the underlying market imperfections (e.g., imperfect capital and insurance markets) may fade into obscurity, rendering the institution inefficient. As far as codetermination is concerned, the German electorate appears to support it; it coincides evidently with the general taste for consensus in decision-making one observes everywhere in the country. If this taste is strong enough, how can one argue with it? As much as I would like to believe that it is a hindrance to the efficient operation of small enterprises, I cannot help but think that mobile capital will demand a "price" for the luxury of codetermination, namely a lower equilibrium wage. Those who want codetermination will have to pay for it.

More generally, I am not convinced that Germany's institutions will be useless when IT technologies consolidate. One already hears of disgruntlement among employees in American new economy companies and it seems that unionization or at least more effective worker representation is just around the corner, as soon as the current phase of creative destruction has passed. Regardless, the response of national policymakers to labor market challenges posed by the information age remains in the normative realm. We should not be coy: Europeans appear willing to accept significant unemployment as the price to be paid for a slow, plodding adjustment to the whatever steady state the new economy holds in store. It strikes me that even with the joblessness rates observed today in the democracies of Germany, France, and Italy, the political heat to reform labor market institutions is virtually nonexistent. What is so miraculous to me about the Dutch miracle is not that institutions matter, but that this country was able to pull off such a systematic regime change of its labor market policies – but only after the pain had exceeded the threshold value. Meanwhile, recent sharp employment cuts observed in U.S. high-tech companies should give pause to consider that European tastes for stable, slow adjustment to a new economy may be more rational than they might sometimes appear.

References

Agell, J., and K.E. Lommerud (1992). Union Egalitarianism as Income Insurance. *Economica* 59(235): 295–310.

Burda, M.C. (1995). Unions and Wage Insurance. CEPR Discussion Paper 1232. Centre of Economic Policy Research, London.

Burda, M.C., and B. Dluhosch (1999). Globalization and European Labor Markets. In H. Siebert (ed.), *Globalization and Labor.* Tübingen: Mohr Siebeck.

Schmidt, C., and K. Zimmermann (2001). *The Evaluation of Labour Market Policies.* Berlin: Springer.

Aaditya Mattoo and Ludger Schuknecht

A WTO Framework for the New Economy

1. Introduction

If international trade in new-economy-related products is allowed to flourish, the benefits will come, first, in the form of more competition and lower costs. In addition to these "standard" gains, trade in new economy products can play an important role in generating so-called endogenous growth effects. The development and dispersion of new-economy-related products and technologies due to trade can facilitate human capital formation and dissemination, learning by doing, and technology transfers.

This paper will address two broad questions: first, what categories of international trade are particularly conducive to realizing the benefits of the new economy and how important is such trade already? Second, how well developed and liberal is the international trade regime, as defined in the context of the World Trade Organization (WTO), and what are the main challenges ahead? To address these questions, the paper will draw upon a set of descriptive statistics and a critical assessment of the legal-institutional framework of the WTO.

In the context of the first question, the study will look at trade in information and communications technology (ICT) products, as well as the trade which was enabled (or at least strongly boosted) by the ICT "revolution", i.e., electronic commerce in goods and services. In the context of the second question, concerning the WTO framework, we distinguish trade in three types of products. First, trade in most new-economy-related goods is covered by the so-called Information Technology Agreement (ITA). Second, trade in software and digitizable media products is still largely conducted in physical form and is, therefore, covered by the rules governing trade in goods, i.e., the General Agreement on Tariffs and Trade (WTO 1994/5). However, such trade will increasingly be conducted on-line through electronic means. This raises the question of how trade in such products

Remark: We are thankful to comments by Francesco Mongelli and by participants of the Economic Policy for the New Economy Conference conducted in Paderborn in May 2001. The project was started while both authors were working at the WTO. Any views expressed here are those of the authors and should not be attributed to the WTO or to their new employers.

should be characterized – as trade in goods (covered by GATT) or as trade in services (covered by the General Agreement on Trade in Services, GATS). Third, the growing use of electronic communications and transmission has given rise to new services and has facilitated enormously the trade in many existing services, which are covered by GATS rules.

We put particular emphasis on discussing the challenges for further trade liberalization and for creating an appropriate body of rules. Note that the WTO framework today extends beyond the negotiation and binding of tariffs. It consists of a complex body of international trade rules designed to enhance the openness, transparency, and stability of the policy environment for international trade. Two of the most important principles of the WTO framework are the most-favored-nation principle (prohibiting discrimination between trading partners) and the national treatment principle (prohibiting discrimination against foreigners). Rules on contingency protection provide "safety valves" for domestic industry; whereas rules on domestic regulation are designed to ensure that they are not more burdensome than necessary to meet policy objectives. We will also briefly mention the complementary role of international property rights protection via the TRIPS agreement.

The main findings of the study are as follows: trade in new-economy-related products is large, accounting for 15–20 percent of world trade in goods and services, and growing rapidly. As regards trade in goods, the ITA has secured far-reaching liberalization of market access. The rules governing trade in goods are well developed and contingency protection is not being applied much against new economy products. As regards software and other digitizable media products, a decision needs to be taken on whether to treat Internet-based trade in such products as services or as goods. In the services domain, market access commitments and rules need to be further strengthened so as to provide a secure and liberal environment for international trade.

The following three sections discuss trade, trade barriers, and rules for each of the three product groups. Section 5 of the study concludes.

2.   Trade in Goods Covered by the Information Technology Agreement

a.   Trade Coverage and Values

The development and spread of the new economy experienced a significant boost with the signing of the Ministerial Declaration on Trade in Information Products in late 1996. The latter is now better known as the Information Technology Agreement (ITA) and covers trade in semiconductors, telecommunications products, sci-

Table 1: Exports in ITA-Related Product Categories, 1997 and 1999[a]

Country	In millions of dollars							
	1997				1999			
	HS Code				HS Code			
	84	85	90	total	84	85	90	total
Australia	2,707	1,508	533	4,748	11,775	8,199	2,754	22,728
Brazil	4,531	1,783	272	6,587	9,355	7,733	1,715	18,803
Canada	19,445	12,939	2,269	34,653	42,040	28,120	7,478	77,638
China	13,717	24,553	3,998	42,268	27,832	35,238	5,013	68,082
France, Monaco	39,055	30,881	7,062	76,998	45,460	30,469	8,404	84,334
Germany	97,074	55,602	18,696	171,372	69,517	51,836	13,531	134,883
India	1,152	882	121	2,155				
Italy	51,595	15,610	4,710	71,915	26,836	19,815	6,494	53,145
Korea Rep.	14,553	34,048	1,951	50,552	13,999	27,329	4,733	46,061
Mexico	13,154	28,147	2,685	43,987	22,715	35,752	4,048	62,514
Poland	1,584	2,077	131	3,793	7,823	4,970	907	13,699
Singapore	40,671	40,060	2,691	83,423	23,569	39,070	3,815	66,453
U.K.	55,635	36,202	10,528	102,365	55,372	41,004	9,757	106,133
U.S.A.	129,840	96,219	32,814	258,873	169,162	148,652	31,283	349,097
Grand Total	736,808	623,791	145,562	1,506,160	803,995	748,188	157,960	1,710,142
Grand Total percent change 97–99					*9.1*	*19.9*	*8.5*	*13.5*

[a] HS Code 84 includes machinery and mechanical appliances and parts, boilers, nuclear reactors. HS Code 85 includes electrical machinery and equipment and parts, sound recorders and reproducers, television image and sound recorders and reproducers and parts and accessories of such articles. HS Code 90 includes optical, photographic, cenematographic, measuring, checking, precision, medical or surgical instruments and apparatus; parts and accesssories thereof.

Source: WTO (2001).

entific instruments, computers, software, semiconductor manufacturing equipment, and various other products (see Bacchetta et al. 1998).

By November 2000, 54 members (countries or separate customs territories) covering at least 93 percent of world trade in such products had signed the ITA (WTO 2000: G/IT/Rev.16). The information technology sector at that time was already one of the most important sectors in the world. The trade value covered was around $500 billion in 1996, about 10 percent of world trade of that year. The exact trade volume, however, is not known, as there is agreement on the broad product coverage but countries apply different interpretations at the margin. This means that there is no exact list of tariff lines that are covered by the ITA. Moreover, there are continuously new products, the classification of which is not always immediately obvious and uniform.

Table 1 nevertheless tries to give an idea of the importance of ITA-related trade by showing trade values for the three 2-digit HS code headings which capture almost all of the ITA-related trade. Table 1, however, exaggerates the relevant trade, as only category 85 is mostly covered by the ITA. Trade (exports) in this category alone increased from \$624 billion in 1997 to \$748 billion in 1999, or about 11 percent of total trade in goods and services. This is an increase of 20 percent, and about twice as fast as the increase in total trade in those two years. Industrialized countries are the most important exporters, but Singapore and Mexico follow closely. Of the other two categories presented in Table 1 and accounting for \$1 trillion worth of trade, only a limited part is covered by the ITA and it is difficult to know exactly how much. But even a small share would already be significant in value terms.

b.   Liberalization Commitments

The objective of the ITA was to eliminate customs duties on all covered products, and most signatory countries had done so by the beginning of 2000. Some countries were granted an extended deadline but in no case will this exceed 2005. Most signatory countries applied tariffs from 0–15 percent for a majority of the affected tariff lines in 1996 (Bacchetta et al. 1998). However, tariffs were much higher for all relevant products in the case of India. Only Iceland, Singapore, and Hong Kong reported a largely tariff-free treatment of such trade already at that time.

The participation of developing countries in the ITA reveals an interesting pattern: while most of the major Asian countries participated, hardly any Latin American countries (only Costa Rica, El Salvador, and Panama) and no African country participated in this Agreement (Table 2). Hence, important trading nations, such as Brazil, Argentina, and South Africa are missing. This is a wasted opportunity because an important way in which the WTO can help is by lending credibility to national reform programs.

Consider the example of two countries which have traditionally had high levels of protection, China and India. Figure 1 shows the commitments that both have made – China under terms of its accession to the WTO and India under the terms of its participation in the ITA – to reduce tariffs in these products virtually to zero in the next five years. This is a good example of a situation where a country strikes a balance: on the one hand it does not want to liberalize immediately but on the other hand it does not want to be held hostage in perpetuity to inefficient domestic

Table 2: Developing Country Members of WTO's Information Technology Agreement

Asia	Chinese Taipei, Hong Kong, India, Indonesia, Israel, Korea, Macau, Malaysia, Philippines, Thailand, Singapore
Latin America	Costa Rica, El Salvador, Panama
Africa	None

Figure 1: Precommitment to Liberalization in Information Technology Products by India and China (Average tariffs for selected products in percent)

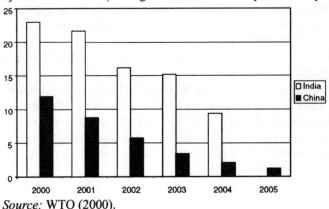

Source: WTO (2000).

industry. More countries could take advantage of this mechanism to lend credibility to their reform programs.

c.   Contingency Protection

Trade involving products covered by the ITA is governed by the GATT rules for all trade in goods. While the ITA has resulted in duty-free trade for most of the world's new-economy-related trade in goods, the GATT nevertheless permits member countries to introduce contingency protection in the form of antidumping and safeguard measures. The Uruguay Round resulted in a significant development of the rules underlying the application of both types of measures.

Antidumping measures are unilateral remedies which a member may apply after an investigation and determination by that member has revealed that an imported product is being "dumped" and that the dumped imports are causing material injury to a domestic industry producing the like product. Antidumping has become the most prominent means of contingency protection and is also increasingly being used by developing countries (Miranda et al. 1998).

New-economy-related products can be the target of antidumping investigations and there have been a number of very prominent cases in the past. The high antidumping duties of the European Union against various Asian DRAM producers illustrate the vulnerability to antidumping protection especially in sectors with high fixed costs and significant price volatility. It is difficult to assess what percentage of antidumping cases affects the new economy but, in general, one can argue that trade in "old" rather than new economy products was the main target of antidump-

ing cases. In the European Union, to our knowledge, there were only two prominent cases over the 1990s: DRAMs and microdiscs. By 2000, only duties on
microdisc imports from a number of countries remained in place (European Commission 2000). These two cases compare to a total of 257 initiated by the European Union during the 1991–1998 period.

The Agreement on Safeguards (which clarifies and reinforces GATT Article
XIX) defines safeguard measures as "emergency" actions with respect to increased imports of particular products where such imports have caused or threaten
to cause serious injury to the importing member's domestic industry. Measures are
in fact temporary suspensions of concessions or obligations and they can consist
of quantitative import restrictions or of duty increases to higher than bound rates.
The total number of safeguard cases and the trade value covered is very small and
new economy products do not feature among them.

d.   WTO Rules as Constraints on Protection

The importance of duty-free trade in the ITA sector needs to be seen in the context
of the broader legal framework of the GATT. On the one hand, as mentioned, this
implies the option to seek contingency protection. On the other hand, the GATT
secures market access through a number of other disciplines on trade-related policies, of which only the most important are discussed here.

In essence, the rules for the "physical" trade in goods are quite well developed
but significant challenges arise in the context of the electronic delivery of products
which so far have been traded as goods on carrier media such as software and various digitizable media products. This particular issue will be dealt with in the following section.

We have already mentioned the most-favored-nation and national treatment
principles (GATT Articles I and III). A further constraint on protection arises from
Article XI, which in principle prohibits the application of quantitative restrictions
on imports and exports. A number of exceptions to this rule, however, permit
countries to take trade-restricting measures necessary to pursue legitimate policy
objectives to protect, inter alia, human life and health. Article XX of the GATT
1994 allows such exceptions but it also stipulates that measures taken must be applied in a nondiscriminatory manner and must not amount to a disguised restriction on trade.

The WTO Agreement on Technical Barriers to Trade (TBT) seeks to ensure
that technical regulations do not pose unnecessary obstacles to trade, i.e., that they
are not more trade-restrictive than necessary to fulfill the legitimate objective
(Articles II.2 and II.3). Moreover, where technical regulations exist, they must be
applied in line with the most-favored-nation principle (Article II.1), which forbids

discrimination between sources of imports, as well as in line with the principle of national treatment (Article II.1), which prohibits discrimination against foreign suppliers. It also encourages the harmonization and mutual recognition of technical regulations, as well as transparency in rules and administrative practices. These issues are of great relevance to new-economy-related trade, especially electronic commerce.

The subsidization of goods trade is also subject to important disciplines in the WTO framework under the Agreement on Subsidies and Countervailing Measures (SCM Agreement). Under Article 1 of the SCM Agreement, a subsidy shall be deemed to exist where there is a financial contribution by a government or any public body within the territory of a member which confers a benefit. The list of financial contributions specified in the agreement includes grants, loans, equity infusions, loan guarantees, fiscal incentives, the provision of goods or services, and the purchase of goods. In order for a financial contribution to be a subsidy, it must be made by or at the direction of a government or any public body within the territory of a member.

The SCM Agreement prohibits two categories of subsidies: export subsidies and subsidies contingent on the use of domestic over imported goods (subject to special and differential treatment for developing country members and members in the process of transition to a market economy). With respect to export subsidies, Article III.1(a) of the agreement refers to an Illustrative List of Export Subsidies subject to the prohibition. Most specific subsidies may be subject to dispute settlement challenge in the WTO if they cause adverse effects to the interests of another member. In addition, a member may impose countervailing measures on imports benefiting from actionable subsidies.

In this context, the Agreement on Trade-Related Aspects of Intellectual Property Rights (TRIPS) is also worth mentioning. The TRIPS Agreement does not deal with trade barriers per se, but rather aims to secure the recognition and enforcement of intellectual property rights (IPRs) across borders. The TRIPS affects trade in new-economy-related goods, as many of these goods have significant intellectual property components. It covers the following areas of the IPRs: (a) copyright and related rights (i.e., the rights of performers, producers of sound recordings and broadcasting organizations); (b) trademarks, including service marks; (c) geo-graphical indications, including appellations of origin; (d) industrial designs; (e) patents, including the protection of new varieties of plants; (f) the layout designs of integrated circuits; and (g) undisclosed information, including trade secrets and test data. Most of these rights are important for the development and dissemination of communication infrastructure and access equipment, for the development of copyrighted material, and for the protection of trademarks and domain names (Bacchetta et al. 1998).

The three main features of the agreement include, first, minimum standards of protection to be provided by each member. Members can provide more extensive protection of intellectual property if they so wish. The second main set of provisions deals with domestic procedures and remedies for the enforcement of intellectual property rights. Thirdly, the agreement makes disputes between WTO members about respect of the TRIPS obligations subject to the WTO's dispute settlement procedures.

3.   The Special Case of Digitizable Software and Media Products Trade

a.   Trade Coverage and Values

In this section, we discuss trade in software and digitizable media products, which has traditionally been conducted physically as trade in goods and which can now be undertaken across networks in digital form. The product categories affected include film, various types of printed material, video games, and various recorded information (such as software or music) on carrier media (such as tapes, CDs, CD-ROMs, and diskettes). Most importantly from a new economy perspective, software is included in the product group. The reason why we treat this product group separately is the fact that the categorization of such products if delivered electronically is one of the key challenges for the WTO framework. Depending on whether electronic trade of such products is treated as goods or as services, different market access commitments and rules apply – as we discuss below.

First, it is important to note that trade in digitizable media products and software is small, but growing. Table 3 provides a product breakdown in 1990, 1996, and 1998. Recorded world trade in these products amounted to less than $50 billion in 1998, or less than 1 percent of total world trade. Printed matter and recorded tapes, CDs, packaged software, etc., accounted for 60 percent of the total.

While the overall numbers are relatively small, trade in several products has increased rapidly in recent years. Average annual trade growth for software and digitizable media products was about 8 percent between 1990 and 1998. Trade growth in recorded media such as CDs and packaged software was higher, at an average annual growth rate of 13 percent, and reached about $15 billion in 1998. For most countries, imports of software and digitizable media products amounted to less than 2 percent of total trade. The EU (including intra-EU trade) accounted for 45 percent of world imports or about $20 billion in 1996. Other industrialized and emerging market countries account for much of the remainder of world trade.

From these figures, we can conclude that trade in software and digitizable media products is currently not very large. But this may change in the near future as

Table 3: World Trade in Software and Digitizable Media Products, 1990–1998[a]

Commodities (incl. SITC Code)		1990[b,c]	1996	1998	1998	Average annual growth rate 1990–1998 (in percent)
		(in millions of dollars)			(in percent of total)	
Cinematograph film (883)	imports	308	354	295	1	–0.6
	exports	292	375	382	1	3.4
Printed matter (8921)	imports	7,421	10,621	10,917	22	4.9
	exports	7,138	11,099	10,697	23	5.2
Newspapers, journals, etc. (8922)	imports	3,488	4,662	4,977	10	4.5
	exports	3,286	4,775	4,580	10	4.2
Advertising material (89286)	imports	3,014	3,254	3,554	7	2.1
	exports	2,789	3,865	4,054	9	4.8
Other printed matter (892)	imports	2,862	5,387	6,523	13	10.8
	exports	2,958	5,138	6,656	15	10.7
Video games (89431)	imports	2,642	3,753	6,339	13	11.6
	exports	384	2,939	3,383	7	31.3
Recorded magnetic tapes (8986)	imports	1,696	1,924	2,085	4	2.6
	exports	1,613	1,719	1,382	3	–1.9
Other recorded media (8987)	imports	5,533	14,136	14,630	30	12.9
	exports	5,413	13,774	14,530	32	13.1
Total	imports	26,964	44,090	49,320	100	7.8
	exports	23,873	43,729	45,663	100	8.4

[a] Re-exports and intra-EU trade included. – [b] Chinese Taipei not included; accounted for 1 percent of imports and exports in 1996. – [c] Discrepancy between imports and exports possibly due to categorization problems.

Source: Compiled by Mattoo et al. (2000), based on UNSD (various issues).

access to personal computers (PCs) and the Internet increases further and the available bandwidth expands. Electronic trade in such products is likely to benefit from this, possibly at the expense of physical trade. In fact, downloading of software is already feasible and may already be done to a significant scale. The Internet-based transmission of music and films (which contain more data) is also likely to be more widely available in the near future.

If physical trade continues to grow at 10 percent, it will reach $100 billion by about 2005. However, by that time a significant share of such trade may be conducted online rather than as "physical" trade on carrier media.

b.   Liberalization Commitments

Market access conditions for the physical trade of such products are currently quite liberal. As mentioned above, software is covered by the ITA and should therefore be traded duty-free in most countries. Mattoo et al. (2001) have calculated the weighted average tariffs applying to this product group in 1996. For industrialized countries, they ranged between 0 percent in Japan and 4.2 percent in New Zealand, below the average for post-Uruguay merchandise trade (Finger et al. 1996). In developing countries, tariffs are below the average for all merchandise trade as well. Only Morocco, Korea, and India reported average applied tariffs between 20 and 30 percent; all others for which data are available featured lower barriers. With the implementation of the ITA, tariffs would now be even lower as software is now largely duty free.[1]

Furthermore, a number of countries only impose tariffs on the carrier media and not on the information content. With the latter normally being much more valuable than, say, the CD or disc, tariff barriers are indeed very low. Note, however, that in some cases antidumping protection (such as in the case of microdiscs in the EU) may raise protection significantly above what is specified in the tariff schedules.

As mentioned, a growing amount of trade in software and digitizable media products seems being conducted on-line. For this type of trade, the WTO decision not to impose tariffs on electronic commerce from May 1998 applies and no duties can be imposed. The WTO decision, thereby, creates an important policy distinction: these products that are otherwise identical are treated differently on the basis of the way they are delivered. Thus, music or software imported in electronic form is exempted from duties but is in some countries subject to duties when imported in physical form.

c.   Challenges for WTO Rules Regarding Trade in Software and
        Digitizable Media Products

As regards the legal framework provided by WTO rules, physical trade in software and digitizable media products will face the same GATT-based environment as other trade in goods and as described in the previous section.

There may, however, be some doubt about how electronically delivered software and media products should be classified. Some argue that their intangible state implies that they are best treated as services subject to GATS rules. Others argue that since their physical counterparts are covered by GATT, they too should be

---

[1]   A precise update of the 1996 tariff calculations, however, would require a considerable amount of work, looking at numerous tariff lines for a large number of countries.

covered by the same rules. An example cited in support of the latter argument is that of a book, a product which is clearly identified in the customs classification systems for goods. The argument would be that since a book in physical form is a good, it makes sense to treat the electronic transmission of a book's contents as trade in goods, just as if the book had entered through normal customs channels at the frontier.

However, there are also reasons to believe such products are services. Perhaps most importantly, it is very difficult and often perhaps impossible to distinguish between the on-line transmission of a piece of music which substitutes for a CD (a good) or which is intended as an audiovisual service.

Guidance could also be sought from the statistical convention for balance of payments purposes, which distinguishes between standardized and nonstandardized products. A book or a mass consumption "over-the-counter" software package, for example, is a standardized product and considered to be a good. But customized data on a CD, or customized software, would be treated as a nonstandardized product and classified as a service. But this distinction may not be easy to make in practice (Bacchetta et al. 1998).

We do not seek to provide an answer to how electronically delivered software and media products should be classified, although for purely practical reasons much confusion and costly bureaucracy and litigation could perhaps be avoided if all electronic deliveries were considered services.

There are also, however, important legal and economic implications of the alternative classification choices arising from the 1998 decision not to levy duties on electronic commerce and from differences in liberalization commitments and rules between the GATT and the GATS. First, treating media products "as if" they were goods would generally imply a more liberal regime for cross-border trade in such products than if they were treated as services. The next section will discuss in detail the degree of liberalization commitments in services.

Second, there are many differences between the legal frameworks of the GATT, covering trade in goods, and the GATS, covering trade in services, but three differences in particular have a crucial bearing on the regime for electronic trade and delivery of software and digitizable media products (see Table 4). The first difference is with respect to the national treatment rule, which obliges countries to treat foreign products no less favorably than domestic products. In the GATT, national treatment is a general obligation, but it applies only to internal measures, such as internal taxes and regulations, and not to border measures, such as customs duties. In the GATS, national treatment applies to all measures affecting the supply of a service, but it is not a general obligation; it only applies to sectors that a member has explicitly scheduled and these, too, may be subject to limitations.

The second difference is a consequence of the first: the GATT envisages the use of customs duties on imports where members have not bound their tariffs at

Table 4: A Comparison of the Key WTO Rules for Measures Affecting Goods and Services Trade

	National treatment	Customs duties	Quotas
GATT rules for goods trade	General obligation, permitting no exceptions, but applies only to internal measures.	Allowed where members have not bound their tariffs at zero.	Not allowed except in certain emergencies.
GATS rules for services trade	Not a general obligation, applies only to sectors that a member has explicitly scheduled and these, too, may be subject to limitations. But applies to all measures affecting the supply of a service.	Not allowed only if a member has committed to providing national treatment without limitations. Allowed otherwise.	Not allowed only if a member has committed to providing market access without limitations. Allowed otherwise.

zero, whereas the GATS has little to say about customs duties, or taxes in general, except that a member's tax regime must be consistent with its national treatment commitments. Finally, the GATT contains a general prohibition on quantitative restrictions (except in certain emergencies). In the GATS, quantitative restrictions are prohibited only in sectors where a country has made a commitment to provide market access without limitations.

As a consequence of these differences, the treatment of a product can differ significantly depending on whether it is classified as a good or a service. Imports of a good cannot be subject to quantitative restrictions or to any discrimination through internal taxation and domestic regulations. They could, however, be subject to tariffs up to the level bound by a member in its schedule. Therefore, if certain electronically delivered media products were to be classified as goods, then the 1998 decision on duty-free electronic commerce would ensure free trade.

However, the services trade regime depends largely on the specific commitments made by a member. In this context, a commitment not to impose customs duties has limited legal value. Consider two alternative possibilities.

If a member has made a commitment to provide national treatment in a particular sector, then all discriminatory taxes (including customs duties by definition) are already prohibited and so the new commitment to duty-free electronic commerce adds nothing. If a member has not made a commitment to provide national treatment, then it remains free to impose discriminatory internal taxes other than customs duties. The decision to abstain from customs duties on electronic commerce may then have limited value.

But there is a more serious problem with the proposal. Banning only customs duties could increase reliance on quotas which are allowed under the GATS (unless a member has committed not to use them).[2] It may, of course, never be technically feasible to impose either customs duties or quotas on electronic trade, in which case the proposed standstill is irrelevant. But if it were to be technically feasible to impose such measures, then there is no good reason why customs duties should be banned while quotas are allowed. Why would we want to prohibit the use of an economically superior instrument of protection while allowing the use of an inferior instrument?[3]

The WTO work program on electronic commerce identifies a number of other issues where the rules to be applied to electronic commerce in software and digitizable media products depend on whether such products are considered goods or services (WTO 2000: G/C/W/158). Among the issues identified are customs valuation, the application of the Agreement on Import Licensing Procedures, standards, rules of origin, and classification issues in the context of the categorization debate. Some of these issues have been discussed in the previous section on rules for goods trade or will be picked up in the following section on rules for services trade.

In sum, software and digitizable media products would face quite different liberalization commitments and rules depending on whether they are classified as goods or services. The strength of the proposal for duty-free treatment of electronic commerce is that for the limited class of electronically delivered media products, it may ensure that trade in the future, as at present, is free of restrictions – provided it is agreed that such products should be treated *as if* they are goods. The weakness of the proposal is that it has legal and economic shortcomings when seen together with the prevailing regime for services which constitute the bulk of electronically transmitted products.

---

[2] Permitted restrictions include limitations of the number of service suppliers, the value of transactions or assets, the number of operations or total quantity of output, the number of natural persons that may be employed, the nature of legal entities permitted to supply services, and the extent of participation of foreign equity in an enterprise (GATS, Article XIV).

[3] In fact, given past patterns of liberalization, precisely the opposite move should be encouraged where feasible, i.e., a conversion of quotas to tariffs which would be gradually reduced – though the agricultural experience also demonstrates the danger of over-tariffication.

4.   Trade in Services

a.   Trade Coverage and Values

The new economy has resulted in the emergence and rapid growth of a number of new services, including many types of telecommunications and computer services. These new services (in conjunction with the necessary hardware) have facilitated trade in many other services. In fact, in the new economy the borderline between nontradables and tradables is shifting constantly, so that fewer and fewer services should really be considered nontradable. Many business services, such as legal, accounting, and architectural services are now traded across borders as are many financial services including financial information, trading in securities etc. Internet-based audiovisual services trade, on-line education or telemedecine are just a few more services which did not exist only a few years ago.

Global cross-border exports in various services which are closely related to the new economy and which are at least partly already traded electronically exceeded $373 billion in 1999 (Table 5). This is almost 30 percent of total services trade and over 5 percent of total world trade. The most important traders are the major industrialized countries. Several developing and transition economies also report significant services trade. In fact, Singapore's services exports in the four sectors displayed in Table 5 have almost reached the value of Japan's exports in the same categories. India, China, and Korea report trade in the same order of magnitude as Spain.

It is also noteworthy that the new economy does not only facilitate cross-border trade in services, referred to as mode 1 trade in the GATS. Other modes of services supply included in the GATS definition of services trade are also likely to benefit through, for instance, better and cheaper communication. These include "consumption abroad" (mode 2), consisting most obviously of tourism; "commercial presence" (mode 3) or foreign establishment trade, which includes trade conducted through foreign affiliates of a service provider; the movement of natural persons (mode 4), i.e., individual service suppliers or employees of service suppliers.

b.   Liberalization Commitments

The appropriate route to secure barrier-free new-economy-related services trade is to negotiate fully liberal commitments under GATS on market access (which would preclude quantitative restrictions) and on national treatment (which would preclude all forms of discrimination, including discrimination through regulation and internal or border taxation). This raises the question: how far are we from this goal?

Table 5: Cross-Border Services Trade to a Great Extent Already in Electronic Form, Selected Sectors 1999 (in millions of dollars)

Countries		Communi-cations	Computer & informa-tion	Financial & insur-ance	Other busi-ness services
Developed countries					
Australia	exports	858	420	1,036	1,679
	imports	998	348	921	1,957
France	exports	966	758	2,411	19,806
	imports	900	640	2,479	14,753
Germany	exports	1,762	2,726	6,536	24,006
	imports	3,240	4,334	4,975	34,643
Italy[a]	exports	674	288	3,560	16,247
	imports	1,429	783	4,917	20,727
Japan	exports	765	1,257	1,963	15,811
	imports	1,407	2,962	5,052	26,032
Netherlands	exports	1,305	1,098	825	17,905
	imports	1,345	971	1,274	13,710
Spain	exports	584	2,039	2,155	7,106
	imports	575	1,156	2,254	9,537
United Kingdom	exports	2,368	2,986	17,782	28,068
	imports	2,828	846	1,235	9,737
United States[b]	exports	3,594	4,102	19,176	44,375
	imports	8,242	541	11,588	28,857
Developing countries					
Brazil[a]	exports	157	6	323	3,160
	imports	230	310	150	3,169
China	exports	590	265	370	4,886
	imports	193	224	2,023	7,098
India	exports	...	...	242	8,788
	imports	...	...	614	7,266
Korea, Rep. of [a]	exports	656	5	197	6,575
	imports	1,133	90	252	7,705
Poland[a]	exports	431	29	1,515	1,277
	imports	354	124	1,210	1,901
Singapore	exports	...	...	486	13,361
	imports	...	...	803	7,038
Global total	exports	21,342	24,930	71,729	254,536
	imports	25,994	16,073	60,164	245,714

Global total of all four selected services trade sectors	exports	372,536	
	imports	347,945	

[a] Data for 1998 instead of 1999. − [b] Excludes cross-border affiliates trade. − ... data not available.

Source: IMF (1997).

Our main interest is in services that are at the heart of the new economy, including, e.g., communications and computer services. Furthermore, trade in a broad range of services is likely to be boosted strongly through developments in the information and communications technology sectors. These sectors include, e.g., business, entertainment, and financial services. When analyzing the commitments relevant to the new economy, we focus on cross-border supply (mode 1), though it must be borne in mind that consumption abroad (mode 2) may also be relevant because the distinction between modes 1 and 2 is not always clear (as discussed in the next section). In examining the level of commitments for the different sectors and modes of supply, three degrees of liberalization commitments can be distinguished. First, there are "full" commitments assuring unrestricted access. These are reflected in a "none" entry against a particular mode of supply in the schedule. Second, there are "partial" commitments which refer to the entries that are conditioned in some way by a limitation. Third, there are "no" commitments which are expressed by an "unbound" entry against the relevant mode, and offer no guarantee of market access.

Commitments on mode 1 for the relevant service sectors are surveyed in Table 6. The first column in this table indicates the relevant sector, while the second column shows the number of countries which have made commitments on at least one subsector of the sector. The third, fourth, and fifth columns indicate the level of market access commitments made on cross-border supply in the sector. The last three columns provide the same information for national treatment commitments.

Several broad features emerge. In only 5 of the sectors considered here were commitments made by more than half of the WTO membership of 130 (at that time). These sectors are professional services, other business services (which include advertising), insurance services, banking and other financial services, and travel agencies and tour operators. In professional services, however, even though there are commitments from 74 members, less than a fifth assure unrestricted market access and national treatment. In software implementation and data processing, of the total WTO membership of over 130, only 56 and 54 members, respectively, have made commitments; and only around half of these commitments guarantee unrestricted market access, and a similar proportion unqualified national treatment.

The table may present a somewhat pessimistic picture of the true economic significance of commitments for two reasons. First, the table counts each country as one and does not take the relative economic importance of countries into account. Secondly, the table counts each subsector as one, and does not take into account differences in their economic importance. However, despite these qualifications, our findings do suggest that there remains significant scope for widening and deepening the scope of these commitments.

Table 6: GATS Commitments on Cross-Border Supply for Selected Service Sectors (percent)

Sector/Subsector	Number of countries	Market access[a]			National treatment[a]		
		Full	Part	No	Full	Part	No
Business services							
A. Professional	74	19	17	64	14	10	76
B. Computer and related	62	40	22	37	25	9	66
C. Research and development	37	37	14	49	24	7	68
D. Real estate	18	50	36	14	30	18	53
E. Rental/leasing	39	28	14	56	20	9	70
F. Other business	71	16	14	71	13	8	80
Communication services							
A. Postal	6	67	33	0	67	33	0
B. Courier	33	39	33	27	42	33	24
C. Telecommunications	57	11	25	63	12	14	75
D. Audiovisual	19	11	23	66	14	10	77
Distribution services							
A. Commission agents	21	10	70	20	10	75	15
B. Wholesale trade	34	27	55	18	30	55	15
C. Retailing	33	24	52	24	21	55	24
D. Franchising	22	64	36	0	59	36	5
E. Other	3	50	50	0	50	50	0
Educational services							
A. Primary education	21	45	25	30	40	40	20
B. Secondary education	23	45	41	14	41	50	9
C. Higher education	20	60	30	10	40	50	10
D. Adult education	20	50	45	5	40	55	5
E. Other education	12	33	67	0	42	58	0
Financial services							
A. All insurance and insurance-related	73	17	31	52	21	23	56
B. Banking and other financial	73	15	24	61	18	19	63
C. Other	8	13	38	50	13	38	50
Tourism and travel-related services							
A. Travel agencies/tour operators	86	50	17	33	50	19	31
B. Tourist guides	52	55	8	38	51	13	36
C. Other	13	38	31	31	46	31	23
Recreational, cultural, and sporting services							
A. Entertainment	28	63	11	26	67	11	22
B. News agency	14	71	21	7	57	43	0
C. Libraries, archives, museums, and other cultural	13	54	23	23	54	31	15
D. Sporting and other recreational	34	54	23	23	54	31	15
E. Other	1	100	0	0	100	0	0
Computer and related services							
A. Consultancy service related to the installation of computer hardware	51	57	20	24	51	22	27
B. Software implementation	56	54	27	20	48	29	23
C. Data processing	54	54	26	20	46	31	22

[a] Full: full commitment; Part: partial commitment; No: no commitment. Percentage may not add up to 100 due to rounding.

The above discussion and table suggest that there is an urgent need for more sophisticated indicators of market access in services trade. This task is rendered particularly difficult by the fact that there are four modes of supply for many sectors and subsectors and that most barriers, such as limits on equity holdings, turnover, branches, etc., are difficult to quantify. Harms et al. (2001) have attempted to develop such an indicator for the most important subsectors of financial services, by weighting the modes and the protectionist implications of different types of protection. Despite the limited commitments, the GATS is an important first step towards securing open markets. Furthermore, the obligation for WTO members to continue negotiations as of the year 2000 suggests that deeper and wider commitments are likely.

c.   WTO Rules as Constraints on Protection

As mentioned above, there are two dimensions through which the multilateral trading system can promote trade in services, and thereby reduce the costs and improve the quality and access to such services. First, we need liberal market access conditions. The prevailing environment has been discussed in the previous section. Second, the WTO framework also provides disciplines on regulatory policies which could more or less directly infringe on trade in services. The GATS is, therefore, an important conduit in promoting trade in services because it provides a framework for WTO members to commit to predictable, stable, and open access conditions.

It is important to note that the "traditional" instruments of contingency protection such as antidumping and safeguards are not (yet) available in GATS. This enhances the predictability of market access and prevents policy backsliding. However, a few "escape clauses" are available in the GATS as well. Article XII allows adopting or maintaining restrictions on which a country has undertaken specific commitments in case of serious balance of payments and external financial difficulties. The so-called prudential carve out can be used to (re)impose restrictions in financial services for prudential reasons (see the GATS Annex on Financial Services). Moreover, "members may modify or withdraw any commitment in its Schedule at any time after three years have elapsed from the date on which that commitment entered into force." However, subsequent negotiations should lead to compensatory measures that lead to a no less favorable general level of commitments (Article XXI).

If members commit to providing market access and national treatment limitations, they are not allowed to impose quantitative restrictions or discriminate between domestic and foreign services suppliers of "like" services. "Each Member shall accord to services and service suppliers of any other Member, in respect of all measures affecting the supply of services, treatment no less favourable than that it accords to its own like services and services suppliers" (Article XVII.1). This means, for example, that members cannot impose differential requirements or tax treatment on foreign telecommunications providers or other service providers. On the other hand, if members have entered national treatment limitations, they provide scope for differential treatment (see Table 4).

The GATS specifies disciplines regarding members' regulatory policies, especially regarding discriminatory and trade-restrictive effects of regulation, mutual recognition, and the behavior of monopoly suppliers. Two types of regulations may become particularly relevant here: (a) qualification and licensing requirements for professionals and institutions (perhaps most relevant in various professional services); and (b) approval requirements for foreign suppliers. Moreover, there are provisions for general and security exceptions (Articles XIV and XIV-bis). These two issues pose important challenges and, together with other challenges, will be discussed in more detail in the next subsection.

d.   Challenges for the GATS

There is a considerable need to clarify and strengthen GATS rules especially regarding electronic trade in services. The WTO acknowledges this need in its Work Programme on Electronic Commerce (WTO 2000: S/C/8, S/C/13) and we will discuss the following key challenges: confirming the principle of technological neutrality, clarifying the classification of services and modes of supply, and strengthening disciplines on domestic regulation.

Technological Neutrality

Confirming the principle of technological neutrality in the GATS is perhaps the single most important step needed to ensure that the rules of the agreement apply to electronic commerce. Technological neutrality implies that members agree not to make policy distinctions between products on the basis of the means of delivery. There are indications that WTO members are close to confirming this principle. In the Interim Report to the General Council by the Council for Trade in Services on the Work Programme on Electronic Commerce (WTO Document S/C/8, dated 31 March 1999, see WTO (2000)), technological neutrality is among the "issues on which a common understanding appeared to be emerging."

It is important to see why this principle matters, and why it cannot be taken for granted. If the principle of technological neutrality is not accepted, the application of key GATS rules – market access, national treatment, and most-favored-nation (MFN) treatment – to electronic delivery is called into question. First, note that the market access provision of the GATS prohibits certain quantitative restrictions in scheduled sectors (unless they are explicitly specified). A prohibition on the *electronic* delivery of a service does not amount to a quota on the total value or volume of a service, provided there are other means of delivering the service across borders. Such a restriction is therefore not precluded by commitments to provide market access – unless it is agreed that a commitment to allow market access implies that the supplier is free to choose any technical means of delivery.

In the application of the MFN and national treatment rules, the concept of like product is crucial.[4] Suppose, for example, a member allowed legal services to be supplied cross-border through mail delivery, but not through electronic delivery. If identical products delivered by different means of conveyance were not deemed like products in a legal sense, then such a regime would be deemed nondiscriminatory. Hence, for the MFN and national treatment provisions to operate in defense of electronic commerce, it is necessary that products be deemed alike regardless of the means by which they are transported.[5]

But is there really a need for an explicit agreement on technological neutrality, can it not simply be presumed? The answer is negative for three reasons. First, the classification of a service under GATS, i.e., the definitions in the underlying United Nations Central Product Classification, are sometimes not technology-neutral. That is, the definition may describe exhaustively the means of delivery without mentioning electronic means.[6] Secondly, in the negotiations on basic telecommunications, an explicit understanding was reached on the principle of neutrality to overcome these definitional doubts and to clarify the coverage of scheduled commitments. The understanding established a presumption that unless indicated to the contrary, the description of a basic telecommunications service in a member's schedule of specific commitments encompassed the full spectrum of ways in which the service in question might be supplied. A commitment on voice telephony, for example, would cover radio-based as well as wire-based technologies unless otherwise indicated. The fact that there was a need for such an understanding in one sector suggests that it may be necessary for WTO members to affirm the principle more generally.

---

[4]   Some of these issues have been discussed also in Hart and Chaitoo (2000).

[5]   In the sphere of goods, a comparable case would be one in which garments transported by road would be subject to one regime and those transported by air would be subject to another. In order to justify this differentiated regime against a charge of MFN inconsistency, garments entering by road and identical garments entering by air would have to be deemed unlike products. While most would regard such distinctions as bizarre in the case of goods, they are perhaps less obviously so in the case of services.

[6]   Alternatively, it may be silent or less than fully explicit on this question, leading to competing interpretations of the intention behind a specific commitment in a member's schedule.

Finally, and somewhat ironically, the decision on duty-free electronic commerce serves to undermine the notion of technological neutrality. The requirement to treat the electronic delivery of software services differently from the delivery of software services through other means (e.g., by mail on a diskette) does call into question the principle that "likeness" of products is not conditional on identical means of delivery.

Classification of Services

Even though all services fall within the scope of the GATS, two classification issues still need to be addressed. The first we have already encountered, and relates to the basic question of how services are to be defined. In particular, should trade in all intangibles including electronically delivered software and media products be classified as services? If it were agreed to do so, there would be a need to enhance the existing classification[7] so that members could make explicit liberalizing commitments for products such as books and music delivered through the Internet. One simple approach could be to have a single category for all electronically delivered media products, but other more differentiated approaches are possible.

The second classification issue concerns services that did not exist when commitments were made but that have emerged especially with the development of the Internet. Examples include "home-ticketing" (i.e., booking and teleprinting of transportation or entertainment tickets) or Internet access services. Given that the GATS approach to product definition is based on a positive listing, it is questionable whether the "other" category that exists within most clusters of services activities could legitimately be considered to encompass new services. Again, there is a need to create scope in the classification for countries to make liberalizing commitments with respect to these activities.

As mentioned, such classification issues would also become important if electronically delivered software or media products were categorized as services. For several such products corresponding services categories are not obvious. If new

---

[7] No compulsory or universally agreed classification system exists for services under GATS. In many instances, members have chosen to follow the nomenclature developed for GATS purposes (GNS/W/120), which in many sectors is based on the provisional Central Product Classification (CPC) of the United Nations. The CPC nomenclature was not, however, used as the classification basis in a number of sectors, including financial services, telecommunications, air transport, and maritime transport. Nevertheless, the mention of a CPC heading in the first column of a GATS schedule can clarify the product description, and hence the precise scope of a commitment. While the intention behind the CPC is to provide an exhaustive classification system, in practice resort is often taken to the description "other services". The version of the CPC on which the GATS classification of services is based was issued in 1989. It could not anticipate subsequent technological developments. A revised CPC is now available and may lead to a revision of the GATS classification in the new round of negotiations.

categories were created, the liberalization commitments applying to these categories would have to be clarified.

Modes of Supply

There is also a need to clarify the assignment of electronic services trade to modes of supply. It is not clear whether services that are delivered electronically across the border fall within the scope of mode 1 of the GATS, i.e., cross-border supply, or mode 2, i.e., consumption abroad. Let us first consider in turn why the distinction is not already clear and then examine why it matters.

In the agreed upon scheduling guidelines,[8] the modes of supply are essentially defined on the basis of the origin of the service supplier and consumer, and the degree and type of territorial presence which they have at the moment the service is delivered. The distinction between modes 1 and 2 hinges upon whether the service is delivered from the territory of one member into the territory of any other member (mode 1) or whether the service is supplied in the territory of one member to the service consumer of any other member (mode 2) (GATS Article I.2). This, however, is not a very clear distinction. It sometimes becomes difficult to determine in an unambiguous manner where the service is delivered. The physical presence of the consumer is not a criterion for determining the place of delivery of a service. One simple solution would be to require a physical movement of the consumer to the territory of another member for a transaction to be classified under mode 2, but other solutions, such as collapsing the two modes together are also possible.

The distinction between the first two modes matters for at least two reasons. First, the levels of commitment made by WTO members on the two modes often differ, and are frequently more liberal with respect to mode 2.[9] Therefore, the classification of some electronic deliveries under the first mode would imply a less open trade regime is assured than if they were classified under the second mode. Secondly, the modal distinction may correspond to a jurisdictional distinction and therefore affect the choice of regulatory regime under which a transaction is deemed to take place. Classification as mode 1 could be taken to imply that regulations of the consumer's country apply, since the transaction is presumed to take place in its territory; classification as mode 2 could imply that regulations in the territory of the supplier apply. In general, the latter choice has a more liberalizing impact than the former.

---

[8]   See WTO document MTN.GNS/W/164 of September 3, 1993 (WTO 2000).

[9]   It is also relevant that GATS rules require a country to allow cross-border capital flows if they are an essential part of the delivery of a service through mode 1, but do not impose a similar requirement with respect to mode 2 – a distinction that is particularly important in financial services.

Domestic Regulation

Among the current impediments to services trade, those posed by domestic regulations are often much more important than those created by explicit barriers like tariffs and quotas. It is, however, difficult to address regulatory barriers to trade without infringing on the freedom of governments to pursue legitimate public policy objectives. Neither the GATT nor the GATS attempts to pronounce upon the legitimacy of regulatory objectives as such. Rather, the WTO's focus is upon how regulatory objectives are met, seeking to ensure that regulations do not serve as a surrogate means of discrimination or protection.

Two key provisions shape the GATS approach to regulation. First, Article XIV (drafted similarly to the GATT general exceptions provision, Article XX) permits members to take measures, in specified circumstances, that would otherwise violate GATS obligations. The reasons for taking such measures include: the protection of public morals, and of human, animal or plant life or health; the maintenance of public order; ensuring compliance with laws and regulations, including those dealing with the prevention of deceptive and fraudulent practices, the non-fulfillment of contracts, the protection of privacy and confidentiality, and safety. Article XIV states that such measures must not be applied in a manner that constitutes "a means of arbitrary or unjustifiable discrimination between countries where like conditions prevail, or a disguised restriction on trade in services." In the context of electronic services trade, Article XIV would provide any necessary legal cover for measures required to protect privacy, prevent dissemination of socially undesirable material, and to deal with fraud.

Since the general exceptions provision covers most issues of concern, it should be possible to strengthen GATS rules dealing with the trade-restrictive impact of other domestic regulations. In the context of electronic commerce, market failure due to informational problems would seem to be the most important reason for regulatory intervention. Is a doctor in another country adequately well-trained, or is a financial institution in another country sound? While such motives for regulation are legitimate, the difficulty is in distinguishing between the necessary and the protectionist. Article VI of the GATS defines a number of disciplines regarding the application of regulations. For instance, it requires that in areas where specific commitments have been made, all "measures of general application" affecting trade in services (for instance, licensing or qualification requirements for all service providers, domestic and foreign) must be administered in a reasonable, objective, and impartial manner.

However, Article VI of the GATS does not as yet stipulate a clear test to determine whether a particular regulation is more burdensome than necessary to achieve the stated objective. Such a provision (notably in the Agreement on Technical Barriers to Trade) has proved important in the goods context to address regulations that are excessively trade-restrictive. It is important that the progress be made in the work program stipulated under Article VI to develop any necessary disciplines to ensure that "measures relating to qualification requirements and procedures, technical standards and licensing requirements do not constitute unnecessary barriers to trade in services."

5.   Conclusion

In this study, we have argued that new-economy-related trade is important in quantitative terms. Perhaps 15–20 percent of world trade – over $1 trillion – is involved. This includes information and communications technology goods, software and digitizable media products, and the cross-border trade of services that is either directly part of the new economy (such as computer services) or that is likely to be boosted strongly by new communications technologies (including the Internet).

Existing liberalization commitments under GATT provide much support to the development and dissemination of new-economy-related trade in goods where free or almost free trade is prevalent. The electronic delivery of software and digitizable media products (and services) is duty-free thanks to a 1998 decision not to impose tariffs on electronic commerce. One challenge is to determine the appropriate classification of electronically delivered software or digitizable media products.

The classification issue is particularly important given the difference in rules and commitments between the GATT and GATS. First of all, liberalization commitments in services trade under the GATS are still quite limited in many countries. Secondly, much more needs to be done to clarify and develop the structure of rules under the GATS. For instance, some uncertainty remains about technological neutrality, classification of new services, the assignment of trade to modes, and the potential rules on domestic regulation. The negotiating parties in the WTO are aware of these challenges, and new negotiations in services should also result in more developed rules and more liberalization commitments. The clarification of some of the cross-cutting legal issues may, however, have to wait until the next negotiation round.

References

Bacchetta, M., P. Low, A. Mattoo, L. Schuknecht, H. Wager, and M. Wehrens (1998). *Electronic Commerce and the Role of the WTO*. Geneva: WTO.

European Commission (2000). *Achtzehnter Jahresbericht der Kommission an das Europäische Parlament über die Antidumping- und Antisubventionsmaßnahmen der Gemeinschaft*. Brüssel: KOM(2000) 440.

Finger, J.M., M.D. Ingco, and U. Reincke (1996). *The Uruguay Round. Statistics on Tariff Concessions Given and Received*. Washington, D.C.: The World Bank.

Harms, P., A. Mattoo, and L. Schuknecht (2001). Explaining Liberalization Commitments in Financial Services Trade. Mimeo. Washington, D.C.

Hart, M., and R. Chaitoo (2000). Electronic Commerce and the International Trade Rules. *The Journal of World Intellectual Property* 2(6): 911–937.

IMF (International Monetary Fund) (1997). *Balance-of-Payments Statistics*. Washington, D.C.: IMF.

Mattoo, A., R. Perez-Esteve, and L. Schuknecht (2001). Electronic Commerce, Trade and Tariff Revenue: A Quantitative Assessment. *The World Economy* 24(7): 955–970.

Miranda, J., R. Torres, and M. Ruiz (1998). The International Use of Antidumping: 1987–97. *Journal of World Trade* 32(5): 5–71.

Panagariya, A. (2000). E-Commerce, WTO and Developing Countries. *The World Economy* 23(8): 959–978.

United Nations (1986). Standard International Trade Classifications. Series No. 33, Revision 3. New York: UN.

UNSD (United Nations Statistical Division) (various issues). COMTRADE. New York.

WTO (World Trade Organization) (1994/5). *The Results of the Uruguay Round of Multilateral Trade Negotiations. The Legal Texts*. Geneva: WHO.

WTO (World Trade Organization) (2000). *Online Documents Database*. www.WTO.org.

WTO (World Trade Organization) (2001). *Market Access Applied Data Base*. Geneva: WTO.

Eli M. Salzberger

Cyberspace, Governance, and the New Economy: How Cyberspace Regulates Us and How Should We Regulate Cyberspace

In the last couple of years the role cyberspace is playing in social, political, and economic activity has been increasing (indeed, accelerating), and despite the current slowdown in the new economy, which is strongly connected to cyberspace, it is likely to continue in substituting more and more traditional institutions and social, political, and economic structures. The effects of cyberspace on human activity in markets and outside markets challenge the traditional analysis of markets and central intervention in them. These effects can alter not only our analysis of the economy, but also our analysis of the state and collective decision making. Existing constitutional, legal, and economic doctrines and rules may have to be adjusted.

This paper will attempt to highlight some of the effects of cyberspace in this regard. It will do so by dealing, first, with the traditional microeconomic model as a paradigm for analyzing commerce and economic activity (Section 1). Within this section (which is based on an earlier work [Elkin-Koren and Salzberger 1999] and a forthcoming book [Elkin-Koren and Salzberger, forthcoming]) my main focus will be to examine the characteristics of the market in cyberspace, analyzing possible market failures in comparison to market failures in the nonvirtual world. Second, I will address the more general effects of cyberspace on the public sphere and on the organization of communities, especially on the entity and institutions of the state (Section 2). Subsequently, I will examine what the major effects of the above analyses are on the governance of cyberspace itself (Section 3). I will end with a short – more philosophical – comment on the possible effects of cyberspace on economic science and on the underlying assumptions of traditional economic thinking (Section 4).

1.   Cyberspace and the Traditional Analysis of Markets

The most important general premise of economic theory is that open competition within a perfect market will lead to the most desirable social outcome, namely a state of efficiency. This general premise was advanced by the economic approach to law in several directions, the two most important of which being (1) analyzing the emergence of the state, its central government, and its institutional structure as derived from problems of collective actions that are market failures of sorts, and (2) defining in what circumstances the central government is justified to intervene in shifting market solutions, circumstances which again are related to market failures.[1]

Traditional economic theory discusses four major market failures: monopolies, public goods, lack of information, and external effects. Later in the development of the market approach, and following Ronald Coase's pathbreaking 1960 article "The Problem of Social Cost" (Coase 1960), the framework of these market failures shifted (especially within the law and economic framework) to a more general setting of transaction costs. Note that these four (or five) categories of market failures are not inclusive; particular issues can be analyzed in more than one framework. For instance, some phenomena can be analyzed either as an externality or as a public good. The following discussion, however, adheres to the doctrinal analysis, and examines separately the traditional market failures, as applied to cyberspace.

a.   Monopolies

Under conditions of perfect competition, producers and consumers see the price as fixed, and therefore set their quantity of output or input at a level at which their marginal costs or benefits equal the price. A single producer (monopoly) or a single consumer (monopsony) sees a changing price curve, and therefore sets her output or input in a way which maximizes her profit, leading to an inefficient level of production or an inefficient market solution. The same premise applies to circumstances in which a very small number of producers (cartel) or consumers coordinate their market actions. Antitrust laws are meant to replace monopolies with

---

[1]   See Cooter (1997a), who asserts that in the 1970s economists, drawing upon the analysis of externalities and public goods, reached a remarkable consensus concerning the intellectual framework for analyzing and justifying state regulation of the economy. According to this framework, a prima facie case for public intervention requires a demonstration of the failure of a free market. See also Breyer (1982: 5–35) and Schultze (1977: 35–46), who conclude that regulation may be the best alternative when there are market failures.

competition where possible. They do so by preventing the creation of monopolies, prohibiting mergers, or limiting price coordination. When a monopoly is a natural situation due to the scale of the market, or in the case of public utilities, the monopoly is allowed to operate but it is closely regulated by the government or by other official agency. Sometimes monopolies are even created by the government in order to remedy other market imperfections. Such is the case, for example, with a patent system.

Cyberspace has several features that are likely to decrease traditional monopoly problems, and hence reduce legitimate central intervention in the market, but on the other hand it may create new types of monopoly problems that might call for innovative solutions. In addition, the global nature of cybermarkets questions the traditional territorial treatment of antitrust issues. Some of these features are described next.

One of the important sources of monopolies in the nonvirtual world is high entry costs and the substantial initial investment needed to establish a business in the market. These features can characterize a natural monopoly, a condition where the fixed costs involved in production are very large, so it is more efficient for a single provider to serve the market. But they can also characterize unnatural monopolies. This factor of entry barriers and high fixed costs, combined with tactics of short-run price cuts by existing market players to prevent new entries, maintains existing monopolistic powers. In cyberspace, entry costs can be significantly lower, and short-term tactics to prevent new entries into the market may prove less effective. This is true not only for products and services provided in cyberspace itself, but also for products and services which are provided in the nonvirtual world following an Internet transaction.

Consider, for instance, the publishing business. Entering such an industry in the nonvirtual world of printed materials requires major investments, such as purchasing and operating a printing press, purchasing paper, and paying distributors for shipment and handling. In cyberspace, almost everyone can become an independent publisher. With the click of a mouse one can distribute text to millions of Internet subscribers.

Another source of monopoly problems is the size of the market. The emergence of many nonvirtual monopolies has to do with market scale. A very small market may not justify more than one provider of a certain product. Cyberspace has no fixed borders. The cybermarket is a global marketplace. This applies fully to the increasing number of products and services provided in cyberspace, but it is also true for products and services provided in the nonvirtual world via cyberspace. National boundaries cannot apply to the increasing share of the former type of products, and are much less effective than in the case of traditional transactions of the latter type. Thus, protective policies such as customs and other trade barriers are becoming less potent. Such barriers can be easily bypassed in cyberspace by shifting the "location" of the transacting players.[2] Consequently, monopolies, which in the nonvirtual world result from the size of the local market, are likely to disappear.

In this respect the feasibility of on-line business may affect also monopolies which currently operate in the nonvirtual world. For instance, virtual bookstores such as Amazon push nonvirtual book chains such as Blackwell, Dillons, and Barnes & Noble into the cybermarket, and this in turn may affect the monopolistic powers of local bookstore chains that do not step into cyberspace. Thus, economies of scale are likely to scale down significantly, diminishing monopolistic powers.

Our analysis so far tends to point to a significant decline in the market failure of monopolistic powers, which indicates fewer justifications for central intervention in the market. However, other features of cyberspace may operate in an opposite direction, increasing monopolistic power and introducing new types of monopoly problems that may require innovative solutions.

One such feature has to do with connectivity and interoperability.[3] The use of any network, especially a global network that consists of a large number of independent networks, relies heavily on the use of shared standards that facilitate interoperability. Interoperability requires products and technologies used on the net to have functional characteristics that permit their functioning in connection with other technologies. Such technologies operating in cyberspace should be able to communicate with one another, to process input created by other products, or to create an output that is processable by other on-line procedures. Connectivity and compatibility requires some level of shared use of technological standards. Consequently, any new technology introduced into cyberspace must be compatible with other existing systems operating in cyberspace. It must conform to specifications of existing technologies, which are often held by private parties as trade secrets,

---

[2]   Consider, for instance, attempts by territorial states to tax on-line transactions. As Internet services are increasingly being delivered through wireless systems to portable computers, it is becoming more difficult to ascertain the location in which a taxable service or product has been provided. Furthermore, taxing on-line transactions would require an increasingly higher level of control over on-line transmission. Taxing such transactions would require tax collectors to monitor on-line transmission and to distinguish between transactions in virtual goods (such as computer program or a news article) and merely information exchange. Though such actions may be technically feasible, they may involve undue invasion of privacy.

[3]   Band and Katoh (1995: 585–588) assign two meanings to the term interoperability. One dimension is interchangeability, namely, "the degree to which one product can substitute for another." Another dimension of interoperability is connectivity that refers to "the degree to which a product can participate in a joint activity without requiring other connected products to alter their mode of operation."

patents, or other types of intellectual property.[4] A firm that controls the standards controls a bottleneck, which establishes its monopolistic power. It may further allow leveraging a monopoly from other markets into cybermarkets.

For instance, Microsoft controls the operating systems of most personal computers that often are connected to cyberspace. It owns the intellectual property rights in the technologies essential for anyone who wishes to develop a product that will be accessible by Internet users. The recent antitrust legal action handed out against Microsoft concluded that Microsoft has incorporated its Web browser (Explorer) into its operating system, thus attempting improperly to drive Netscape's Web browser out of the market.

A related feature of cyberspace that may increase monopoly effects has to do with network externalities. Network externalities emerge when the use of one product is more beneficial the more people use it. The more widespread the use of a word processor becomes, the more beneficial it becomes to any of its users. If we all use the same word processor, we may save the time involved in converting files, the costs of correcting errors, and even the costs caused by the inability to process digital files created by another program. Network externalities are typical of a network environment such as cyberspace, since this environment is based on connectivity and compatibility. Once an on-line product becomes widespread, it gains value not merely owing to its technological superiority but also, and sometimes only, owing to its prevalence.[5] Network externalities may limit competition by increasing the costs of entry. They provide a significant advantage to first comers, who may establish their products as the standard for future goods.

Finally, the cost of learning new technologies may further limit competition. Cyberspace is a sophisticated technological infrastructure that is used by consumers without any intermediaries. Every new product that users must operate involves costs of learning and adapting to the new method of work. Consequently, the costs of switching to a new technology may sometimes be prohibitively high. This may further increase entry costs and may have a restraining effect on competition.

To summarize, cyberspace reduces the traditional nonvirtual monopolistic problems, but it creates new ones. These special monopolistic effects in cyberspace are strictly related to technology and standards. The identification of such monopolistic power is different from identification of monopolies in the nonvirtual world, and the traditional remedies of price and quantity control may not be

---

[4]   Lemly and McGowan (1998) argue that intellectual property rights in standards constrain the ability of consumers to switch network standards, and increase control exercised by standard owner over access and pricing.

[5]   Microsoft Word uses a Hebrew standard that is accessible only by Microsoft Explorer and not by the competing browser Netscape. Thus, domination over the word processors market allows MS to dominate the market for browsers in Hebrew and to increase the costs of entry (or entirely prevent entry) by a competing browser.

efficacious to remedy these problems. Setting standards or shifting some technologies to the public domain may be a better method to tackle the new monopolies. In addition, the monopolistic problems of cyberspace are of a global nature. Thus, the shape and the type of legal intervention and institutions that may be justifiable cannot derive from the traditional territorial-based market analysis of supply and demand. The new monopolies of cyberspace, therefore, require fresh economic thinking and global institutions.

b.   Lack of Information

The hypothesis about competitive markets, which result in optimal production and distribution, is contingent on the assumption of full information. Information refers to knowledge of prices, preferences, and quality. Lack of such information, and especially asymmetry in information (e.g., where the seller knows more about the quality of her product than the buyer), are likely to lead the market to a failure. Thus, central intervention is required. It can be through production of information by the government, as well as intervention in the voluntary market exchange, for example, by imposition of duties of disclosure.

Cyberspace is almost all about information. The sophisticated engines of the Internet provide us with lots of information which in the real world is difficult and costly to obtain.[6] Information may be collected, accumulated, stored, and produced more efficiently. When a rational person plans to purchase a good in the nonvirtual market, a necessary preparatory activity is to inquire at shops and suppliers about prices and other sale and product conditions. This is not an easy task. It requires time and resources. A rational person will make such inquiries until the marginal benefits from further inquiries equal the marginal costs of such activity. In any case, these are imperfections of the market.

The equivalent picture in cyberspace is very different. With the tip of a finger the cyber-customer can run various software programs that compare prices, quality, contractual clauses, and other pieces of information with regard to the desired commodity. Some of these programs can even go further and conduct the transaction. Likewise, as the production and distribution of information are easier and cheaper than in the nonvirtual world, customers who were not satisfied with the product can easily make their dissatisfaction common knowledge (or vice versa). Although this activity in cyberspace is not totally costless, in the same time frame one can obtain significantly more information for a much smaller investment.

---

[6]   But see Elkin-Koren (2001). Elkin-Koren finds that search engines cover only small portion of information in cyberspace, and the share covered is partly the result of intentional selection effected by many sorts of considerations.

Game theory analysis distinguishes games that are played once from repeated games. Many one-off games tend to result in inefficient solutions, as defection is likely to occur; most repeated games, by contrast, tend to result in efficient outcomes, as cooperation will be chosen by the players. This general and simplified statement can distinguish cases where central intervention is not desirable (repeated games) from situations in which central intervention is required (one-off games). The flow of information in cyberspace can shift typical one-off games into repeated games, thus eliminating the need for central intervention into the market.

Consider the following example: a tourist who is planning a journey in which she will stay one night in every city she visits. She considers the hotels to book into. Since she is staying only one night in each hotel, her contractual relations can be characterized as a one-off game. Her travel agent shows her pictures of possible hotels and short descriptions of them. She might be shown several options and select from them. If the hotel does not meet her expectations or its description turns out to be inaccurate, but not to such a degree that our tourist would consider a lawsuit, or even complaining to her travel agent, the game is over. Other potential tourists will not benefit from this information. They will be engaged in separate games, ending similarly. Hotels are motivated to take advantage of this situation.

Booking a hotel through the Internet is a different story. The tourist can examine and compare more options; the details provided on the hotels are more comprehensive, including a variety of pictures, virtual tours, etc. They are provided by several sources, such as travel agencies, the hotels themselves, independent tourist operators, and the general public. Many sites on the Web allow tourists to read opinions of former guests, unedited, thus more likely to be independent and impartial (which is not always the case with printed tour guides, for example). This fact tends to shift the booking contract from a one-off game to a repeated game, in which the collective body of tourists can be considered as a player. Under such circumstances, central intervention due to lack of information or asymmetric information does not seem to be justified.

While some costs of information, such as collecting and communicating it, are reduced in cyberspace, other information costs may increase and new types of costs may appear. Such costs are the costs related to determining the reliability of information distributed in cyberspace. We have seen that the relatively low costs of on-line publishing business allow literally every user to become an information provider. Everyone can post information and make it accessible to millions of users around the world. The provision and distribution of information in cyberspace is decentralized. Cyberspace does not create the same bottleneck effect that characterizes traditional methods of communicating information. The ability to communicate directly at low cost reduces the need for intermediaries (such as publishers and the mass media industry). The absence of intermediaries causes proliferation of information. Information previously unavailable because its distribution was not cost effective may become available.[7]

Decentralized sources of information create a problem of ascertaining the reliability of such information. Distribution of information in the physical world includes clues indicating reliability. If one reads an article published by the *New York Times* one can assume that writers took standard steps to certify the reported facts. If one reads news on flying cows in a tabloid one is less likely to assume it really happened. How can you know whether things you read on the Internet are reliable? Well, to some extent one may use the truth traits one uses in the nonvirtual world. Thus, if one reads the article on the NYT Web site, one may rely on it, at least, if the site is indeed operated by the NYT. This is not the case if one downloads the article from an unknown source.[8]

However, even information from the NYT Web site cannot be considered as totally reliable. Information that is presented digitally is very easy to change. While printed information is fixed, digitized information may be easily manipulated. Thus, if one reads a court's decision on the Internet, one ought to check whether any changes were inserted to the original text. If we turn back to the tourist example, a potential tourist may not easily determine whether information posted on behalf of guests is indeed authentic, or whether it was originated by the hotel agents or was altered by them. This may lead to a tendency to confirm information with other sources, which does not exist in the nonvirtual world and which is likely to increase the costs involved in information seeking.

These changes in the availability of information and the costs of information suggest that central intervention should assume a different nature in correcting such market failures. For instance, rather than imposing disclosure duties, it may be necessary to standardize authentication means on the Internet, or facilitate name registries, document identification means, etc.

The most significant change in cyberspace regarding information has to do with the increasing costs of selecting and processing information, and making it

---

[7]   The high cost involved in mass distribution in the nonvirtual world (establishing a printing press or a broadcasting network) dictates the type of information that is distributed. Providers invest in providing information for which they can charge (sell copies, charge for use, sell commercials). Thus, information for which potential market is too small, is not produced at all.

[8]   Domain names are used for identifying Internet Protocol (IP) addresses on the Internet. IP numbers indicate the "location" of the server ("host") which is connected to the Internet. Since numbers are long and therefore hard to remember they were replaced by names. Domain name registries coordinate the assignment of top-level domain names (the InterNIC for a .com address, and local registries for countries address such as .uk, .il). Several commentators believe that domain names should incorporate trademark law and protect the public interest in identifying the source of goods and services and distinguish it from the goods or services provided by others. See Loundy (1997) and Johnson and Post (1997).

comprehensible. Processing the vast volume of information involves higher costs. While some sorting and processing may be done automatically, reducing the costs incurred by human actors, market players would still have to make more choices and thus spend more time and resources on processing information.

In other words, the changing market circumstances in cyberspace that increase the availability of information shift attention from the traditional lack of information to information overflow. It shifts the problem from availability of information to the limits of human cognition. Full information may no longer be perceived as an optimal market trait, and policies may not be designed to facilitate full information. The most significant impediment to perfect competition in cybermarkets seems to be the ability of humankind to process mass information and to continuously and intensively make choices and determine preferences. Simply searching for lack of information and information asymmetries may not be sufficient for addressing the types of information problems emerging in cyberspace.

c.   Public Goods

Public goods create another market failure. A public good is a commodity with two distinctive but related characteristics: nonexcludability and nonrivalry. Public goods are not likely to be produced and supplied by the market, and if they are privately provided they are likely to be undersupplied. Thus, government intervention is necessary in order to guarantee the optimal supply of public goods, either by subsidizing the private provision of the good or by producing it itself. Indeed, some economic theories justify the mere creation of the state as a solution to this market failure.

Cyberspace significantly reduces the public goods failure with regard to commodities supplied in cyberspace itself. Information is such a public good. In the nonvirtual world, its consumption is nonrivalrous and the use of information cannot be efficiently excluded (Landes and Posner 1989; Menell 1987, 1989). This is because information has no physical boundaries, and its duplication and distribution involve relatively low costs. The marginal costs of exclusion are often greater than the marginal costs of provision, so it is inefficient to spend resources to exclude nonpayers. Such free riding reduces incentives for investment in generating new information, and without government intervention information tends to be undersupplied.[9]

One form of government intervention in the real world is through intellectual property laws. These laws stimulate creation by providing creators with a legal right to exclude. They allow creators to use the power of the state to exclude non-

---

[9]   The production of information (generating a database, identifying genes responsible for a certain decease, gathering news) involves high cost. Consequently, in the absence of a mechanism that will prevent free riding and secure a return on such investment, information producers will tend to undersupply it.

payers, and to deter potential free riders. By legally excluding nonpayers, the law facilitates creators' ability to reap returns on their investments by collecting fees for the use of their works.[10]

Cyberspace is a virtual world in which almost everything boils down to information. Every interaction among users over email and group chats is in fact interactive exchange of informational signals. Surfing the Internet is data mining. Internet advertising distributes information over Web sites. The main commodities that are exchanged in cyberspace are informational products such as texts, music, data, or computer programs. The rich human interactive environment of cyberspace is merely the creation, processing, and transmission of information. Consequently, the share of public goods out of all property in cyberspace is far greater than in real world. According to traditional economic theory, this means a need for massive intervention by the government. Is this really the case?

Cyberspace transforms the way information is produced and distributed. Information is no longer embodied in physical objects such as paper or CDs. Information in cyberspace is delivered without the usage of any physical medium; instead it involves transmission of electronic signals.[11] However, such delivery is more tangible than oral communication, since every communication in cyberspace can be reduced to a discernible form.[12] Electronic delivery of information involves low cost, and does not require any large investment in the production of copies and establishing distribution channels. Distribution of copies in cyberspace is performed routinely by all users from any workstation connected to the net. Furthermore, disseminating information may not involve any distribution of copies, but instead providing access to a copy.[13]

---

[10]   Although intellectual property laws induce production of information by allowing nonpayers to be excluded at the same time, they keep this monopoly limited to serve its ultimate purpose of maximizing access to information. The law thus regulates access to information by balancing incentives to create and enhancing the accessibility of information.

[11]   See Landow (1992: 23). Once materials are posted on a Web site any user may access such materials and often download the file. One may simply post files on her Web site for remote retrieval by the public. On dissemination by access, see Elkin-Koren (1996: 250–254).

[12]   See, for instance, Gibbons (1997: 482), who argues that "freedom of speech implicates a property right in what is spoken, as speech in cyberspace is always reduced to tangible form; thus, creating a copyright (property) interest in pure speech."

[13]   For instance, digital networks provide remote access to large databases on mainframe computers. Information may be available to users by downloading from a bulletin board or a database. Another way of dissemination by access is by making files available on the network for the use of the general public. Anonymous FTP (File Transfer Protocol) is the posing of files for remote retrieval by the public, in a publicly accessible directory. Anyone is able to log in anonymously and retrieve the files in the public access directory. See Landow (1992: 23).

How does this affect the economic analysis of information as a public good? The first impression is that cyberspace tends to convert types of information which are private goods in the nonvirtual world to a public good in cyberspace.[14] Because of low costs of copying and distributing information on the Internet and the dematerialization of information, prevention of unauthorized use of the information and tracking down of violators are less likely to occur. Thus, we may expect a growing manifestation of free riding, which characterizes public goods.

But the more significant point is that cyberspace enhances the ability to exclude and control the distribution of information to the extent that makes it no longer a public good. The nature of information in cyberspace, as discussed above, allows the application of cost-effective self-help technical measures to control the consumption and use of information. Such means make information into an excludable commodity. Indeed, the creation of digital copies involves very low cost. Yet distribution of copies is no longer the sole way of generating profits. One shift is from selling copies to charging for access. The technical frontiers, for example, permit collecting a fee for access to a Web site and charging per use for the information provided. It allows temporary entrance permits and restrictions on use, blocking the possibilities of copying information or forwarding it, and more (Bell 1998, Dam 1999).

The results of this analysis seem to be ideal: on the one hand, cyberspace is causing a significant increase in the production and distribution of information, and, on the other hand, information can no longer be regarded as suffering from the public good deficiencies. Thus, government intervention is not required or desirable.

This, however, is not the full picture. The development of exclusion measures is likely to encourage users to develop counter-code-breaking and counter-hacking tools. This in turn will lead to sophistication of the exclusion tools and a continuous technological race between the two sorts of devices. Such a race may divert funds that might otherwise be invested in more productive directions. In other words, this infertile race is mostly just waste. It may require central intervention, which is very different from government intervention in the traditional public goods framework. Here the government will not be called upon to provide the public good or the legal means of exclusion to enable its production by private firms.

---

[14]   See Trachtman (1998: fn 38–39) and accompanying text. Trachtman admits that this analysis may not be conclusive and that information which is ordinarily distributed in physical form already has public good characteristics. Yet, he argues that cyberspace accentuates these characteristics.

Central intervention may be required here to halt or control the technological race between exclusion tools and their countertechnologies.[15] This approach is reflected in recent U.S. copyright legislation that prohibits the manufacture and distribution of the means of circumventing technological measures protecting the rights of a copyright owner.[16] Such an approach overlooks the significance of the technological race and competition between security systems and hacking technologies as driving forces of technological innovation, and more importantly, it overlooks the public interest in increasing the amount of information available to the public.

This discussion demonstrates the shortcomings of the public good analysis in cyberspace. The public good analysis takes technology as a given. It assumes a static technological state of the art that is the outcome of external market processes. Technology, however, is not static. The technologies available in cyberspace are rapidly changing. The extent to which information in cyberspace is a "public good" is not clear-cut. It depends, among other factors, on the technological state of the art. Consequently, the public good analysis may not be very conclusive in determining when government intervention is necessary. Indeed, conclusions regarding justification for government intervention vary among commentators[17] and legislators.[18] Furthermore, technological development and innovation does not occur out of its own internal logic. It is the outcome of a complex interaction between accumulated knowledge and other social institutions such as laws and markets. At a minimum, technological development should not be perceived as external to market processes, but as a mutable component that not only affects market processes, but is also shaped by the market. The traditional public good

---

[15]   See Dam (1999). Dam argues that it is inevitable that countertechnologies which defeat self-help systems will arise. He believes that such a race will require government intervention in prohibiting circumventing means, though suggesting that regulation should carefully drafted to avoid hindering technological development altogether.

[16]   Digital Millenium Copyright Act (DMCA). The DMCA further prohibits manufacturing or making available technologies, products and services used to defeat technological measures controlling access. 17 U.S.C. § 1201(a)(2), (b) (1998).

[17]   Several commentators (e.g., Jane Ginsburg) believe that information in cyberspace is more vulnerable. Other commentators (e.g., Pam Samuelson, Mark Lemley, Julie Cohen) emphasize the increasing power of copyright holders to control on-line uses of their works. For further discussion of excludability of information, see Radin (1996).

[18]   See, for instance, National Information Infrastructure Copyright Protection Act (NIICPA), H.R. 2441, 104th Cong., 2d Sess., 1995, which is based on the U.S. Department of Commerce, Information Infrastructure Task Force: *The Final Report of the Working Group on Intellectual Property Rights: Intellectual Property and the National Information Infrastructure* (1995 White Paper). The report emphasized the threat introduced by the Internet to the interests of copyright holders, and therefore recommended expanding the rights granted to owners for on-line distribution.

analysis cannot incorporate such considerations. As in the case of monopolies, I believe that this analysis is insufficient for defining the role of law in cyberspace.

d.   Externalities

Externalities are another type of market failure and their presence in particular market situations justifies government intervention. Externality is an effect on a market whose source is external to the market. In other words, it is a situation in which the welfare of market players is influenced by other market players, not through the market, or not through voluntary exchange. Positive externalities occur whenever an activity generates benefits that the actor is unable to internalize (some of the population is immunized, having a positive impact on the health of those who are not). Negative externalities occur when one's activity imposes costs on others (a polluting factory). When externalities exist, parties involved in an activity do not internalize the precise value of their actions on others. Consequently, their actions do not correspond with the total social welfare and thus result in inefficiencies. The role of regulation in such circumstances is to facilitate the internalization of the external costs or benefits involved in the activity to secure an optimal level of activity.[19]

Externality as an analytic concept involves several assumptions. It relies on a dichotomy between external/internal effects, and therefore necessitates a distinction between them. In order to determine what effects should be considered an externality, it is first necessary to define the relevant market (or community). Effects that fall outside the scope of a particular community are considered an externality.

Another assumption involved in the externalities analysis has to do with hierarchy of units and subunits. Externalities are defined by reference to a unit in which internal and external utility can be measured. Such basic units may be local communities, associations, corporations, unions, or even contracting parties. Subunits are part of a broader scope unit, for which total welfare is measured. It is crucial for the economic regulatory approach to externalities to determine what is the relevant social unit in which social welfare ought to be measured. Maximizing a community's welfare may have negative or positive externalities that affect the welfare of outsiders. The question then becomes, what is the community and who are the outsiders? For instance, if we take the state as the basic unit, state intervention will be justified in regulating the activity of local governments when such ac-

---

[19]   For instance, by taxing an actor whose activity imposes negative externalities or subsidizing an activity that involves positive externalities. These remedies and the general analysis of externalities can be attributed to the French economist Pigou (1920).

tivity imposes externalities on other communities within the state jurisdiction.[20] If we take states as self-regarding subunits, federations or international bodies become the relevant units for measuring total welfare. Thus, the absence of environmental protection in one state may inflict negative effects on neighboring states.[21]

Defining the social unit (and therefore what should count as an externality) is essential for the market analysis, since this analysis is related to questions of jurisdiction and enforcement.[22] The definition of the social unit will determine which body (local government or state government, firm or unions, states or international bodies) should have the power to regulate any particular behavior. In other words, questions of externalities are in fact questions of jurisdiction.

Cyberspace challenges some of the assumptions underlying the viability of externality analysis, since it blurs community (and market) boundaries. Territorial borders often define such boundaries and the territorial state is often the unit in which total utility is measured. Yet territorial borders may no longer serve in cyberspace to define community boundaries. Cyberspace reduces the effect of physical location.[23] It creates virtual communities that do not exist in any particular geographical location. Participants in on-line exchanges often do not even know (and sometimes cannot know) the physical location of the other party. Cyberspace is therefore "everywhere if anywhere, and hence no place in particular" (Lessig 1996: 1404).

The borderless nature of cyberspace can have very different implications for the analysis of externalities in the traditional unit of state and for the analysis of externalities in cyberspace itself. When the basic units are the traditional geographical units, cyberspace can be held to increase externalities. For instance, if a neo-Nazi site operates in Holland, its offensive content is equally accessible to users around the world, thus creating externalities in all jurisdictions. If Finland's

---

[20]   For example, a polluter in one community may affect individuals in other communities. Such externalities are not internalized by decision-makers in the regulating community. This will often lead to inefficiencies (when the total welfare of both units is thought of). From the perspective of accumulative welfare, such regulation will lower total utility and will therefore be suboptimal.

[21]   On economic analysis of international law, see Dunoff and Trachtman (1999), who argue that the international arena ought to be seen as a market in which self-regarding units (mostly states) interact to trade in power in order to maximize their basket of preferences.

[22]   Trachtman (1998: 578) argues that "the role of jurisdictional rule is to internalize externalities to the extent desired or alternatively to provide clear enough allocations of jurisdiction that it may be reallocated (and externalities thereby internalized to the extent worthwhile) through transactions between states."

[23]   Post (1996: 158) argues that cyberspace destroys the significance of physical locations which serves as a definitional basis for law-making sovereignty.

laws allow anonymous remailers[24] within its jurisdiction, users who reside in other states, including those states that prohibit such remailers by law, may use remailers located in Finland to send anonymous messages (Hardy 1994). Such messages may allow users to violate their local laws or to engage in a harmful activity without being caught, i.e., to impose an externality on their local law.

This observation, and especially its implications for the enforcement of laws of the territorial states in cyberspace, has led some scholars to suggest that cyberspace should be considered an independent jurisdiction.[25] The argument goes like this: territorial rules that affect on-line activity produce externalities, which influence the welfare of individuals in other jurisdictions (Johnson and Post 1997). To prevent such spillovers, cyberspace should be looked at as an independent unit for which the net defines its community boundaries. Utility should be maximized within this community, and attempts to regulate it by territorial governments are no longer justified.

This argument is valid insofar as municipal regulation can increase externalities in other jurisdictions because of cyberspace. It is, however, insufficient regarding externalities caused by cyberspace in the context of geographical units, regardless of the intervention of municipal authorities into the activities in cyberspace. In other words, even self-regulating cyberspace (which might be justified for other reasons, such as efficiency of self-regulation in cyberspace and the narrow effect of market failures) is likely to increase externalities in physical jurisdictions.

On-line communities overlap with real-world communities, without the possibility of a clear distinction being drawn between them. Individuals who occupy the Internet necessarily live in physical communities. People who send email, use chat rooms, sell computer programs, and consume on-line music also live in physical communities. Their willingness to purchase a book in the neighborhood bookstore may be affected by their visit to an on-line bookstore that may offer books at a lower price. A libelous message posted on-line may have a harmful effect on one's career in the real world. Visits to pedophilic Web sites may affect users' behavior towards their nonvirtual neighbors. Users who read about their government's actions over the Internet may change their views regarding their representatives. In other words, on-line experience may affect prices and markets, social relations, community standards, and politics in real-world communities. Consequently, spillover effects necessarily occur between virtual and real-world communities.

---

[24]   Remailers are simply intermediary computers that strip off identifying information from the original message (name and address).

[25]   Johnson and Post (1996: 1370) believe that cyberspace is a "world in which the effects of conduct has been decoupled from the physical location in which the conduct occurs."

A separate level of analysis focuses on externalities within cyberspace, or where the relevant unit of analysis is cyberspace itself. Here, the complexity of defining the basic unit and subunits for analysis is amplified by the low costs of exit and the dynamic nature of overlapping cybermarkets and communities. Cyberspace is a network of networks. It consists of overlapping on-line communities, such as discussion groups on USNET, LISTSERVES, subscribers to a service provider, members of the WELL (Hafner 1997), users of on-line chat rooms, players of games on a Web site, or subscribers to ICQ. Such communities may vary in the level of their members' homogeneity (Lemley 1998), the duration of membership (one-time players or a long-term relationship between members), or the communication structure of interaction among community members (moderated or non-moderated, open and public or intimate). Various communities may adopt different (even contradictory) sets of norms from which users may choose. It has, therefore, been suggested by some scholars that the coexistence of communities will facilitate a market for norms. Users will join on-line communities in which community rules ultimately suit their preferences.[26]

Diversified communities also exist in the real world. What makes cybercommunities different is the malleability of communities and the ease of changing membership. Members may simultaneously belong to a large number of on-line communities and may also switch communities. This is because the costs of "virtual exit" (Burk 1998) in cyberspace are relatively low compared with costs of exit involved in leaving one community and moving to another in the real world.[27] Consequently, communities in cyberspace are dynamic to an extent that makes it difficult to treat them analytically as identifiable units. The low costs of exit suggest that externalities in cyberspace may be substantially reduced. If a community adopts a policy that inflicts positive externalities on another community, its members will join the other community as well. If a rule of community A imposes costs on community B, members of community B will move to community A. In other words, if the costs of switching from community A to communities B–Z are zero, members of community A will internalize the costs and benefits that may be imposed by their actions on outside communities.

To sum up, applying the framework of externalities in the context of cyberspace results in two very different outcomes. Within cyberspace, our analysis tends to conclude that externalities cannot be regarded as a market failure that jus-

---

[26]   Post (1996) demonstrates this argument by the example of AOL in Cyberpromotions; the rule imposed by AOL (No Spam) represents the collective will of the subscribers. When it does not, subscribers will "vote with their electrons" by switching to another provider.

[27]   Compare, for instance, the cost of moving to a new neighborhood, changing a club, or switching jobs with the cost of leaving an unsatisfactory on-line service or migrating to a new on-line community.

tifies central intervention. With regard to the traditional geographical units, the analysis tends to conclude the opposite, namely that cyberspace increases externalities, but also that the conventional solution of central intervention to internalize the externalities would prove ineffective. Given the diffuse and dynamic nature of communities in cyberspace and the increased overlap among on-line communities, it is unclear whether conventional externality analysis can continue to be a useful analytic tool. In the absence of a clear definition of communities the analysis does not offer a solution to the question of whether the government (and which government) should intervene to correct the effects of externalities.

e.   Transaction Costs

Transaction costs were not considered in the traditional microeconomic model as a separate market failure.[28] Indeed, what is analyzed today under the category of "transaction costs" overlaps with some of the traditional market failures, especially externalities and lack of information. The focus on transaction costs within the economic approach emerged following Ronald Coase's 1960 seminal paper on the *Problem of Social Cost*. The paper criticized the conventional theory with regard to externalities, arguing that in a world with no transaction costs, contractual negotiations between the parties will eliminate externalities and will drive the market to efficient solution without central intervention. Only when transaction costs are not zero is there a need for such intervention. In this analysis, Coase referred mainly to costs of negotiation.

A decade later Calabresi and Melamed (1972) took the analysis a step further, expanding the notion of transaction costs to include also enforcement and adjudication costs. They put forward a model in which assignments of property rights and enforcement methods are determined according to the structure of transaction costs. The current paradigm of transaction costs economics is much broader. It is associated with the neoinstitutional school, which views the transaction as the basic unit of economic analysis, and hence attributes attention to various factors surrounding this unit as transaction costs. These include information, enforcement, governance structures of firms, and political and other collective decision-making structures.

This wider framework of transaction costs economics is of great importance to cyberspace. As argued before, the application of traditional market economic analysis to cyberspace is at least incomplete, as basic assumptions of the traditional analysis, such as the existence of a defined market, and the existence of central government with various intervention powers and enforcement abilities, cannot be applied to cyberspace. The market of cyberspace, its community, and its govern-

---

[28]   A historical survey of transaction cost economics can be found in Mercuro and Medema (1997: 147–156).

ance are different from the territorial state. The new transaction costs economics recognizes that all these factors cannot be exogenous to the economic analysis and must be taken as integral components of the discussion.

The effect of cyberspace on transaction costs is controversial. Some argue that transaction costs in cyberspace are lower.[29] They emphasize the reduced costs of searching for information, exchanging information, and the fast and efficient transmission of information. Thus, parties may efficiently search the web for information on their counterparts: other businesses in which they are engaged, the background of their executives, or the history of their products. Parties may efficiently find out what other products or services are available, at what price, and under what terms. If transaction costs in cyberspace are lower, cyberspace is likely to facilitate more transactions.

Others believe, however, that transaction costs in cyberspace may remain intact.[30] The human (cognitive) cost of engaging in a transaction, paying attention, learning the different options, defining preferences, or making choices may remain the same. In fact, if the volume of transactions increases, due to the decrease of transaction costs of the first type, then transaction costs of the second type may increase. That is something we all experience on a daily basis. The vast volume of information available at all levels requires an increasing portion of our time to

---

[29]   For example, Sunstein (1995: 1783) asserts that "the economic point is obvious, for the costs of transacting – of obtaining information and entering into mutually beneficial deals – will decrease enormously, and hence it will be much easier for consumers to get what they want, whatever it is they want." See also Easterbrook (1996) and Trachtman (1998).

[30]   One study suggests that the assumption regarding reduced transaction costs in cyberspace is questionable. See Bailey and Brynjolfsson (1997). In this preliminary analysis, the authors check if there is a price differentiation between the physical market and the Internet market. Their study examined the on-line bookstore Amazon, which has dominated the on-line book sales since 1995. The researchers studied the on-line competition between Amazon and Barnes & Noble, which launched its first virtual bookstore in March 1997. Unlike Amazon, Barnes & Noble already had physical bookstores since 1965. It was predicted that when users enjoy perfect information and transaction costs are very low, competition will lower the price. Yet, contrary to those predictions, prices increased. Indeed, the researchers found that when Barnes & Noble first entered the on-line market, Amazon lowered its prices. However, in June 1997, Amazon started increasing its prices and comparing them to those of Barnes & Noble's. Among other things, the authors suggest that the increase in price is due to high search costs.
        Another study suggests that transaction costs involved in processing on-line transactions are not lower. See a report by Ice group *Amazon.com: Prototype of a New Millennium Company?*, which analyzed Amazon. Results for the second quarter of 1998 found that Amazon was generating a loss on each on-line transaction. The report noted that processing orders on-line was not cheaper than more conventional distribution methods, as was generally perceived. An average order costs Amazon $40.81 to process, yet the average order value was $35.59, generating a $5.22 loss for every order processed. http://www.nua.ie/surveys/ viewed on 21. 8. 1998.

process it. The second (cognitive) type of transaction costs may also decrease with the increasing availability of technological means that undertake some of these functions. Such tools may automatically perform some of these "cognitive" tasks – such as sorting information, comparing options by various measures, and reflecting preferences in choices.[31] Nevertheless, users' attention will be necessary for defining preferences for automated agents, for providing them with enough information, and for monitoring their output.

The Calabresi–Melamed framework focuses on the structure of transaction costs as determining the efficient method of protection of entitlements. More specifically, it considers the protection of entitlements by property rules versus such protection by liability rules. Property rules ought to be preferred when negotiation costs are lower than the administrative costs of an enforcement agency or court determining the value of the entitlement. In such a case central intervention ought to be minimal. Entitlements will change hands through a voluntary exchange in the market, where the state's role will be only to prevent bypassing the market using the tools of injunction and criminal law. The persons who hold the entitlement are protected by a property rule granting them an injunction which prohibits the injurer from causing them any harm. Thus the injurers can cause damage only if they buy off the victim.

Liability rules ought to be preferred when the costs of establishing the value of an initial entitlement by negotiation are higher than the costs of determining this value by an enforcement mechanism. In addition, liability rules might be preferred in order to avoid bargaining costs. Lack of information or uncertainty as to the cheapest avoider of costs is likely to point us, according to Calabresi and Melamed, in the direction of liability rules as well (for a detailed account, see Polinsky 1989: 21–25). Liability rules involve additional central intervention by a state organ deciding on the objective value of the entitlement. In this case, if the victim has the entitlement, he has the right to be compensated, but he cannot prohibit the injurer from causing harm.

Cyberspace has two important features relevant in the context of the Calabresi–Melamed model. First, negotiation costs, which include the costs of identifying the parties with whom one has to negotiate, information costs, the costs of getting together with the relevant party, and the costs of the bargaining process are significantly lower than in the nonvirtual world. Second, enforcement can be a hundred percent effective with no involvement whatsoever of police, courts, or other central institutions. Effective enforcement can be achieved through codes of access (Lessig 1996: 1408; Reidenberg 1998). Instead of injunction against trespass, a cyberian can implement a system of passwords. Instead of trying to enforce rules

---

[31]   See Allen and Widdison (1996), who discuss the legal implication of systems that perform human cognitive tasks that are associated with the exercise of free will, such as making choices, forming intentions, and manifesting consent.

of behavior, one can use software which defines the terms upon which one gains access.[32]

This effective enforcement by the code refers to property rules and not to liability rules. It seems that enforcement of the latter rules in cyberspace by courts in a conventional manner is much less effective than in the nonvirtual world, as it is always possible to cross geographical boundaries and to disguise the physical identity of the infringer. The traditional territorial-based jurisdictional rules face a major problem in having to deal with activity in cyberspace. This activity is almost always multijurisdictional, and cyberians do not even know through which jurisdictions the bits into which their activity in cyperspace is translated physically pass. Courts might be so ineffective that the idea of Virtual Magistrates, who are likely to be much more familiar with cyberspace practices, has been put forward (see Gibbons 1997: 535).

The discussion above leads us to the conclusion that the application of the Calabresi–Melamed model to cyberspace would result in strong preference for property rules over liability rules, and since these property rules can be self-enforced by technological means; no central intervention would be required. This is an interesting conclusion, as it means that even when transaction costs are not zero, central intervention may not be desirable. Support for this conclusion can be found from a different direction – the transaction costs of exit. Johnson and Post (1996: 1398) argue that these costs are so low that the regulation powers of governments and the desirability of such regulation are decreased (for an opposing view, see Lessig 1996: 1406).

If cyberspace reduces transaction costs, we are likely to see more competition over the terms of transactions. Low transaction costs will allow suppliers to collect information about consumers' preferences and to tailor contract terms accordingly. Lower search costs will allow consumers to search and compare various contract terms for the same good. If, in the real world, consumers do not have any incentives to bargain over the terms of a contract, as the costs of negotiation are prohibitively high, automated protocols in cyberspace may create demand for new transaction terms. It is, therefore, predicted that we will see more tailor-made contracts and more diversity in terms. Furthermore, if transaction costs in cyberspace are lower, economic justification for the enforceability of standard form contracts is weakened. Such contracts lack the efficiency attributed to transactions conducted by assenting parties.

The tentative conclusions from the application of transaction costs analysis to cyberspace are similar to those which result from the application of the traditional market failures analysis – a significant decrease in the role and justification of cen-

---

[32]   This is the case for products and services provided in cyberspace itself. However, even for products supplied in the nonvirtual world, the cybertransaction can significantly lower these costs.

tral intervention. However, transaction costs analysis takes the state of technology as given. It does not take into account the possibility of a change in technologies as a result from the legal rules. Indeed, the technologies relevant to Coase's examples were not likely to change significantly as a result of the choice or change of legal rules. This is not he case with cyberspace, where technologies are constantly changing and the results of Coasian analysis may be different with each technological state of the art. This is an apparent shortcoming of the transaction costs economic approach when applied to cyberspace.

f.   Conclusion

In this section, I have tried to examine whether and how cyberspace modulates the traditional microeconomic analysis of markets and its implications for central intervention. Although this analysis is far from exhaustive, I believe that the main conclusion that can be drawn from it is that whether we look at cyberspace as the relevant market or whether we look into the traditional geographical markets (local, national, international) and the effects of cyberspace on them, the traditional analysis of competition, market failures, and the role of central intervention has to be significantly modified.

Cyberspace is predicted to eliminate or at least notably diminish some of the common market failures. Some of the traditional public goods (i.e., information) or monopolies are such failures. Some of the nonvirtual market problems of lack of information, externalities, and transaction costs are such failures. On the other hand, cyberspace creates some market deficiencies, which are less notable in the traditional markets. The technological race between enforcement measures created by the architecture of cyberspace and countermeasures is the most significant example. Costs involved in verifying information is another.

2.   Cyberspace and the Public Sphere

The traditional models of the economic approach, analyzed above, are constructed on presuppositions which take as exogenous the existence of states, the borders between them, their central governments, and their enforcement power (despite the fact that the justification for the state and its central government can be presented as a remedy to market failures, especially to the problem of public goods). These models also assume that there are territorial jurisdictions with central governments able to intervene effectively in the market through financial policies and regulation. These assumptions do not hold in cyberspace and the existence of cyberspace may also question their application to traditional markets.

Cyberspace breaks territory-based markets. The strict correlation between markets and states, or between forums which facilitate private contracts and public forums of collective decision making, does not exist in cyberspace. It seems, therefore, that, before we can draw conclusions as to the regulation of cyberspace as a market, it is necessary to examine the simultaneous effects of constitutional, public law, and political features of cyberspace with its private law characteristics. The aim of this section is to raise some preliminary thoughts in this regard.

a.   The Weakening Concept of the State

Liberal theories of the state from Hobbes to Rawls presuppose that markets correspond to states which are basically territorial units. A social contract or other forms of collective action are carried out by citizens of a specific territorial unit which becomes a state or other form of a national unit. Central government, its organs, and structure are analyzed in a territorial context. One of the most interesting features of cyberspace is the bankruptcy of this territorial conception of community.

Cyberspace is neither a conventional territorial entity with central government, nor a traditional economic market. It breaks the territorial units on several levels. First, markets in cyberspace are global. A user sitting physically in North America can do business with another user located in Asia. For that matter, no differences exist between this transaction and a virtual transaction she conducts with a user just across the street. Second, not only business, but also community activities – discussion groups, political groups, entertainment, and so on – cross geographical borders, developing new common and distinct cultural and social norms which are aterritorial. In fact, cyberians can simultaneously find themselves members of several communities that are very different. Third, virtual activity, when translated to actual electronic bits that are transferred from one user to another, may cross many borders. Communication between two next-door neighbors may pass through several other countries. Cyberspace users cannot even know through which jurisdiction their activity is directed (Burk 1996).

The basic assumption of most political theories, and certainly political theories that can be associated with the economic approach, is that human beings are social creatures and that collective action can benefit the well-being of all individuals. Beginning with ancient Athenians' notion of democracy, through Thomas Hobbes' minimal social contract and the philosophical ideals of the American founding fathers' extensive social contract, to Rawls's theory of justice, the bedrock of the liberal theory of the state has been contractual or consensual collective decision making.[33] But based on this thin rationale for the state, with the technological

---

[33]   The same idea is reflected by the Pareto criterion within the framework of microeconomic theories.

advances of cyberspace, one can think about new forms of communities, which are neither territorial nor excluding. The traditional state might still be needed to supply public goods, which cannot be produced by cyberspace, but other public goods (such as education and culture) can be provided by different sorts of virtual communities. Hence, cyberspace is likely to weaken the traditional states' structures and the state domination of our public and private lives.

Another feature of cyberspace is that cyberspace does not require the same general applicability and exclusivity of rules that characterize rules of legal regimes in the nonvirtual world. At least since the rise of the positivist theory of the law,[34] we view the law as hierarchical, territorial, and backed up by the physical ability of enforcement through sanctions. Legal norms are created on the authority of higher legal norms. Regulations are valid because statutes authorize their construction. Statutes are valid as long as they do not conflict with constitutional norms. The highest legal norm – the constitution – derives its power from the basic norm, which represents either force or social convention.[35] Legal norms claim a monopoly on power and superiority over other types of norms. The power of the state to enforce legal norms makes this superiority possible,[36] hence arises the perception of law as territorial and corresponding to political regimes, which own physical enforcement powers.

Cyberspace seems to fundamentally change this picture of law. It allows the co-existence of competing rule systems. Not only may rules be created from the bottom up, but they may also apply simultaneously in different spaces, and may apply only to users who enter virtual spaces.[37] Rules have to be generally applicable, but they are generally applicable only to users who choose to enter their domain. Thus, conflicting rules may exist, with no hierarchy between them.

Cyberspace allows the development of diversified regimes that will be shaped indirectly by way of interaction between sysops defining the terms of use, and users making choices regarding their preferred system and services (Johnson and Post 1997: 78). Internet service providers, list moderators, or Web site owners will adapt their rules to the wishes of users, and users who disagree with such rules will be able to leave and find an alternative regime that better serves their interests and

---

[34]   See especially Kelsen's (1945) theory of the law.

[35]   While Kelsen wrote about meta-legal basic norms, Hart (1961) wrote about the rule of recognition, which reflects social convention as the unifying element of a legal system.

[36]   This idea was first expressed as part of a legal theory in the 19th century by Jeremy Bantam and John Austin.

[37]   "The Internet is not physical or tangible entity, but rather a giant network which interconnects innumerable smaller groups of linked computer networks... The resulting whole is a decentralized, global medium of communications – or 'cyberspace' – that links people, institutions, corporations, and governments around the world" ACLU v. Reno, 929 F. Supp. 824, 830–31 (E.D. Pa. 1996).

values. The advantage of cyberspace is that it can facilitate the coexistence of different regimes. Thus, rules and norms may be generated by the "invisible hand." Under such vision of "market of rules," users of cyberspace may choose the laws that apply to them (Johnson and Post 1996: 1389–1391).

The feasibility of such diversified regimes depends, however, on the ability to control exit. This is because for rules to be effective it would sometimes be necessary to make users accountable for their on-line behavior – be it infringement of a regulatory norm or violation of contract terms and conditions. Such accountability requires a mechanism of identification because users' on-line identities are represented by IP addresses or domain names. These virtual identities may not be easy to monitor and apply sanctions to, since they may be multiple and unsteady. Users may escape responsibility for on-line harm by changing their IP address. Some may also use different addresses for different purposes, thus escaping any sanctions applied against them – such as restricting their access to an on-line area. User accountability, therefore, requires a technical ability to link the virtual representations of users and their physical entities. However, a central identification system may threaten users' privacy and allow service providers (registries, ISPs) a high degree of control over on-line activities. This potential control may threaten the civil liberties of users. Furthermore, if such identification and control mechanisms are available they may be used to place users' on-line behavior within the jurisdiction of their local governments.

For all the difficulties, there is no question that cyberspace is transforming the traditional, hierarchical, and monolithic system of law in the direction of plurality of normative systems, the rupture of hierarchies, the overlapping of norms, and their dissociation from the territorial nation-state.

b.   The Changing Nature of Central Government

Even if the traditional national-state is here to stay, cyberspace ought to make us rethink very entrenched notions of central government and its organization. The liberal-economic theories of the state (as well as practical thinking), despite the contractual-consensual rationale of collective action, have acknowledged the obstacles concerning the application of these principles to the daily life of communities and the need for more efficient day-to-day collective decision-making processes.

The two solutions offered by modern democratic states are representative democracy and majority decision making. The Athenians' resort to majority rule and decisions by lottery were methods to overcome the difficulties of consensual decision making (although the latter remained the ultimate goal). So do the modern developments of representative democracy and the tools designed to overcome its fallacies such as the separation of powers.

Representatives acting on behalf of their constituents save the costs of frequently measuring public preferences on each and every issue and the prohibitively high costs of coordinating massive numbers of people. Cyberspace significantly reduces the costs of communicating and processing individuals' preferences. It makes it possible to efficiently collect information from individuals by asking them to click their preferences directly onto the screen.[38] It reduces transaction costs involved in collecting information about preferences. Cyberspace also facilitates fast and cost-effective information processing that allows real-time feedback on public preferences and choices. This, in turn, reduces the need for agencies. The reduced costs of coordination and communication diminish the extent of collective action problems. If transaction costs involved in coordination are low or nonexistent, there is no need for representatives – intermediaries – to reflect the aggregated will of their constituents. Individuals may directly communicate their preferences on each and every matter.

In addition, low transaction costs may allow individuals, who cannot become organized in the nonvirtual world, to become organized. Cyberspace reduces the cost of identifying relevant parties, communicating, acting together, and spreading information that concerns all. This can lead to increased democratization and decentralization of rule-making processes, in whose various stages cyberspace allows groups and individuals to participate.[39] This may allow citizens to take a more active part in governance, and to effectively monitor government actions.[40]

From the perspective of economic theory, two important problematic phenomena which exist in representative democracy ought to be mentioned, as they are toned down significantly in cyberspace. The first is agency costs, which are associated with representative government.[41] These costs are the result of ineffective monitoring of representatives by their voters and the ability of the former to act in a self-interested manner without being penalized by the voters (or the costs of the penalties being smaller than the political or personal gains). The easy and rela-

---

[38] Consider, for instance, an issue on the current agenda – whether to charge a fee for Internet domain name registry. It is possible to pose this question to all Internet users at low cost. It is also relatively easy to collect the information and process the results. If different parties have different agendas on this issues, they can also communicate their propaganda to users.

[39] Legislative bodies, for example, may efficiently collect public comments on bills posted on the Internet. Technology will make it possible in the future not only to consult the public but also to delegate to the public the actual decision-making powers.

[40] See also Trachtman (1998), who argues that cyberspace reduces transaction costs of coordination in the private sector and in the public sector.

[41] For a basic analysis of political agency costs, see Musgrave and Musgrave (1980).

tively cheap access to information and the lower costs of collective deliberation and action in cyberspace are likely to increase the effective monitoring level and thus reduce these agency costs.

The second phenomenon of representative democracy is the power of interest groups to rent seek, and make gains through pressure on the representatives at the expense of the general public. Interest groups are able to succeed in their actions because of the costs of collective action. These costs allow only small groups to organize – groups whose potential gain from collective action is higher than the costs of organization (see the classical text, Olson 1965, and in the legal context, see Farber and Frickey 1991: Ch. 1). Cyberspace, as indicated above, tends to lower the costs of collective action, which in turn enables broader interest groups to organize, bringing more equality to the political markets and diffusing the impact of narrow interest groups.

Thus, cyberspace allows the decentralization and democratization of rule-making processes in that it facilitates effective participation of people in setting the rules. Rules may be increasingly created from the bottom up, and therefore reflect the need for diversified social and economic interests by increasingly complex societies (for further discussion of the advantages of decentralization, see Cooter 1997b). A legal regime in which individuals are able to directly communicate their preferences has several advantages over a legislative process exercised by elected representatives. Individuals are able to reflect their preferences directly, and hence more accurately. This reduces the chances of mistaken assessment of public preferences and therefore inaccurate setting of the rules.

A majority rule is yet another solution to the impediments to consensual collective action. The economic reasoning for the resort to majority rule is best represented by the model of collective decision making set by Buchanan and Tullock's *Calculus of Consent* (1962). This model can be considered as one of the classical presentations of a normative analysis of collective decision making in the framework of the consensus principle. It is a good reference point for the analysis of collective action in cyberspace.

Buchanan and Tullock distinguish external costs of collective decision making from internal costs. The former is the total costs to individuals negatively affected by the decision. These costs diminish, as the majority that is required for reaching a decision increases. In unanimous decision making these costs are zero as rational individuals will not consent to decisions which harm them. A dictator's rule inflicts the highest external costs on the members of his or her community. The internal cost function reflects the costs involved in the decision-making process itself. It is shaped in the opposite direction to the external cost function: dictatorial rule is the least expensive to operate. As the majority required for passing a decision increases, so do the costs involved in the decision-making process. Consensual rule is the most expensive to operate. The optimal decision-making rule is the one which minimizes the sum of the two types of costs. Buchanan and Tullock show that in most areas this optimal rule is a simple majority, but there might be special types of decisions (e.g., decisions which touch upon basic human rights) in which the optimal decision-making rule is a qualified majority. The Buchanan–Tullock model is one of the few modern justifications for majority rule.

The application of this framework to cyberspace is interesting. Its results depend on the definition of the cyberian community. If we regard all of cyberspace as the unit of analysis, we believe that the external cost function will not change notably in comparison with the nonvirtual world, while the internal cost function – the decision-making costs – will decrease significantly. Collective decisions, as already mentioned above, are cheaper to arrive at because of lower information costs, negotiation costs, and communication costs.[42] If the marginal cost function of decision making as related to the majority required for deciding is more moderately sloped, we can expect the optimal decision-making rule to be greater than a simple majority. Hence, the democratization in cyberspace is reflected not only by weakening the dependency on representative structure and the agency costs it is associated with, but also by shifting the decision-making rule from simple majority towards unanimity. This can increase the total well-being of the members of the community.

So far, we have viewed cyberspace as one community. If, however, we view cyberspace as a conglomerate of communities, a change will also occur with regard to the external costs function. This is because of the exit option, which is much easier to opt for in virtual communities. The availability of this option is likely to decrease the external cost function in addition to the internal cost function. This might not change our conclusion regarding the optimal decision-making rule, as this conclusion is contingent on the marginal cost functions. But, in any case, the analysis of cyberspace as a conglomerate of communities will lead us to an even greater total advantage from collective action.

3.   Law and Enforcement

Another way in which cyberspace transforms the law as an institution, and therefore the traditional functions of the state, is connected to enforcement. On the one hand, conventional enforcement (by the state apparatus) is much less effective in cyberspace, as it is always possible to cross geographical boundaries, to disguise

---

[42]   See also Sunstein (1995: 1783), who argues that cyberspace, in contrast to the Madisonian vision of the state, enables large-scale substantive discussion which brings us closer to the deliberative democracy or the Republican vision of the state.

the physical identity of the infringer etc. (see also Hardy 1994). On the other hand, cyberspace introduces new methods of enforcement that challenge traditional thinking about enforcement and transforms its meaning. In a sense, technology in cyberspace allows efficient enforcement to a degree that does not exist in the non-virtual world.

The most significant change in the context of enforcement is the ability to regulate behavior using the infrastructure of cyberspace. The computer programs, communications design, and network architecture that constitute cyberspace are not neutral. They reflect a certain social order, shape behavior and social interaction among users, and define the potential choices of actions available to users in cyberspace (Lessig 1999).

Consider privacy, for instance. The privacy of users' correspondence, their on-line chats or the list of Web sites they visit may be protected by either the law or the code. Laws that protect privacy define certain behaviors, such as unauthorized invasion of individuals' private mail, as illegal. The law may impose liability for damages on invaders, inflicting negative incentives to discourage a behavior that is not socially beneficial. Invasion of privacy may be also enforced by criminal law. But these conventional enforcement means might not be effective in cyberspace because of territorial jurisdiction, identification problems, and more. In cyberspace, privacy might instead be protected by the code, which may, for instance, allow the use of encrypted messages to protect the privacy of senders. Such self-help means render privacy protection laws unnecessary because these devices simply prevent the undesirable behavior.

Another example is copyright laws. Copyright law prohibits the creation of copies without the authorization of the copyright owner. A copier will pay the owner damages for the infringing copies she has made. In cyberspace, some programs may simply prevent the creation of uncompensated copies by using copyright management systems (Bell 1998), encryption, digital watermarks, etc. Such means may replace reliance on copyright laws.

Enforcement by the code is very different from the enforcement of rules in real-world legal regimes. Rather than defining undesirable behaviors by the law, or providing incentives for a desirable behavior, regulation by the code makes it possible to prevent certain behaviors altogether (see Lessig 1996: 1407–1408; Reidenberg 1998). Whereas traditional enforcement of legal rules is ex post, enforcement by the code is ex ante. Enforcement by the code does not require any law enforcement institutions such as courts and the legal system. It is self-executed and self-implemented. The same system that provides the service (such as the computer program that facilitate access to a Web site) also defines the terms of access and the terms of use – such as copying, and permitting others – such as browsing.

Enforcement by the code, therefore, is more efficient. It involves relatively lower costs than enforcement by the legal system. It does not involve the costs of identifying, seizing, and prosecuting violators. The costs of implementing self-help means of enforcement are lower than the administrative costs of maintaining the bodies of the legal enforcement system, such as the police and the courts. But it is not without cost: it involves the costs of developing a technology and preserving its technological superiority. In addition, the financial structure of enforcement costs is different: costs of self-enforcement by the code are usually borne by users, whereas the burden of administrative costs of the legal enforcement system is usually distributed among taxpayers.

Regulation by the code further differs from the enforcement of rules in that it entails perfect performance. It does not offer users any choice of whether to go by the rule or to violate it (Reidenberg 1998: Part III; Lessig 1996: 1408). The architecture simply prevents any undesirable behavior from occurring. Consequently, the level of enforcement and its success does not depend on the extent to which the public comprehends and internalizes the rules. However, this type of enforcement violates an important legal principle, namely that laws ought to be publicized and accessible to the public.

To the extent self-enforcement is perfect, it is likely to reduce the price of goods and services. Consider, for instance, the price of copyrighted works. The price has to cover not only the large investment in creating and marketing the work, but also the costs of enforcement and the expected loss from failure to enforce the rights of the copyright holder. If the expected market for a music publisher is substantially reduced due to the creation of unauthorized copies, the publisher will raise the price per copy in order to cover its expenses. If enforcement by the code prevents the creation of unauthorized copies, it will reduce the price of copyrighted works (Bell 1998).

These differences between the traditional system of law enforcement and enforcement by the code raise conceptual issues regarding the notions of enforcement and regulations. The literature on technological self-enforcement regards the code as a type of regulation.[43] A preliminary question is of course whether it is justified to talk about regulation by the code and enforcement by the code as part of the law. Economic theory may treat technology as simply design or an architectural constraint because the notion of regulation under economic analysis of law assumes a choice. The underlying assumption of the economic approach to rules is that rational agents are able to control their behavior. They are motivated by their wish to maximize their utility. Rules are sometimes necessary to correct an otherwise distorted set of incentives (due to market failures), and provide individuals with appropriate incentives so they will choose to act efficiently. If a design

---

[43] Reidenberg (1998) endorses the lex informatica embodied in the code as the new and modern version of the lex mercatoria of merchants in the middle ages. Trachtman (1998) refers to these approaches that endorse regulation by the code as "new medievalists."

simply prevents a certain behavior, we can no longer talk about regulations and incentives, since there is no longer a choice by individuals for the law to promote or prevent.

On the other hand, enforcement by the code can be violated by countercoding technology. If we view such technological developments as possible, and the only question about their materialization is one of choice and costs, it is feasible to argue that from the perspective of economic theory, the differences between traditional enforcement analysis and the analysis of enforcement by the code are not so significant as they might appear, and that we may regard the enforcement by the code as part of a legal regime after all. If this is the case, the question about publicity and accessibility of the code is a very crucial one.

To summarize, cyberspace is likely to transform our understanding of law. The way in which law is created is under change, with the introduction of greater decentralization and democratization. The way in which law is enforced is also changing, with the replacement of the traditional enforcement institutions – police, courts, etc. – by enforcement by the code. Cyberspace is leading to globalization, effectively decreasing municipal regulations and territorial sovereignty.[44] This may cause transformation not only of law but also the framework of the nation-state. In the future, technological zoning will create new communities, from which different laws might emerge, but which will be in increasing competition with the nonvirtual community (Lessig 1996: 1409). All these issues bring us to the major current practical question: should cyberspace be regulated by traditional means, and if yes, how?

4.   Should Cyberspace Be Regulated, and if So, How?

The regulation of cyberspace has become a hotly contested issue worldwide. Legal economists are using an existing economic framework to support nonintervention policies (Easterbrook 1996: 215–216). If cyberspace approaches the zero transaction cost world, legal economists would argue, it will be necessary to keep the law out of cybermarkets. Furthermore, the technological gallop not only renders legislation unnecessary, it also makes it dangerous. When technology develops quickly, the risk of errors in legislation becomes significantly higher. I beg to differ. The pertinence of the economic framework to cyberspace may be crucial to policy choices. However, the analysis in the two previous sections ought to lead us to the following interim conclusions which are different from the conclusions of those using the existing economic framework:

---

[44]   On the American jurisdiction rules and their inapplicability to cyberspace, see Burk (1996).

1. Cyberspace challenges the current paradigms of the state, the law, and the economic markets, and therefore it requires fresh thinking and new analytical frameworks. This conclusion stands in sharp contrast to Easterbrook's (1996) assertion that to talk about the law of and in cyberspace is just like talking about the "Law of the Horse." Cyberspace does not, according to Easterbrook, alter the basic tenets of legal theory or of the economic analysis of law. Those principles can be applied to cyberspace just as they are applied to any specific legal situation. So, just as Dean Casper of the Chicago Law School refused to offer a course on "The Law of the Horse" there was no justification to reconstruct legal theory just because we had entered an era of extensive usage in computer networks.

Easterbrook's stance overlooks the possible paradigmatic shifts that cyberspace brings about. Thus, as I have tried to show, cyberspace creates new frameworks for market and nonmarket activities, which at the moment exist alongside the traditional markets and political organizations, but in doing so, they also affect the traditional structures. The features of cyberspace undermine the presuppositions of traditional economic theory as well as traditional political and legal theory, and therefore, they require new solutions.

2. The question "should cyberspace be regulated?" is a misleading one. As demonstrated in the previous section, cyberspace is already regulated, not only by traditional laws but primarily by the code. In this regard, it is important to point at the changing forces behind the architecture of cyberspace. The Internet was founded by the academic community. It was originally devised in a way that allows the open flow of information and democratic and egalitarian access and use, for no profits. In recent years economic forces have discovered cyberspace, and its architecture has been changing towards less free, less egalitarian, profit-motivated, power-motivated goals. Lack of traditional legal intervention does not mean lack of regulation. It means that we give our consent to the change of norms governing cyberspace through the code. This is a possible choice of regulation but it is indeed regulation and indeed a choice. Examination is required whether the new regulation by the code tackles the new market failures that were pointed to in the first section. My tentative answer to this question is negative.

Because of the very different features of cyberspace as a market and as a public forum, different from the features of the nonvirtual world, it is very possible that different sort of regulation is required to cybermarkets, as well as cybercommunities.

3. An important feature that emerges from our analysis, in the first section, of cyberspace as a market is its global nature. Therefore, central intervention attempts at the state level will prove to be unsuccessful and inefficient. The nature of the transactions in cyberspace does not even enable locating a transaction in a specific physical location. Even if such location can be pointed at,

as long as there are differences between intervention of various jurisdictions, we are likely to witness a constant shopping around for the better jurisdiction. Since the exit option in cyberspace is very cheap, traditional jurisdictional regulation will be ineffective.

The conclusion, therefore, is that regulation of cyberspace (either through the code, or by more traditional means) ought to be carried out on a global level.

4. As we noted in the previous section, one of the problems of regulation by the code is lack of publicity and accessibility of the law by the general public. Even if our conclusions are that cyberspace ought to be regulated by the code, rather than by law, this point has to be remedied, by public debate and information as to the choices made in this regard. An appropriate global institution has to be formed to carry out the tasks of regulating cyberspace and openly deliberating the possible choices in fulfilling this task.

5. As we have seen in the previous chapter, one major characteristic of cyberspace is self-enforcement. What are the implications of self-enforcing means (technological or social) for the question: when and how should the (traditional) law intervene? The code and the legal system overlap in that both legal regimes simultaneously apply to the same people. They may conflict with one another. They may compete with one another.

Under standard economic analysis, a law enforcement system is considered a public good that must be provided by the state. Furthermore, the state requires a monopoly over enforcement means. In most circumstances the state will not allow competing enforcement entities (including international law) to exercise their power in a way that threatens its monopoly over enforcement. Enforcement by the code is a private good. Should enforcement functions, traditionally reserved for the legal system, be privatized in cyberspace? To address this question, it is necessary to consider several aspects of enforcement by the code.

It is arguable that in cyberspace self-enforcement methods by the code are more efficient and should therefore replace any exercise of power by the territorial states. Furthermore, the costs of enforcement by the traditional legal system in cyberspace may be prohibitively high. Global access imposes increased costs of enforcing rules of the territorial state outside its jurisdiction (Post 1996, Reidenberg 1998). Access and on-line activities are not tied to any geographical place, and may constantly switch locations. Violators may effectively act from another jurisdiction and thereby defeat enforcement attempts.[45] Globalized access may further increase the costs of enforcing rights outside the jurisdiction, the costs of resolving conflicts with laws, and uncertainty about the legal rules.

---

[45]   For instance, relocating a Web site with materials considered illegal under one jurisdiction in a different jurisdiction (Lessig 1996).

On the other hand, the traditional enforcement systems of governments may also use cyberspace to regularly monitor their citizens, thus reducing enforcement costs. Monitoring on-line activity may involve lower costs than monitoring real-world activity. Enforcement agencies may efficiently collect information in cyberspace not otherwise available to law enforcement agencies. This may reduce enforcement costs outside cyberspace. However, technologies that allow encryption and anonymity may increase the costs of identifying and tracing law violators.

The power of code designers may be reduced by market effects. The use of self-enforcement measures is also subject to market rules. Copy protection that did not allow the making of any copies of a computer program turned out to be a failure. Similarly, Web sites which make use of technology that secures the privacy of visitors advertise it through a rating system, presumably because it makes their sites more attractive. Internet businesses that do not provide a security system would not be able to attract customers. Thus, the power of code designers to develop the rules for cyberspace is not unlimited. The market effects may mitigate abuse of technological advantages only in the absence of market failures.

But if, for instance, a company exercises a monopoly power, then its technology becomes the standard and consumers may not be able to avoid restrictions on use and access by switching to a different program that reflects different rules. A decision on whether to allow competing regulations by the code should take into account this new and dynamic scheme of power relations.

Enforcement by the code depends on technological and market advantages. The efficacy of technological protection of copyrighted works depends on the absence of circumvention means. For every protection measure there is always a countertechnology to crack it. The development of cybertechnologies is dialectic in the sense that it has always involved developing measures to bypass, remove, or disable other technological measures. Consequently, perfect enforcement and full compliance depend on the resilience of the technology to circumvention means. This may change over time, and in cyberspace it changes rather quickly.

If enforcement is left to the code, it is likely that social resources will be invested in developing measures and antimeasures. This may contribute to technological development, in that some inventions sometimes have other uses. To the extent that resources are redirected to the race of merely developing protection and defeating measures, they represent economic waste,[46] and the law of the real-world legal system may arguably be necessary to prevent it.

---

[46]   Compare to the waste involved in a pre-property regime in which every member has to exercise self-protection measures to prevent the taking of what she considered to be her property.

In other words, intervention by regulation might be needed as a second-degree enforcement control.[47]

6. The simultaneous existence of self-enforcement measures in cyberspace and the traditional legal system requires some thought be given to the interface between them. Should the law intervene in such self-help methods of enforcement? Of what nature should such intervention be? The traditional role accorded to the law under standard economic analysis of law is to correct market failures. In the case of a market failure the role of law will be to alter the payoff functions of players in the market (Basu 1998). In other words, when market processes do not function efficiently due to a market failure, the law will change the incentives attached to individuals' choices of action, and will thereby affect the strategies adopted by individual players in the market.[48] In cyberspace, the target of regulation may become the technologies that affect users' behavior rather than the behaviors themselves, largely owing to the information problem discussed above.[49] The law may provide negative incentives to circumvent such systems to prevent the waste involved in the technological race for security and antisecurity means.[50] Legislation may also prevent implementing a certain technology altogether.[51]

From our market failure analysis of the first section, it seems that the major market failures that can characterize cyberspace are connected with technology: technological monopolies and waste as a result of technological wars – especially of exclusion and circumvention. But the sort of global central intervention that is required is not straightforward at all. On the one hand, such intervention ought to protect inventors and providers from hacking and illegitimate copying or use. On the other hand, it ought to prevent the providers and inventors from monopolizing technological standards and from obliging the consumers to purchase other products that they did not intend to buy from this

---

[47]   See, for instance, in articles 11 and 12 of the World Intellectual Property Organization [WIPO] Copyright Treaty signed in December 1996, according to which contracting parties agreed to provide adequate legal protection against the circumvention of effective technological measures used by copyright owners to protect their rights to the works. Attempts to regulate technologies are risky in the sense that they impede innovation.

[48]   This includes imposing fines, liability rules, providing a public good, etc.

[49]   See Reidenberg (1998), who suggests that lex informatica should become the target of regulation instead of direct regulation of the behavior itself – for instance, the promotion of technical standards.

[50]   For example, proposals in the U.S. Congress to prevent the development of circumventing technologies that may tamper with copyright management systems provide such systems with immunity by law.

[51]   The law may prohibit a program that allows invading private exchanges (reading all emails from any workstation). The law may, however, do nothing, and thus require individuals who wish to protect their privacy to encrypt their messages.

particular provider. In addition, the intervention has to try to preserve the original aims of the creators of cyberspace, providing for more open, democratic, and pluralistic societies. The *American Digital Millennium Act* is an example of imbalance intervention which favors the big and rich (American, mostly) producers and providers, and which diminishes the amount of free informational flow. This is a good example of why a global response is to be preferred to national one.

7. The principle that laws ought to be public assumes that the law can affect the behavior of people, so they should be aware of it. Enforcement by the code involves serious problems of information about the rules that are embodied in the code itself. Users may not have perfect information regarding the rule that is implemented by the code. The rule, as well as the code, is not directly accessible to people.[52] Users may learn what a particular program or a design does and does not do from the way it functions. This takes time and often some expertise. It may be difficult, for instance, to find out whether Internet browsers or programs used on Web sites collect and store information on Internet users.[53] One goal of central intervention, therefore, is to provide the public with information as to the regulation of cyberspace, especially if this regulation is done through the code rather than the traditional methods.

5.   A Final Note on the Economic Approach Itself

Cyberspace provides an opportunity to test the economic approach as an analytic framework, and to examine its usefulness in defining when the law should intervene and how. Cyberspace is often perceived as a concrete version of a Coasian ideal world, approaching the zero-transactions-costs state, in which the rule of law does not matter and optimal allocation through bargaining can be achieved. But are the traditional models of law and economics really useful to define the scope of legal intervention in cyberspace? Applying economic constructs to cyberspace highlights some of the problematic presuppositions made by the economic analysis of law regarding the state and its institutions, the legal system, and the changes in the state of technology. The technological gallop not only challenges legislative efforts. It also affects the foci of economic analysis and requires an adjustment of

---

[52]   Take, for instance, the network services provided by Microsoft when it launched its network, services that allowed automatic reading of users' information on their hard drive without their knowledge.

[53]   Another example is provided by Lemley (1998). Filtering systems allow users to rate third-party sites. Such filtering systems may embody different judgments regarding what should be considered appropriate material. It is very difficult to get perfect information on how the program operates and which sites it would block.

its framework. How should the economic model adapt itself to cyberspace? What can cyberspace teach us about the economic analysis of law?

One can describe the economic approach as comprising three generations, which can be perceived as separate paradigms of sorts: the traditional Chicago school economic analysis of law, transaction cost analysis, and neoinstitutional economic analysis of law and of legal institutions.[54] The Chicago school views the microeconomic model as the suitable theoretical framework for the analysis of all legal questions, including those which are not traditional market issues. The tools of microeconomic theory – the curves of supply and demand – can be applied to analyze the market for children for adoption, or the market for crimes, or the market for laws in general, as they are applied to the market for apples or cars.

The Chicago framework does not distinguish between rational individuals and other, more complex, market players such as firms, governments, or agencies. The state and its structure and institutions are perceived as exogenous to the analysis. Markets and states are assumed to correspond to each other. I already elaborated in previous sections why these assumptions cannot hold for cyberspace. Especially the strict correlation between markets and states, or between forums which facilitate private contracts and public forums of collective decision making, does not exist in cyberspace. This can indicate low, or even a lack of, relevancy of this paradigm to the analysis of regulation of cyberspace.

A transitional generation in the development of the economic approach towards law is transaction cost analysis. Its starting point is, in fact, an extension of the Chicago school; this extension eventually brought about the third generation of neoinstitutional law and economics. The heart of transaction costs analysis is the Coase theorem, which undermines the categorization of the traditional market failures and especially the analysis of the remedies to correct them. Coase's analysis points at transaction costs as the sole factor which diverts the market from efficiency, and thus the sole factor to take on board when legal rules are considered. The concept of transaction costs, which was originally used to analyze the interaction between individuals in the market, was soon broadened to include the analysis of the emergence of institutions, their internal decision-making process, and their external interactions. In doing so, the methodological tools used for the analysis were expended and hence the shift towards the third generation.

---

54   As some of the roots of the neoinstitutional law and economics can be traced back to the 18th century works of Borda and Condorcet, the term "generation" is being used here not merely on chronological bases, but more as an indicator for the width and complexity of the economic analysis. As the science of economics is based upon the transformation of real world reality into a simplified setting which is the basis for applying rigorous models of analysis, the presuppositions which set the framework for the modeling can determine the complexity of the analysis and thus the precision of its results. In this sense, the Chicago school can be labeled as first generation law and economics, while neoinstitutional law and economics can be labeled as third generation.

The Coasian model of transaction costs assumes, however, a given technology that affects efficiency. The efficient outcome depends on the availability of technologies and their costs. Transaction costs analysis takes as given that one party may exercise technology that may increase the value of the resource or may lower the costs inflicted by harmful use, but it does not take into account the possibility of technologies changing as a result of the legal rule. Coase did not take on board the possibility that legal rules might have a direct effect on technology, as this factor in his example of straying cattle which destroy crops growing on neighboring land is indeed remote. It is not so in the cyberian world.

Indeed, in cyberspace, technologies are constantly changing and the analysis may be different with each technological state of the art. The substance of a legal rule may affect technological development. The introduction of new technologies has a dialectic relationship with other processes. The apparent shortcoming of the economic approach is that it takes technological development as static, and overlooks the correlation and reciprocity between technological developments and legal rules. Technology should therefore become endogenous to the analysis, and the economic discourse should be expanded to address it.

The third generation of economic analysis of law, which can be associated with the neoinstitutional paradigm, is the broadest framework of economic analysis insofar as it incorporates institutional structures as endogenous variables within the analysis of law. Thus, neoinstitutional analysis views the political structure, the bureaucratic structure, the legal institutions, and other commercial and noncommercial entities as affecting each other. Political rules intertwine with economic rules, which intertwine with contracts. However, even here I believe that the developments in cyberspace may require some fresh thinking on the level of the whole project. Two points ought to be mentioned.

First, neoinstitutional law and economics emphasizes the connection between the political and institutional structures, on the one hand, and market activity, on the other hand. One of the most significant features of the cybermarket is its development against the background of a lack of concrete political and institutional structure. One of the most innovative characteristics of cyberspace is that norms are developed there from the bottom up, and that central intervention may prove to be ineffective. The borders between private and public, between markets and hierarchies, are not as clear as in the nonvirtual world. These features pose some challenges which have never been addressed, even by the neoinstitutional approach. This approach can show how certain political structures may influence markets and laws; it has not shown how a lack of structures may do the same.

Second, cyberspace accentuates some weaknesses that exist in the shadow of the neoinstitutional endeavor with regard to the nonvirtual world and that are brought to light in the virtual world. One of the major points of criticism against the whole project of economic analysis is that it is based on the assumption of rational behavior. I do not wish here to repeat and elaborate the general criticism along this line against this presupposition, but a few words about the special challenges posed by cyberspace to this paradigmatic assumption are in place.

Economic analysis assumes that the players have preferences that are exogenous to their contractual and collective public activity; it also assumes that perfect information will enhance rational choices by players that will meet their individual preferences. One of the important features of cyberspace is that it provides almost unlimited information. In fact, lack of information can no longer be held as affecting irrational behavior. But perhaps the contrary is true. There is so much information that a need for information processing tools arises. In the nonvirtual world there are significant gaps in information, and on the other hand there is diversity within society and between societies that creates different sets of information that are affected by given preferences – political, cultural, and linguistic. By contrast, cyberspace is characterized by uniformity. The whole world becomes a small, global village, with a common language and cultural identities. Ironically, this combination of endless information and homogeneity might affect the independence of individuals in general and their preferences in particular.

While some argue about individual preferences in the nonvirtual world as being exogenous to the political process and to the economic markets, cyberspace requires us to internalize even the analysis of individual preferences. Fresh thinking, if not a fresh paradigm of economic analysis, has to emerge in which these basic presuppositions with regard to rationality and preferences are internalized. Such thinking would help us to assess whether cyberspace is a forum that creates much more free choice or a tool for suppressing independence – in fact, limiting freedom of choice, whether technology sets new horizons for individual and collective well-being or patterns our individual character, our self, by the same universal agents for everyone; whether it enhances communication of diversities, or causes the disappearance of the diversity which in the nonvirtual world fosters the definition of the unique self, leaving us with a brave new homogeneous human being.

References

Allen, T., and R. Widdison (1996). Can Computers Make Contracts? *Harvard Journal of Law and Technology* 9:25–52.

Bailey, J., and E. Brynjolfsson (1997). In Search of "Friction-Free Markets": An Exploratory Analysis of Prices for Books, CDs and Software Sold on the Internet. Paper presented at the 25th Telecommunications Policy Research Conference. Alexandria, VA, September 27–29.

Band, J., and M. Katoh (1995). *Interface on Trial, Intellectual Property and Interoperability in the Global Software Industry.* Boulder, Col.: Westview Press.

Basu, K. (1998). The Role of Norms and Law in Economics: An Essay on Political Economy. Working Papers in Law and Economics. The Law School, Berkeley.

Bell, T. (1998). Fair Use v. Fared Use: The Impact of Automated Rights Management on Copyright's Fair Use Doctrine. *N.C.L.R.* 76:557–619.

Breyer, S. (1982). *Regulation and Its Reform.* Cambridge, Mass.: Harvard University Press.

Buchanan, J., and G. Tullock (1962). *The Calculus of Consent.* Ann Arbor: University of Michigan.

Burk, D. (1996). Federalism in Cyberspace. *Connell Law Review* 28:1095–1136.

Burk, D.L. (1998). Virtual Exit in the Global Information Economy. *Chicago-Kent Law Review* 73:943–995.

Calabresi, G., and D. Melamed (1972). Property Rights, Liability Rules and Inalienability: One View of the Cathedral. *Harvard Law Review* 85:1089–1128.

Coase, R. (1960). The Problem of Social Cost. *Journal of Law and Economics* 3:1–44.

Cooter, R. (1997a). Normative Failure Theory of Law. *Cornell Law Review* 82:947–979.

Cooter, R. (1997b). Symposium: Normative Failure Theory of Law. *Cornell Law Review* 82:951–978.

Dam, K.W. (1999). Self-help in the Digital Jungle. *Journal of Legal Studies* 28(2):393–412.

Dunoff, J., and J. Trachtman (1999). Economic Analysis of International Law: An Invitation and a Caveat. *Yale Journal of International Law* 24:1–59.

Easterbrook, F. (1996). Cyberspace and the Law of the Horse. *University of Chicago Legal Forum* 207–216.

Elkin-Koren, N. (1996). Cyberlaw and Social Change: A Democratic Approach to Copyright Law in Cyberspace. *Cardozo Arts & Entertainment Law Journal* 14:250–295.

Elkin-Koren, N. (2001). Let the Crawlers Crawl: On Virtual Gatekeepers and the Right to Exclude Indexing. *Dayton Law Review* 26:179–209.

Elkin-Koren, N., and E.M. Salzberger (1999). Law and Economics in Cyberspace. *International Review of Law and Economics* 19(4):553–581.

Elkin-Koren, N., and E.M. Salzberger (forthcoming). *Law, Economics and Cyberspace* (Edward Elgar).

Farber, D., and P. Frickey (1991). *Law and Public Choice – A Critical Introduction.* Chicago: University of Chicago Press.

Gibbons, L.J. (1997). No Regulation, Government Regulation, or Self-Regulation: Social Enforcement or Social Contracting for Governance in Cyberspace. *Cornell Journal of Law and Public Policy* 6:475–551.

Hafner, K. (1997). The World's Most Influential On-line Community (and it is not AOL), WIRED.

Hardy, T. (1994). The Proper Legal Regime for Cyberspace. *University of Pitt. L. Rev.* 55:993–1055.

Hart, H.L.A. (1961). *The Concept of Law.* Oxford: Clarendon Press.

Johnson, D.R., and D. Post (1996). Law and Borders – The Rise of Law in Cyberspace. *Stanford Law Review* 48:1367–1402.

Johnson, D.R., and D. Post (1997). And How Shall the Net Be Governed? A Meditation on the Relative Virtues of Decentralized, Emergent Law. In B. Kahin and J. Keller (eds.), *Coordinating the Internet*. Cambridge, Mass.: MIT Press.

Kelsen, H. (1945). *General Theory of Law and State*. Cambridge, Mass.

Landes, W., and R. Posner (1989). An Economic Analysis of Copyright Law. *Journal of Legal Studies* 18(2):325–363.

Landow, G.P. (1992). *Hypertext, the Convergence of Contemporary Critical Theory and Technology*. Baltimore, Md.: Johns Hopkins University Press.

Lemley, M. (1998). The Law and Economics of Internet Norms. *Chicago-Kent Law Review* 73:1257–1294.

Lemley, M., and D. McGowan (1998). Legal Implications of Network Economic Effects. *California Law Review* 86:470–559.

Lessig, L. (1996). Symposium: Surveying Law and Borders: The Zones of Cyberspace. *Stanford Law Review* 48:1403–1411.

Lessig, L. (1999). *Code and other Laws of Cyberspace*. New York: Basic Books.

Loundy, D.J. (1997). Primer on Trademark Law and Internet Addresses. *John Marshall J. of Computer and Info. Law* 15:465–491.

Menell, P. (1987). Tailoring Legal Protection for Computer Software. *Stanford Law Review* 39:1329–1372.

Menell, P. (1989). An Analysis of the Scope of Copyright Protection for Application Programs. *Stanford Law Review* 41:1045–1104.

Mercuro, N., and S. Medema (1997). *Economics and the Law – From Posner to Post-Modernism*. Princeton: Princeton University Press.

Musgrave, P., and R. Musgrave (1980). *Public Finance in Theory and Practice*. New York: McGraw-Hill Book.

Pigou, A.C. (1920). *The Economics of Welfare*. London: Macmillan.

Polinsky, A.M. (1989). *An Introduction to Law and Economics*. Boston: Little, Brown and Company.

Post, D. (1996). Governing Cyberspace. *Wayne Law Review* 43:155–173.

Post, D., and D. Johnson (1997). The New Civic Virtue of the Net: Lessons from Models of Complex Systems for the Governance of Cyberspace. *Stanford Tech. L.* 1:10.

Olson, M. (1965). *The Logic of Collective Action*. Cambridge, Mass.: Harvard University Press.

Radin, M.J. (1996). Property Evolving in Cyberspace. *The Journal of Law and Commerce* 15:509–526.

Reidenberg, J. (1998). Lex Informatica: the Formulation of Information Policy Rules Through Technology. *Texas Law Review* 76:553–593.

Sunstein, C. (1995). Emerging Media Technology and the First Amendment: The First Amendment in Cyberspace. *Yale Law Journal* 104:1757–1804.

Schultze, C.L. (1977). *The Public Use of Private Interest*. Washington, D.C.: Brookings Institution.

Trachtman, J. (1998). Cyberspace, Sovereignty, Jurisdiction and Modernism. *Ind. J. Global Legal Stud.* 5:561–581.

Comment on Eli M. Salzberger

Peter Johnston

1.   A New Strategy for Europe

IT and communications infrastructures are already widely deployed and are increasingly changing business, work and our daily lives: 45 percent of European workers use a computer for their work, 74 percent of "white collar" workers, and 20 percent also use a computer at home for work. Over 120 million Europeans now use the Internet (30 percent of the world total), and this is likely to rise to over 200 million by 2003. Over 230 million (65 percent of Europeans) now use digital mobile phones, and these will become Internet access devices within 2 years: Further technology developments will accelerate and broaden these changes.

This transformation is now at the center of the European Union's strategy, agreed upon in Lisbon in March 2000, to become *the most competitive knowledge-based economy in the world, with sustained growth, more and better jobs, and greater social cohesion.*

The e-economy transformation is a triple one: to networked services; to knowledge as our key resource; and to global business and markets.

There are good reasons to believe that all three elements will increase growth, productivity, and wealth. However, superposition of a knowledge economy on established industrial and agricultural activities will also increase wealth and earning differentials – both *between* countries and *within* countries: software engineers have greater earning potential than manual workers in all countries.

Policies which maximize participation in the knowledge economy will lead to higher growth, and the proportion of the population (both within the EU and globally) which can be engaged in knowledge economy activities can also be much greater than was achieved in the last (20th) century in industrial economies. The affordability and geographic spread of access to knowledge work and markets for services is greater. More people will have access to the Internet via mobile phones in 2005[1] than the 750 million that had access to telephones in 2000. As many as 2½ billion people may be able to afford and use mobile Internet access in 2010.[2]

---

[1]   Nokia now estimates that over 1 billion people will have mobile phones by 2002.

[2]   Internet will by then be accessible from wireless (3G and Wireless LAN), fixed telephony, Cable (digital) TV, and optical fiber connections.

The key objective of the Lisbon strategy is therefore to engage as many people as possible in knowledge economy work, both within the EU and worldwide. The E-Europe Action Plan will accelerate this by cutting access costs, by increasing digital literacy, and by providing public access in all communities.

However, we must recognize that the transformation to a knowledge economy changes growth dynamics and governance frameworks. Governance, specifically in and of cyberspace, is discussed in Eli Salzberger's paper. As he describes, new legal issues are raised by the Internet, but these must be kept in the perspective of its new growth dynamic in the new economy, and I can best complement his paper by some observations on this dynamic and on a European perspective on Internet governance and its wider impact.

2.   New Growth Dynamics

The network is the new paradigm. Network growth dynamics are ones of self-reinforcing growth and much of the initial dynamism of Internet and GSM use is attributable to "*Metcalf's law*" that the total value of a network increases as the square of the number of people connected.[3] However, new network capabilities first attract more prosperous and skilled people, and continued expansion to near 100 percent of the population has diminishing economic returns.

In Europe and the United States, after initial expansion has reached about 25–35 percent of the population, the incremental value of further expansion is less, and is continuing to slow. However, in Europe, where tax-and-benefit systems reduce income disparities, there continue to be significant positive value increases to over 90 percent of the population.

The size of networks is also important in itself. The value and diversity of services also grows faster in larger networks than in smaller ones, even when the size of the networked community is stable. This is because innovation itself depends on interaction: The more people interacting in a network, the more new ideas are generated by everyone.

Interoperability is therefore a benefit, both to the participants in different networks, and to the vitality of growth of services on them. It is 10 times better to have everyone connected to interoperating networks than to have one-tenth of the same population connected to each of ten separate networks.

---

[3]   The *"total value"* is associated with the ability to communicate with any (or all) of the other connected people – value associated with each individual or business being a creator *and* user of knowledge (an *e-worker or e-business*).

Digitization is itself a self-reinforcing process: the more information and knowledge (scientific research, cultural heritage, etc.) available over networks in digital form, the wider the base for new creativity and innovation.

Finally, positive *economic feedback*[4] reinforces growth: The more users of network services, the bigger the market, the more revenue and re-investment in R&D, the better the services, and the more users...

However, these same feedback mechanisms can also increase economic and financial volatility. A fall in confidence, by customers or investors, can quickly propagate in an interconnected world. Businesses that have few physical assets are particularly susceptible to changes in consumer preferences and investor confidence. New markets for new services can quickly be overtaken by yet more imaginative offerings; and the fast pace of technology change demands continued high investments in the latest technologies anyway.

This has been well illustrated by recent stock market volatility – is e-commerce just "the froth on the daydream" or is there a deeper crisis in underlying technology developments? The answer is in part "yes." The whole TMT sector is affected – infrastructure suppliers like CISCO as much as e-commerce players. And the fall in investor confidence may well now interrupt the "Moore's law" doubling of computing power every 18 months. But the economic development answer is probably "no." The underlying growth in the sector is still strong.[5]

Despite the deflationary impact of the € 130 billion charged for 3G spectrum licences in Europe, revenue growth and infrastructure investment (although slowed) remains robust.

3.   Internet Governance and Governance in a Networked World

The Internet is therefore not only changing the dynamics of technology development and economic growth. It is also changing ideas and models of governance.

It poses specific new challenges. Cyberspace is intrinsically nonterritorial. Its value depends critically on preserving its interoperability and technological integrity. The Internet is the single largest information system ever built by humanity; and it must preserve its integrity despite continuing fast technology change.

---

[4]   *Feedback Mechanisms in the Evolution of Networks: The Installed User Base and Innovation in the Communications Sector.* ETLA report No 725 of 3/8/2000, from the Research Institute of the Finnish Economy.

[5]   Europe is now the most dynamic ICT market in the world: According to the European IT Observatory, the Western European ICT market grew by 13 percent in 2000 and is still expected to grow by 11 percent in 2001. In 2000, the U.S. ICT market grew by only 8.2 percent, and the Japanese market by only 6.7 percent.

The governance system of the Internet itself has worked and evolved alongside the Internet for 20 years. Its development is managed by a set of nongovernment organizations (NGOs) for which the global ICT business community provides the major financial support and ensures both wide participation and respect for collective agreements. The major governing bodies are:

— *The Internet Society (ISOC),* which is a nonprofit international NGO with over 8,600 members in 170 countries, focused on the 4 pillars of Standards, Public policy, Education and training, and Widening membership. It is the organizational "home" of technical groups (IETF, IAB, IESG and the IRTF) and provides support for training workshops and centers, and for the Internet Societal Task Force. The ISOC is financed by 175 sponsor organizations, mainly ICT companies, and is officially recognized by UNESCO as its NGO partners in the Global Social Policy activities.

— *The Internet Engineering Task Force* (IETF), which is the main technology development and standardization body that ensures interoperability of the whole Internet system. Its activities are supervised by a steering group, and it works within the overall guidance of the Internet Architecture Board. It works over the Internet, and its meetings (every 4 months) are open to all. About 2,000 engineers participate in each; about one-third new each time.

— *The Internet Corporation for Assigned Names and Numbers* (ICANN), which is the body now responsible for "address space" allocation; "domain name" management, and the "root server" system. It is a nonprofit private corporation reflecting the Internet's business, technical, academic, and user communities. Its board is composed of 19 Directors: 9 representing Internet users, 9 representing its supporting organizations, and an independent President/ CEO.

Internet governance is therefore open, networked and participatory, nongovernmental, and dependent on decisions by consensus. However, while those involved in its governance frameworks often like to believe their task is technological, it is clear that the major challenges come from reflections of "real world" concerns:

— Cybersquatting – the acquisition and speculation in domain names related to major brands and trademarks – has arisen from the " land-grab" system of new territory exploitation, modeled on the 19th century settlement of the U.S. western states. The transposition of IPR rights into cyberspace is now further complicated by their transposition from the ".com" space into other new spaces such as ".business."

— The initially dominant "national" top-level domain names (such as .uk or .de for Germany) transposed territorial disputes into cyberspace without consis-

tent national governance systems – with consequential problems such as the separate domains for Taiwan and China, and those associated with the disintegration of Yugoslavia, and with overlapping regional domains such as .EU.
– An implicit new "U.S. imperialism" in domains such as .gov and .mil being reserved for U.S. government and U.S. military sites, and the commercialization of "national" domains such as ".TV" and ".NU," have arisen.
– New monopolies, such as .com, have arisen which can only be broken by new alternative, and nonterritorial, top-level domains such as ".business" and ".museum."

In addition, the necessary transition to the next generation Internet Protocol 6 (IPv6) poses new challenges. With an effectively unlimited "address space" of over 10 to the power of 30 – more unique identifiers than ever could be written down, or stored in computer memories – power shifts from those who control space, to those who control access to it: from ICANN to the network operators and Internet service providers. Cyberspace is of no value unless it can be accessed in a coherent and reliable way.

While Internet governance frameworks such as the IETF provide some defense against the emergence of new monopolies based on proprietary standards, they do not interwork well with traditional legal instruments.

Internet governance frameworks can do nothing about information content, its social acceptability, its authenticity and reliability, etc. Action in these areas has to be left to voluntary measures taken by Internet service providers, portals, and market intermediaries (eBay etc).

Finally, other governance issues, such as consumer protection, privacy, and data protection escape from national jurisdictions, and depend on self-regulation by companies adhering to "codes of conduct" on which there is only weak democratic supervision.

Despite these challenges, open, networked, participatory forms of governance, inspired and facilitated by the Internet, are gaining in popularity. Even in the European Union, the new "open method of co-operation" between member states in their implementation of the Lisbon strategy for accelerated development of a knowledge economy is a major step away from the centralized, legislative approach of the 1980s for creation of the "Single Market." Civil society organizations, and businesses have also been able to strengthen the coherence of their actions – while keeping flexibility and managing diversity.

The issue therefore is not "How to regulate the Internet?" but "How will the Internet affect governance?"

David T. Llewellyn

Financial Intermediaries in the New Economy: Will Banks Lose Their Traditional Role?

1. Introduction

The banking industry is in an era of substantial structural change where a combination of pressures operating simultaneously is changing all aspects of the business: the structure and intensity of competition, new types of competitors (including nonfinancial companies), some banking markets have become more contestable, the business profiles of banks, the way banking business is conducted (manufacture, origination, processing), the nature of the interface between banks and their customers, organisational structures of banking firms, and the structure of the industry.

The objective of this paper is to offer an overview of the banking industry in the context of the emerging "new economy", to pose a series of fundamental questions about the future of banking in the context of the traditional theory of the banking firm, and to consider the nature of the pressures producing structural change in banking. The general context is that, around the world, banks face challenges to their historic monopolies and comparative advantages: banks are no longer the monopoly suppliers of banking services.

In particular, technology is transforming the economics of all aspects of banking business. In this regard, a distinction is made between *incremental* and *paradigm* technology, where the former, while changing in a limited way the way banking business is conducted, does not change the fundamental economics of the industry, while the latter does have this impact.

2. The General Context

Banks have traditionally played a key role in the financial system by acting as financial intermediaries between ultimate savers and borrowers. As asset transformers, they have accepted deposits with one set of characteristics and created assets with a different set. They have also been the central mechanism within the payments system. For these and other reasons banks have traditionally been regarded as "special" within the finanical system.

The nature of what a bank does has changed radically over the past few years, and it is likely to change further in the years ahead. The type of institutions conducting banking business has also changed. With respect to the first issue, banks conduct a much wider range of business than simply taking in deposits and making loans (their traditional financial intermediation business). Banks have become financial services firms, and in many countries off-balance sheet income of banks now exceeds income earned from traditional financial intermediation business. *What* a bank is is no longer clearly defined.

At the same time as banks have been diversifying and redefining their business, a wide range of new types of firm have begun to supply some traditional banking services and, in particular, transactions deposits, savings accounts and a range of loans. Such firms include supermarkets, utility companies, insurance companies, mutual funds and even car manufacturers. There is little, if anything, that banks do that could not now equally be done by markets, nonbank financial institutions, and nonfinancial firms. In other words, banks have lost their traditional monopoly advantages. Banks are even losing their monopoly in the payments system. The idea of a bank as a middleman in the payments process is being challenged by the removal of physical media and the development of electronic media: e-money. Some payments systems exclude banks altogether. This range of issues raises the question: *who* is a bank?

Occasions sometimes arise in the evolution of a particular industry when it is possible to look back and isolate a period when that industry was being transformed: a defining period of significant structural change. Such a period is when the competitive structure of the industry changes, entry barriers decline and new types of competitor enter the industry which often have different cost structures and business structures than incumbents, the underlying economics of the industry changes, challenges are made to traditional ways of conducting business, and new optimum organisational structures emerge. Technology is often a dominant driving force in such periods. In such a period, some firms disappear or exit, while others adapt. It has sometimes been the case in such industries that large incumbents are not necessarily those that subsequently prosper as their dominant position comes to be challenged by new entrants which were not foreseen. The theme in this paper is that banking may be in such a period now.

Four strands of argument emerge in the paper:

- (1) Technology is transforming the underlying economics of the business of banking, the way banking business is conducted, the structure of the banking industry, and the organisational structure of the banking firm.

- (2) Banks have become potentially vulnerable in their traditional business as alternative firms have begun to offer some traditional banking services, and new ways (e.g., markets and financial instruments) have emerged to satisfy customer demands that have traditionally been met through bank products and services.
- (3) Banks have considerably widened the range of services and products they supply and have become less dependent upon their traditional financial intermediation business.
- (4) Banks have come to exploit their core competencies (information, risk analysis, monitoring, etc.) in a variety of ways other than through traditional on-balance sheet business.

Some of the traditional monopolies and inherent comparative advantages possessed by banks are being eroded. The pressures impinging on banks have the potential to transform the structure of the industry, the type of business undertaken by banks, the type and range of institutions conducting banking business, and the way that traditional banking business is untertaken. They are also likely to affect the internal structures of the banking firm as banks move towards a structure of *contract binding*.

A dominant pressure derives from new technology with respect to information, trading, processing and delivery of financial services. As noted by Vesala (2001: 31), "developments in information collection, storage, processing and transmission technologies (IT technologies) have strongly influenced and continue to influence all aspects of banking activity". Industrial history shows that the development of new technology has the potential to have a major impact on any industry. This is most especially the case when technology impacts on the very core of the business; in the case of banking: information, risk analysis, monitoring, processing and delivery. It is largely technology, and what follows from it, that is transforming the banking and financial services industries, and changing the underlying economics of banking and the banking firm.

3.   Are Banks in Decline?

In some respects the relative role of traditional banks in the financial system is declining and the value of the banking franchise is being eroded. There is a substantial literature (mainly related to the banking system in the United States) that discusses these propositions. However, we note that, in general, banks have a more dominant position in the financial systems of the European Union than is the case in the United States. Thus, bank assets as a proportion of GDP are around 240 per cent in the European Union compared with 60 per cent in America. The usual evidence cited for the relative decline in the role of banks includes:

- the "intermediation ratio" has been declining;
- the declining share of bank loans in total corporate sector borrowing;
- the shift towards corporate sector borrowing in the commercial paper market (the immediate competitor to banks);
- the loss of corporate lending business to finance companies;
- the declining share of personal sector savings flows going to banks;
- the spectacular growth of money market mutual funds;
- the trend towards securitisation in many national and international markets;
- the entry of nonbank financial institutions into traditional banking markets;
- the emergence of a new set of nonfinancial companies (such as supermarkets) in the markets for retail and wholesale financial services;
- nonbanks offering payments facilities, and
- the development of in-house company banks.

Banks are no longer the exclusive suppliers of banking services. However, care is needed when translating the banks' loss of share in lending business (particularly to the corporate sector) to the more general notion that banking as an industry, and banks as firms, are in secular decline. The two are synonymous only to the extent that the role of banks in financial intermediation is measured by the volume of assets on the balance sheet, and that banks do not compensate for the loss of some business by diversifying into other areas. A central theme of the paper is that banks have certain core competencies or market advantages (e.g., information, risk analysis, etc.) and that these can be used in a variety of different ways amongst which making loans and holding them as assets on the balance sheet is only one. A distinction needs to be made between the traditional core competencies of banks and the way these competencies are used and in which markets.

In the United States, data indicate that there is no clear evidence of banks being in secular decline when the focus is value added, and when allowance is made for diversification into new business, much of which is conducted off the balance sheet. Boyd and Gertler (1994) make adjustments to balance sheet data to account for the different risk characteristics of different types of bank assets, and apply national income accounts data to the measurement of value added by banks. They conclude that there is no unambiguous evidence that banks are in decline in the United States. Similar conclusions are found in Kaufman and Mote (1994).

As with any firms, banks exist for one of two generic reasons:

- they have a particular expertise enabling them to do what other firms cannot do: they possess certain monopoly attributes and capabilities, or

– they do what can be done by others but they possess certain comparative advantages which give them a competitive advantage in the market place.

It follows that any firm becomes potentially vulnerable if it loses a monopoly power (i.e., others become able to do what was previously the exclusive preserve of the firm(s) in question), or its traditional comparative advantages are eroded, or because alternative firms or markets can provide the same services at lower cost.

a.   Monopoly Erosion

In many ways, banks have lost some of their traditional monopolies. In particular, the development of technology has lowered entry barriers as has the process of deregulation. The emergence of *deconstruction* (considered in detail below) and *consumer unbundling* also means that new suppliers can offer competition to banks because they are no longer required to provide the full range of banking services, or undertake all of the processes involved in supplying banking services. In addition, consumers have more information about a wider range of alternatives to bank deposits for holding liquid funds. For instance, the development of money market mutual funds (some of which incorporate payments facilities) also challenges the traditional monopoly of banks in the supply of transactions balances.

A core competence of a bank is the information base which results from managing customers' bank accounts. However, banks are losing some of their traditional information monopolies, as information technology has the effect of increasing the supply, and reducing the cost, of information to a wider range of suppliers of financial services. This general trend is reinforced by more public disclosure of information by companies and the development of rating agencies.

b.   Comparative Advantage Erosion

New technology and declining entry barriers have also challenged some of the traditional comparative advantages possessed by banks. In particular, disclosure laws have eroded some of the information advantages traditionally held by banks. The development of unit trusts and money market mutual funds also allows consumers to have diversified portfolios even with relatively small investments. With respect to risk analysis, the development of credit scoring techniques means that the credit standing of borrowers can be assessed without the necessity of the information derived through an institution maintaining a borrower's current account.

The growth of rating agencies further challenges banks' traditional information and monitoring advantages. Banks' economies of scale advantages in processing are also being challenged by the emergence of *deconstruction* and outsourcing when much of banks' processing in the value chain is subcontracted to technology companies.

Banks, in addition, are losing their traditional comparative advantages in delivery by virtue of their branch network. New delivery technology undermines this, as some banking services are able to be supplied without a branch network. This in itself is a factor lowering entry barriers.

c.   Lower Costs of Alternative Suppliers

For the same reason, if the costs of alternative suppliers of traditional banking services fall relative to those of banks, the latter become vulnerable. In particular, financial innovation and the power of new technology have tended to increase the relative competitiveness of the capital market vis-à-vis banks. New delivery technology has also lowered the cost of alternative suppliers of financial services (e.g., supermarkets) to the extent that they no longer need to develop a branch network. Further, to the extent that regulatory costs imposed on banks are higher than those imposed on alternative suppliers of some of the services provided by banks, regulation has the effect of increasing the relative competitiveness of nonbank suppliers of banking services. A latter section considers various factors that enable new entrants to complete effectively with traditional banks.

4.   The Existence of Banks

It is instructive to consider the extent to which some of the traditional factors that give rise to the existence of banks (and enhance their role in the financial system) may have become less powerful. The traditional theory of the banking firm (the so-called existence literature) emphasises four key elements:

- information advantages;
- imperfect markets;
- the theory of delegated monitoring; and
- the special role of banks in the payments system.

Given their importance in the theory of banking, and the potential vulnerability of banks, each of these is briefly considered. Other key elements emphasised in the "existence literature" are considered in Llewellyn (1999).

a.   Information Advantages

Several theoretical approaches to the existence of banks focus upon various information problems in financial transactions, and how banks are able to handle them more efficiently than the capital market or bilateral transactions between savers and borrowers. Banks have a comparative advantage over capital markets when information on enterprises and their projects are not easily transferred to open markets, when problems arise over monitoring borrowers' behaviour, when for competitive reasons firms do not wish to make information publicly available, and when borrowers do not wish to be subject to the discipline of continuous open public scrutiny. With personal customers, banks gain valuable information by managing their bank accounts as transactions through the account reflect customers' income, wealth and expenditure patterns.

The information rationale for financial intermediation is that banks can solve ex ante (adverse selection) and ex post (moral hazard) contracting problems more efficiently than can be done either directly between ultimate borrowers and lenders, or through markets.

Several factors are operating to erode some of the banks' traditional information advantages vis-à-vis alternative suppliers of intermediation services. Firstly, technological developments have reduced the cost of acquiring and accessing information for alternative suppliers. Secondly, rating agencies have developed both to make information more widely available and accessible, and to assess information on behalf of potential investors. This is of particular value to capital market transactors. Thirdly, disclosure laws (most especially in the United States and the United Kingdom) have been extended. This means that, in some cases, information which was previously a private advantage to the bank has become more of a "public good".

The development of information technology also increases the availability and access to information to institutions other than banks. There is something of a vicious or virtuous circle: as capital markets become more efficient, firms have a greater incentive to disclose more information in order to secure access to capital market facilities. In turn, this increased supply of information enables the capital market to function more efficiently and to act as a greater competitor to banks in their lending business. As noted by Bisignano (1990: 46), "the comparative advantage that banks have in obtaining and assessing the creditworthiness of borrowers and of resolving the asymmetric information problems, appears to be declining, primarily in those countries with increasingly sophisticated capital markets". In various ways, therefore, banks are losing some of their traditional information advantages that have been the core of their comparative advantage.

b.   Imperfect Markets

One general theory of the banking firm is that banks exist because financial markets are imperfect and incomplete. However, the process of "spectrum filling" (appraoching the Arrow–Debreu state) reduces the number and extent of discontinuities in the range of market instruments. Borrowers now have a wider range of capital market instruments. Van Horn (1985) argues that securitisation and financial innovation take us closer to a world of complete markets. In addition, new information and trading technology have reduced information costs in capital markets relative to bank lending costs.

Technology has also lowered transactions costs in capital markets and, as already noted, has had the effect of reducing information costs and making information more publicly available for the capital markets. In general, the more complete contracts are, the easier they are to securitise. The process of financial innovation generally has this effect, and enables more complete contracts to be constructed. Overall, market pressures have been eroding the market imperfections and incompleteness which have given rise to the banks' comparative advantage over markets (Eisenbeis 1990). The overall result is that markets have become more significant competitors to banks.

c.   Delegated Monitoring

As contracts are necessarily incomplete, borrowers need to be monitored to ensure that their behaviour maximises the probability that loans will be repaid. The question is who is best able to undertake such monitoring, bearing in mind that it is a costly activity. In parallel with analyses which emphasise information problems is a strand of analysis which emphasises the role of banks as monitors of behaviour. In effect, investors (who become depositors in banks) delegate the monitoring role (both in assessing projects and monitoring subsequent behaviour) to banks which have two comparative advantages: (i) economies of scale in monitoring and (ii) an ability to reduce the cost of monitoring by diversification (Diamond 1984). Diamond's model incorporates monitoring costs and shows that, because direct investors would be duplicating monitoring costs, and that to some extent monitoring and evaluation is a public good that no-one has an incentive to provide, financial intermediation can be the most efficient monitoring method. Banks reduce information and incentive problems via monitoring the firm. However, along with the increased availability and lower cost of public information, the development of rating agencies also challenges the traditional role of banks as delegated monitors. As noted by Mayer (1994), monitoring can become a fee-based activity rather than an integral part of the bank loan process.

d.   Payments Advantage

Some theories of the banking firm emphasise the advantage that banks have because they are an integral part of the payments system. However, banks are losing these monopolies. The development of money market mutual funds and unit trusts with payments facilities offers a challenge to the banks' traditional monopoly in this area. Similarly, the development of credit and debit cards erodes this same monopoly, and an increasing proportion of transactions can now be executed without the need for even a temporary stock of funds in a traditional bank account. The development of electronic barter has the potential to undermine banks' traditional monopoly in the payments system.

In general, this is a threat to banks based on a challenge to two traditional assumptions: that transactions require money and that only banks can issue money. Money is a convenient facility as it means that transactors do not need information about the standing of the payer as would be the case if payments were made through the transfer of other assets. However, technology also facilitates the verification of the standing of transactors: a particular example is the development of smart cards. Information can now be easily stored in such cards, which in turn can be issued by a variety of firms other than banks.

Although the use of e-cash has not to date become widespread (European Central Bank 1999), its potential is substantial. For instance, as noted by Vesala (2001), there is potential for diffusion of the use of e-cash stored on chip cards or electronic purses for purchases via the Internet. As the required investment is substantially smaller than with the establishment of EFTPOS terminals, this could accelerate the trend towards e-cash.

5.   Assessment

In various ways, therefore, the related pressures of competition, deregulation, financial innovation and technology have eroded some of the comparative advantages of banks in their traditional financial intermediation business. In addition, new information and trading technology has reduced information and transactions costs in capital markets relative to bank lending costs. Financial innovation and technology (together with the development of rating agencies) are eroding transactions and information costs and market imperfections which have been the basis of banks' efficiency and comparative advantage over capital markets. Also, to some extent, historically regulation exaggerated the comparative advantages possessed by banks because it created something of a protected market environment.

Market pressures are eroding the market imperfections which gave rise to the banks' comparative advantage over intermediation in capital markets. Financial innovation and technology are also eroding transactions and information costs and market imperfections which are the basis of financial institutions' efficiency over direct credit markets.

In effect, banks in some countries are losing their predominant role as deposit takers and lenders to companies. Joss (1996) argues that banks are losing some of their traditional advantages, and that there are categories of traditional lending business (such as standardised consumer credit and large corporate loans) that banks are no longer suited to fund. He argues that "it is mostly borrowers with unique, non-standard credit needs that will rely heavily on banks and finance companies for their funding requirements".

Although the demand for banking services will continue to rise (and probably relative to incomes), this does not mean that institutions called "banks" will automatically be the suppliers of these services. However, neither does it follow that banks will in the future be conducting only the banking business they have conducted in the past, and they will adapt to pressures by changing the way even traditional banking business is conducted.

6.   Three Fundamental Questions

Having outlined some of the traditional analysis and theory of banks and why they exist, three questions are posed:

- Are banks necessary for banking?
- Is banking necessary for banks?
- Will the traditional integrated structure of the banking firm survive?

a.   Are Banks Necessary for Banking?

It would appear that the answer to this is "no" in that there is now little that banks do that could not equally be done by markets, nonbank financial institutions or nonfinancial banking institutions. As entry barriers are eroded, a wider range of competitors has emerged: department stores, supermarkets, companies such as GEC, Virgin Atlantic, a range of "industrial banks", unit trusts and money market funds, telephone companies, etc. Alternative firms can and do provide some traditional banking services. Some life assurance companies have recently obtained banking licences and offer a range of banking services. Some supermarket stores in the United Kingdom (Tesco, Sainsbury, and Safeway) offer limited banking facilities and offer a rate of interest on credit balances significantly higher than traditional banks. The Virgin Group in the United Kingdom also sells a range of financial products and offers some banking services: deposits, loans, mortgages.

b.   Is Banking Necessary for Banks?

Again the answer seems to be "no" except in the purely tautological sense that "banking" might be defined as anything that banks do. Banks do not restrict themselves to "banking" business. Just as insurance companies have diversified into banking, so banks have diversified into insurance. In this respect, while banks' traditional monopolies and comparative advantages are being eroded, and they have come to be challenged in some of their traditional business, this does not mean that the outlook for banks is bleak. Banks can and do respond in two ways: by diversifying their business, and by conducting traditional banking business in different ways. Overall, the traditional distinctions between different types of financial institution have been eroding rapidly and substantially, and even to the extent that it is debatable whether, in a decade's time, there will be clearly recognisable institutions called "insurance companies", "banks", etc.

c.   Will the Traditional Bank Structure Survive?

The traditional banking firm is vertically integrated in that it manufactures and provides the products and services it offers to customers, and untertakes all of the component processes of those products and services. The concept of *contract banking* challenges this traditional structure. The trend has been towards subcontracting bank processes to external specialist companies with the bank being a manager of a set of internal and external contracts. In effect, a bank becomes a broker between the customer and a set of outside contractors whose activities make up the range of banking products and services. This is considered further below.

7.   Secular Pressures on the Banking Industry

Over the next decade, banking as an industry, and banks as firms, are likely to face substantial structure change. The business of banking, the operation of the banking firm, and the structure of the industry are likely to change radically. Two main reasons why the changes in the financial system are likely to be so substantial are: (1) because some of the pressures (notably technology) faced by banks challenge the core of financial business: *information, risk analysis, monitoring, processing* and *delivery*, and (2) because as entry barriers are declining, competition is not only intensifying but coming from new types of competitors. It is largely technology, and what follows from it, that is transforming the banking and financial services industries.

Banks have come to face more intense competition on both sides of the balance sheet: for deposits and loans. On the liabilities side, banks in many countries face increased competition from unit trusts, money market funds and life assurance companies. In many countries (the United Kingdom in particular) the proportion of personal sector assets in the form of liquid deposits is decreasing, while that in illiquid, longer-term insurance and investment products is rising. Some major life assurance companies have recently secured banking licenses in order to compete for traditional deposits.

There is now a wider range of substitutes for bank deposits. Browne (1992: 18) notes the impact of financial innovation, "financial innovation has now provided savers with greater flexibility in managing their portfolios by enhancing the available instrument choice, and by making existing instruments more accessible." Consumers also have more choice and are able to accept some asymmetric information risks in return for a higher interest rate, whereas historically they have, to some extent, been locked in to bank deposits. Financial innovation, and the creation of new instruments, also enable risks to be hedged. Put another way, part of the returns to intermediation have now been appropriated directly by the saver rather than by deposit-taking intermediaries.

It is partly because of these trends that banks in some countries now offer unit trust facilities within their group so that deposits lost by the bank are not lost to the group overall. In effect, an original process of disintermediation (depositors at banks switching to markets) has been followed by a countervailing process of *re-intermediation* as banks have themselves come to offer market instruments for investors.

8. Banking Markets Have Become More Contestable

The power of competition to constrain the behaviour of incumbent firms in an industry is not so much indicated by the degree of competition present at any point in time, but the extent to which the market is *contestable*. A market is said to be contestable if entry and exit barriers are low. The latter will be the case if sunk costs (i.e., costs that cannot be recovered at the point of exit) are low. In such a market environment, competition is not measured by the number of firms currently in an industry. If entry and exit barriers are low, incumbent firms will be under pressure to behave as if they were operating in a market with many competitors.

Banking markets (rather than necessarily the banking industry) have become more contestable. The distinction is made because it is now possible for banking products and services to be unbundled and for new firms to enter some banking markets without offering the full range of traditional banking products and services. Several factors have raised the contestability of banking markets:

— The development of information technology increases the supply, and lowers the cost, of information, and enables new entrants to access and process information.
— Regulatory barriers have been eased as regulation has become less restrictive about the type of firms that are able to offer banking services and products.
— The development of credit-scoring techniques, coupled with greater access to information, enables new entrants to assess credit risks without having the experience gained through managing borrowers' bank accounts over a period of years. This lowers the economies of scope advantages traditionally possessed by banks.
— The proces of *deconstruction* (the ability to decompose banking products and services into their component parts with each supplied by different firms) lowers entry barriers in three ways: (1) new firms can compete without themselves undertaking all of the processes involved in a particular service, (2) it enables entry without the requirement of substantial up-front fixed costs which are involved with some processes, and (3) new firms are able to enter without having all of the necessary expertise as gaps can be bought in from other firms through outsourcing contracts.
— Scale has also become less important to the extent that processes can be subcontracted as, with lower fixed costs through subcontracting, economies of scale can be bought in from specialist providers of processing services. Scale economies are in *processes* rather than *firms*, which means that, if processes can be subcontracted, economies of scale can be secured by firms of varying size. This lowers scale barriers to entry. It also lowers exit barriers, as entry is made without installing heavy infrastructure.
— The emergence of *contract banking* (banks outsourcing some bank processes) also makes it easier for new firms to enter banking markets. A particular implication of outsourcing is that scale become less significant in that a small firm is able to buy in economies of scale from external suppliers of some component services.

- Securitisation also means that loans need no longer be held permanently on the balance sheet of an originating institution.
- As new forms (most especially telephonic) of delivering banking services have emerged and developed rapidly, the branch network (traditionally an entry barrier) has become relatively less significant. New entrants are able to offer banking services without the necessity of an extensive and costly branch network with concomitant heavy fixed costs.
- In some banking markets (notably wholesale lending) the steady globalisation of banking markets has made local marekts increasingly contestable, as large-scale borrowers have access to global banking markets.
- The development of Internet facilities for banking products and services has also enhanced the contestability of banking markets. Above all, the Internet means that search costs for consumers and advertising costs for suppliers have been lowered substantially. It also means that distance between supplier and consumer becomes less significant.
- Many bank products have become increasingly *commoditised* (Santomero 1999) and sold almost exclusively on the basis of price.
- Consumers have become more prepared to "unbundle" banking products (i.e., regard each product as an indepedent transaction rather than as part of a total banking package). This makes banking markets more contestable as new competitors are able to focus on a narrow range of business and need not offer the full range of banking products and services. New entrants are able to compete in those particular markets in which they have a potential competitive advantage.
- Linked with this, consumers have become less conservative about the type of firm (including nonfinancial firms such as supermarkets) they are prepared to deal with when conducting banking operations and buying banking products and services. This lowers reputation and brand barriers to entry.

The key to the increased contestability of banking markets is a combination of: (1) low entry and exit barriers, (2) the process of *deconstruction*, and (3) the growing tendency for consumers to unbundle their demand for banking and financial services. The first makes it easier for new firms to enter. The second means that new entrants do not need to conduct all of the processes involved in banking operations. The third means that new entrants are able to choose their markets and are not forced to offer the full range of banking services.

These considerations are important when judging the nature of the competitive environment in which banks operate. They are also relevant when making judgements about the competition implications of bank mergers. Vesala (2001) observes that new entrants have significantly undercut the prices of established banks and have already significantly influenced pricing in banking markets.

9.   Deconstruction

The process of *deconstruction* also lowers entry barriers into some banking markets. A standard bank loan (such as a mortgage) can be decomposed into three components: origination, management and asset-holding. A loan has to be originated (a borrower located), subsequently administered (interest rate set and collected), and held on a balance sheet. This has traditionally been undertaken as a single process by lending institutions. And yet different agents may have comparative advantages in different parts of the process, and there is no necessary presumption that a single institution is the most efficient at undertaking all three parts of the process. Thus a bank may have an advantage in originating loans (e.g., through the branch network) and administrating them, and yet face a capital or funding constraint in funding the loans and holding them on the balance sheet. In which case it can originate and administer loans which, for a fee, are effectively sold to other institutions which have a comparative advantage (perhaps because of lower funding and capital costs) in holding them as assets. In the United Kingdom, for example, foreign banks are significant holders of mortgage assets which have been originated and administered by building societies. In these cases different institutions exploit their particular comparative advantages. In general, specialist providers are often more efficient than others.

Equally, in some cases the monitoring of borrowers may be undertaken by rating agencies: monitoring does not have to be part of the credit process although this usually is the case with bank loans. As noted by Joss (1966), banks are increasingly looking at core elements of their business on a stand-alone basis rather than a necessary part of an integrated business.

10.   Technology

A central theme is that technology has become one of the major drivers of change in the banking industry. Technology has the power to transform the underlying economics of any industry. A combination of information, trading and processing technology is transforming the fundamental economics of banking just as it has with many other industries. However, unlike in other industries, finance technology is changing the *production, processing*, and *distribution* economics simultaneously. As already noted, the fundamental cores of banking business are: *information, risk analysis, monitoring, processing, trading* and *delivery*. Technology is changing the underlying economics of each of these core business components.

When considering the impact of technology on the banking industry a distinction can usefully be made between *managerial* and *paradigm* technology. With managerial technology, while business operations may change and technology may raise internal efficiency in processes, the technology is by its nature incremental and does not change the underlying economics of the industry in any fundamental way. *Paradigm technology*, on the other hand, does change the underlying economics of the business. While the application of technology in the 1970s, 1980s, and early 1990s was predominantly *managerial* in nature, current technology is different in that recent developments in the application of technology in banking represent a paradigm shift rather than being incremental in nature. This is because, in contrast to many other industries, it is impacting on all aspects of the business: production, distribution, processing, delivery, the way the consumer interfaces with banks and suppliers of financial services, the competitive environment, and also optimal organisational structures. It also has the effect, in some areas, of lowering entry barriers and changing the economics of the branch network and delivery mechanisms. At the same time, some aspects of new information technology are making some banking and financial products more transparent and are lowering consumer search costs.

The power of technology has been decisive: it acts as both a threat and an opportunity to banks. It enables existing services to be provided more efficiently, enables new services to be offered, increases the economies of scale in bank processing, enhances management's access to information, lowers entry barriers in some areas, and changes the economics of delivery. Technology has the power to transform the basic economics of any industry. In this respect, banking is no different from other industries which have been transformed by technology. Technology has the potential to increase the availability and reduce the cost of information. This is a potentially powerful force as it both reinforces and challenges one of the banks' major core competencies: information. Given that banks are ultimately in the "information business", anything that impacts on the availability, cost and management of information must have a decisive influence on their business.

The Internet

One dimension of new technology in banking relates to the delivery system and the Internet in particular. In the course of time, the Internet could become the dominant delivery medium for relatively simple and standard transactions. In the United States, several banks have formed joint ventures with a group of computer companies to provide a "financial services superhighway". Banks are experimenting with electronic shopping malls and several banks and building societies in the United Kingdom offer services through the Internet.

The potential economic impact of the Internet on banking is substantial:

— the marginal cost of transactions is virtually zero;
— distance between consumer and supplier becomes meaningless and of no economic significance, which may result in more cross-border competition;
— consumer search costs are low as information and price discovery are made easier and prices become more transparent;
— it is usually the case that the consumer pays the access costs;
— as an increasing number of rival banks and financial firms open net sites and home pages, the cost of information to the consumer and the search costs for rival services and products become very low, which in itself increases competitive pressures in the market;
— the transactions costs of switching between competitors are reduced, which is likely to have the effect of eroding customer loyalty;
— it further erodes the necessity to have a branch network to supply financial services and further erodes entry barriers;
— incumbency advantages are lowered and small firms are able to compete.

While, for many consumers in the early stages, access to Internet facilities may appear formidable, this will ease as Internet financial directories develop. Several currently exist in the United Kingdom to facilitate easy access for consumers and lower search costs for rival products. Thus, TrustNet, Insurance Mail, Infotrade, and Financial Information Net Directory offer facilities such as comparable data for products and services, general market information, information on the full range of personal financial topics, price and terms quotations, and on-line trading.

11.   New Entrants into Banking

A constant theme of this paper has been the impact of declining entry barriers enabling a wider range of financial and nonfinancial companies to enter banking and retail financial services markets. Such entry strategies are frequently on the basis of joint ventures with banks forming strategic links with partners who are potentially also major competitors. In the United Kingdom, a range of nonfinancial companies have entered banking and retail financial services markets on a significant scale.

a.   Common Characteristics

There are several common characteristics about such new entrants, and which account for their strategies:

— New entrants are able to exploit new forms of delivery almost as easily as their bank competitors.
— New entrants are usually highly focused in the product range, and do not offer the full range of financial services offered by banks: they are able to choose those parts of the business of incumbents in which they judge they have a competitive advantage. Unlike their banking competitors, they are not under pressure to offer the full range of banking and services.
— This focus is partly associated with the banks' pricing policies, which frequently create cross-subsidies: uneconomic services are sustained in part by subsidies from other parts of the business. New entrants, on the other hand, are able to price services without cross-subsidies as, in some cases, they choose products which banks are pricing so as to subsidise other parts of the business. In effect, they are able to "cherry pick". This is particularly evident in the deposit market, where some supermarkets are offering considerably higher rates of interest than banks are. This in turn is partly a reflection of the cross-subsidies within banks: "free banking" is paid for largely through low interest rates on retail deposits.
— New entrants tend to be highly focused within the value chain. With the potential for *deconstruction*, much of the high-cost processing is subcontracted to specialists including, in some cases, bank competitors or partners.
— In many cases, overall costs are lower than in incumbent firms.
— Because of the ability to subcontract large segments of processing, and effectively to buy into economies of scale through specialist processors, new companies are able to operate with comparatively low fixed costs.
— New entrants also avoid legacy costs in that they do not have an existing cost structure based on past technology. In effect, they are able to avoid the transactions costs of re-engineering the business to adapt to current conditions.
— New entrants are able to establish systems consistent with current regulatory requirements. They are not faced with the need to adapt existing systems to new requirements.
— In most cases, new firms are able to exploit the value of a franchise associated with their brand name. The idea of a "brand value" is that it stands for something which is more than the product itself. New entrants tend to be household names associated with companies for which the consumer has a high degree of trust built up through a long association independently of financial services. In effect, they believe they can "brand" the financial products or services being

sold, i.e., the name attached to the product adds value in consumers' minds because of the general reputation of the company. One of the key functions of a brand is "quality certification", which is especially significant in cases where, as with many financial contracts and services, the consumer is unable to determine quality at the point of purchase, and where the post-sale behaviour of the seller can affect the value of the product to the consumer.

— Retailers which have begun to offer retail financial services have very large customer bases.

12.   Capital Markets and *Primary Securitisation*

A useful distinction can be made between what might be termed *primary securitisation* (where corporate borrowers fund directly in the capital market without the intermediation of banks) and *secondary securitisation* (where a portfolio of loans on the balance sheet of banks is packaged and sold into the capital market).

In some models of banking, the existence of banks is viewed as an endogenous response to imperfect and incomplete markets. In a world of zero transactions costs, complete and symmetrically available information, with a complete set of markets to cover all possible future states, there would be no role for banks as financial intermediaries (i.e., their role in accepting deposits with one set of characteristics and creating assets with a different set). Although these conditions are not met in practice, the process of financial innovation and the creation of a wider range of financial instruments (*spectrum filling*) has reduced the degree of market imperfections and incompleteness (Llewellyn 1985, 1992), and the number and extent of discontinuities in the range of market instruments. Borrowers now have considerably more choice of instruments in the capital market than in the past.

A further factor in securitisation has been the introduction of new standardised financial instruments suited for mass trade in secondary markets (Horngren 1990). In addition, the development of new analytical methods for valuing complex contingent claims (particularly the Black–Scholes model in the valuation of options) has contributed to the development of organised markets for standardised options. A further decisive factor has been the rapid development of information technology which, inter alia, has meant that the bundling and unbundling of financial assets into new packages that might be of interest to investors has become feasible for trading in organised secondary markets.

The growing institutionalisation of personal savings has reinforced other factors inducing financial flows through markets rather than banks.

The trend towards securitisation has, therefore, been a product both of changes in the market and economic environment, and shifts in the relative efficiency of bank and capital market facilities. On the other hand, the same process of financial innovation has in several respects also eroded the distinction between banking and capital market facilities: many capital market instruments are based upon floating interest rates, banks have become holders of capital market instruments, many instruments (swaps being an obvious example) straddle banking and capital markets, and others (Note Issuance Facilities (NIFs) and Revolving Underwriting Facilities (RUFs)) combine banking and capital market instruments. It is also the case that banks are involved in the arranging of these facilities for corporate clients and hence it is not business that is entirely lost.

Securitisation does not mean that banks lose business altogether, but that they use their comparative advantages in different ways in the securitisation process: as underwriters, offering parallel loans, through credit enhancement facilities, acting as brokers and arrangers, etc. The nature of banks' business changes in the process, as does the form of remuneration: fees rather than margin.

13.   The Fundamentals of Banking

Our starting point was to identify the fundamentals of the banking firm: i.e., what gives banks competitive advantage. These are essentially: information advantages, risk analysis expertise, processing capabilities, monitoring of borrowers and enforcement of loan contracts, broking potential (bringing various counterparties together), delivery capacity, and acting as the core of the payments system.

These basic elements represent what might be regarded as banks' core competencies. Banks have traditionally used their comparative advantages to specialise in the provision, holding and monitoring of loans that are not readily marketable. However, the same competencies can be used in a variety of other ways. For example, information advantages can be used by a bank to make loans, to underwrite capital market issues of their customers, to conduct broking operations, or as a basis for cross-selling a variety of products and services. They can also be used to signal the credit-worthiness of their customers to the capital market.

There is no unique way in which core competencies can be used. The skill in developing competitive strategies in a changing market environment is to identify the firm's core competencies and then to judge how they can be most effectively exploited. The latter will change over time as market and technology circumstances change. Thus, while banks' core competencies may be enduring, the way they are used to gain competitive advantage is not. Two particular examples of this are to be found in *secondary securitisation* and *off-balance-sheet business*.

14.   Secondary Securitisation

Secondary securitisation is the process through which assets originally held on the balance sheet of a bank are packaged and sold to a capital market institution which is funded by issuing securities. In effect, secondary securitisation is the conversion of cash flows from a portfolio of assets into negotiable instruments which are sold to investors, are secured on the underlying assets, and carry one or more forms of credit enhancement. The securitisation vehicles are not required to hold capital to the extent (if at all) required of banks, as the vehicles do not have deposit-type liabilities. The economics of securitisation is discussed in detail in Pais (1998).

In the United States, over two-thirds of residential mortgages and half the credit card receivables are now funded through wholesale markets via securitisation programmes. In Australia, about half of all housing loans from mortgage originators are funded by mortgage-backed securities issued by special purpose vehicles.

Increasingly, banks have come to securitise a significant proportion of their assets and this has major implications. First, it implies that fee income has become an increasing proportion of banks' total income relative to margin income. Secondly, it implies that the relative size of the capital market and banks in the financing of the corporate sector is shifting towards the capital market. Thirdly, it also implies that the liquidity of banks' balance sheets has increased to the extent that they hold securitised assets on the balance sheet. In effect, the securitisation of assets and the banks' holdings of such assets means that one of the traditional special characteristics of banks (the holding of nonmarketable assets) is being challenged. Fourthly, the nature of banking business is changing as banks become managers of securitised assets (*The Economist* 1992: 94–95).

Securitisation may also mean that banks will increasingly operate as originators and packagers of credit risks which are ultimately assumed by others. In some senses, securitisation undermines much of what banks have traditionally been paid for: analysing nonstandardised credits and holding them in the form of nontradable assets against their own capital.

Primary and *secondary* securitisation mean that, in effect, banks in some business areas have come to use their core competencies in different ways: not to make loans to be held permanently on the balance sheet, but to facilitate capital market intermediation. A measure of the changes occurring in the underlying economics of banking is seen in the United Kingdom, where some banks have ben simultaneously securitising loans (which reduces the required holding of capital) and repaying capital to shareholders. This must reflect that some business traditionally conducted on the balance sheet of banks is now not sufficiently profitable to earn the required rate of return on capital.

15.   Off-Balance-Sheet Business

A second example of how banks may use their core competencies in different ways is off-balance-sheet business. There has been a trend in many countries for off-balance-sheet business and income to rise as a proportion of banks' total business and income. There is a powerful parallel between on- and off-balance-sheet business in two respects: the same basic functions and services are being provided, and the same core competencies (e.g., a bank's information advantage) are being applied. Lewis (1988) shows that this applies to the two major areas of off-balance-sheet business: contingent claims (loan commitments, guarantees, swaps and hedge transactions, and investment banking activities), and financial services (loan-related services, trust and advisory services, brokerage and agency services, etc.). Thus on- and off-balance-sheet business are alternative ways of exploiting the same core competencies. For instance, an information advantage can be used either to make on-balance-sheet loans (with profit earned through the interest margin) or to offer a guarantee or back-up line of credit to a borrower making a capital market issue (with profit earned through fee income).

16.   The Paradigm of Contract Banking

A further dimension where the pressures outlined earlier are having a major impact on the banking firm is with respect to organisational structure. Traditional banking involves a joint production technology that produces deposit, lending and transactions services within a given institution. This structure has faced an increasing challenge from separate production technologies. In this way, technology can fundamentally change the basic economics of the financial firm.

The conventional image of a bank is of a vertically integrated firm providing each of the subcomponents of particular services and products: it provides the whole product or service. However, the basic economics of the banking firm has already begun to change, and the process is likely to accelerate in the years to come. A distinction needs to be made between the services and products the customer ultimately demands (e.g., loans) and the components and processes that go to make up those products and services.

The process of *deconstruction*, common in the manufacture of goods, has not been the norm in banking where traditionally the banking firm has offered an integrated service by providing the service and their components itself. The process of *deconstruction* changes this picture. It enables particular subcomponents of products or services to be subcontracted (outsourced) and supplied by other firms on a contract basis. Similarly, *deconstruction* enables a bank to provide a particular subcomponent of a service to competitors. Thus, a bank may subcontract the administration of its credit card operation and at the same time export to other banks its risk analysis capacity. The potential exists because the economies of scale in bank processes vary. By subcontracting a particular process, a small bank may be able to buy into economies of scale that it could not achieve itself.

What might be termed *contract banking* implies a bank offering a full range of services but where the bank coordinates inputs from a wide range of different companies. The core is a contract the bank has with its customers to supply a set of services or products of a particular standard. In turn, the bank contractor has a set of contracts with a range of internal and external suppliers of the components of these ultimate products and services. The value added by the bank contractor is in the management of these contracts. The concept of *contract banking* is discussed more fully in Llewellyn (1997).

There are several reasons why outsourcing is undertaken and why it has become an increasingly common feature in banking:

— to reap economies of scale that cannot be obtained internally;
— to avoid installing excess capacity to cope with peak-load problems;
— some areas may be too specialist to be untertaken internally;
— a particular expertise may not be available internally and may be uneconomic to acquire;
— increased flexibility in the use of technology;
— to spread costs and risks;
— to break an internal monopoly when services are supplied exclusively internally;
— to change the firm's cost structure: lower fixed costs.

Above all, a major advantage of outsourcing is that it transforms fixed costs into variable costs and hence reduces the requirement for, often large, up-front costs in developing and adapting processing facilities. If a firm conducts its own processing, for instance, it pays and must recoup through the pricing of its products and services both the large fixed and small variable costs of the process. On the other hand, if it subcontracts the process it pays the supplier a proportion of the supplier's fixed costs plus the variable costs. The whole procedure is economic if the higher variable and transactions costs through outsourcing are less than the savings on fixed costs.

In addition, the outsourcing firm may find it economic to outsource even when this condition is not met because of the sharing of risks and the greater flexibility it secures through minimising its infrastructure and fixed costs. In general, firms with low fixed costs and capacity are more flexible than those with high fixed costs and capacity even if its variable costs are higher.

At its extreme, the possibility of the *virtual bank* emerges. This has an interface with its customers and seemingly supplies a set of integrated services and products. And yet it may do nothing itself other than manage a set of contracts with external suppliers. It is a contractor of other firms' products and services and a coordinator of a network of contracts and services. It is, in effect, a broker between the customer and the ultimate supplier of services which go to make up the final products and services demanded by the customer. This may mean that comparatively small *virtual banks* can exist side by side large banks. They may provide the full range of banking services with the customer being unaware that the bank is in truth a network of alliances with specialist providers.

What in practice is likely to emerge is a spectrum of different types of bank. At one end of the spectrum will be the traditional fully integrated bank which, because of the economies of scale in bank processes, will be very large. At the other end of the spectrum will lie the *virtual bank*. In practice, the majority of banks will lie within the polar boundaries of the spectrum, with some services being provided internally and others outsourced. It is ultimately a question of the balance between internal and external contracts and many alternative structures are likely to emerge.

Some outsourcing arrangements involve technology companies, and to date the relationship has been cooperative largely because technology companies have not been in competition with banks. This may change. If banking becomes an integral part of e-commerce over the Internet, the companies that have control over the access technology have a potentially major competitive advantage through recognising the customer at the point of access. If the technology companies were themselves to offer financial services, they would have a competitive advantage comparable to the historic advantage banks have had through the branch network. What starts as a cooperative arrangement could end with technology companies becoming traditional banks' major competitors in at least some banking markets.

Economies of Scale

One aspect of new technology in banking is that economies of scale in bank back-office processing are increasing. However, when combined with the process of *deconstruction*, this does not mean that banks need to be big in order to secure these larger economies of scale. Outsourcing back-office processing can have the effect of effectively buying in economies of scale from outside the firm. This means that small banks can gain economies of scale externally where their own size of operations limits their ability to secure internal economies of scale.

This aspect of technology can be represented in Figure 1 below. AC1 represents the average cost curve of a bank process with traditional technology. With

Figure 1: Technology and Economies of Scale

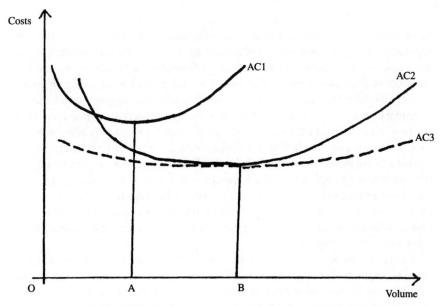

new processing technology, but with traditional organisational structures, the average cost curve shifts to AC2. This implies that economies of scale are greater, the optimum volume of processing rises from OA to OB, but also that, at low levels of processing, average costs of processing may be higher with new than with old technology. This may be because, while variable costs are lower, fixed costs are higher. If organisational structures are changed (e.g., through outsourcing processing to external agencies which have economies of scale because they are offering services to several banks), firms of all sizes can approach the low costs of those largest competitors who are able to secure economies of scale internally. This can be represented by a new average cost curve AC3.

The competitive strategy implication of this analysis is that, while competitive pressures will be forcing banks to lower costs in any way they can and to secure economies of scale where they exist, this does not mean that this can be done only by big banks. One of the implications of new technology, combined with *deconstruction* and outsourcing processes, is that firms of varying size are able to secure economies of scale.

17.   Assessment

In various ways the related pressures of competition, declining entry barriers, deregulation, financial innovation, and technology have eroded some of the comparative advantages of banks in their traditional financial intermediation business. In the process, they have been transforming the fundamental economics of banking.

Regulation in the past to some extent exaggerated the comparative advantages of banks because it created something of a protective market environment. Now, because of deregulation, banks in some countries are losing their predominant role as deposit takers and lenders to companies. Market pressures are also eroding the market imperfections which gave rise to the banks' comparative advantages over intermediation by capital markets. Financial innovation and technology are eroding transactions and information costs and market imperfections which have been the basis of banks' efficiency over direct credit markets. In addition, banks' own cost structures (including the cost of capital) may also have eroded some of their comparative advantages.

Above all, banks are no longer the exclusive suppliers of banking services: there are many traditional activities of banks that can now be undertaken equally well by markets and other types of financial and nonfinancial companies. Banks face competition from a wider variety of competitors (including niche players) whose underlying economics are different from incumbents. Smaller firms and new entrants are also able to challenge the scale advantages of incumbents through outsourcing. In addition, with the exponential development of information, trading and delivery technology, the value added in the banking business is increasingly passing away from banks to specialist technology companies.

The reason why the combined pressures and developments outlined above constitute a "new economics of banking" is because: (1) they impact powerfully on competition and contestability, (2) incumbent banks have come to face competition from new types of competitors, (3) technology is changing all aspects of banking simultaneously, (4) the structure of the banking firm is changing, and (5) technology is transforming the underlying economics of everything that banks do.

On top of all this, there is also increasing pressure from the capital market for banks to focus on the return on capital. Some banks adopt an economic value added (EVA) business strategy. EVA gives emphasis to economic rather than accounting profitability and to the weighted average cost of capital as the hurdle. Four strategies are consistent with such a focus on EVA: (1) raising the rate of return on assets (e.g., cost-cutting, enhanced revenue strategies, consolidation, etc.), (2) developing capital-free (off-balance-sheet) business, (3) removing less profitable assets from the balance sheet (selling subsidiaries, securitising assets, etc.), and (4) returning capital to shareholders.

However, these trends do not necessarily mean a pessimistic outlook for *banking firms* as the business of the banking firm is likely to change towards the provision of a wider range of financial services relative to the traditional financial intermediation and on-balance sheet role. Banks are not so much in decline as re-creating themselves in a different way.

The successful development of corporate strategy is ultimately a question of defining comparative advantages, and developing alternative ways of exploiting such advantages. Thus, while banks may continue to have information advantages with respect to their customers, this does not necessarily mean they are only to be exploited in the form of making loans and/or holding loans on the balance sheet. Information advantages can be exploited in many other ways such as servicing the capital market. While banks may lose market share in some of their traditional markets, they will gain and develop other business and use their core competencies in different ways.

References

Bisignano, J. (1990). Structure of Financial Intermediation, Corporate Finance and Central Banking. Mimeo. Bank for International Settlements, Basle.

Boyd, J., and M. Gertler (1994). Are Banks Dead? Or Are the Reports Greatly Exaggerated. Federal Reserve Bank of Chicago. *Quarterly Review* 18(3): 2–23.

Browne, F. (1992). Efficiency and Financial Fragility in Irish Banking: Causes, Consequences and Policy Recommendations. Research Paper 4/R/92. Bank of Ireland, Dublin.

Diamond, D. (1984). Financial Intermediation and Delegated Monitoring. *Review of Economic Studies* 51(166): 393–414.

The Economicst (1992). Time To Leave: A Survey of World Banking. May 2.

Edwards, F. (1993). Financial Markets in Transition: Or the Decline of Commercial Banking. In Federal Reserve Bank of Kansas City (ed.), *Changing Capital Markets: Implications for Monetary Policy.* Kansas City.

Eisenbeis, R. (1990). The Impact of Securitisation and Internationalisation on Market Imperfections: Implications for Regulatory Reform and the Structure of the Payments System. In E. Gardener (ed.), *The Future of Financial Systems and Services.* London: Macmillan.

European Central Bank (1999). *The Effects of Technology and the EU Banking Systems.* Frankfurt: ECB.

Horngren, L. (1990). Some Policy Implications of Securitisation. Mimeo. Sveriges Riksbank, Stockholm.

Joss, R. (1996). Developments in the Business of Banking. In Reserve Bank of Australia (ed.), *The Future of the Financial System*. Sydney.

Kaufman, G.G., and L.R. Mote (1994). Is Banking a Declining Industry: A Historical Perspective. *Economic Perspectives* (Federal Reserve Bank of Chicago) 18(3): 2–21.

Lewis, M.K. (1988). Off-Balance Sheet Activities and Financial Innovation in Banking. *Banca Nazionale del Lavoro, Quarterly Review* (167): 387–410.

Llewellyn, D.T. (1985). *Evolution of the British Financial System*. London: Institute of Bankers.

Llewellyn, D.T. (1992). Financial Innovation: A Basic Analysis. In H. Cavanna (ed.), *Financial Innovation*. London: Routledge.

Llewellyn, D.T. (1997). Contract Banking and Its Implications for Building Societies. Project Paper 5. *Economics of Mutuality and the Future of Building Societies*. London: Building Societies Association.

Llewellyn, D.T. (1999). *The New Economics of Banking*. SUERF Studies 5. Amsterdam: SUERF.

Martin, P. (1998). A Long Goodbye. *Financial Times*, December 1, page 6.

Mayer, C. (1994). Financial Systems, Corporate Finance and Economic Development. In G.R. Hubbard (ed.), *Asymmetric Information, Corporate Finance and Investment*. NBER, Chicago: University of Chicago Press.

Pais, E. (1998). *Asset Securitisation in Europe*. London: HMSO.

Santomero, A.M. (1999). Bank Mergers: What's a Policy Maker To Do? *Journal of Banking and Finance* 23 (February): 637–645.

Van Horn, J. (1985). Of Financial Innovation and Excesses. *Journal of Finance* 40(3): 621–631.

Vesala, J. (2001). *Technological Transformation and Retail Banking Competition: Implications and Measurement*. Bank of Finland Studies 20. Helsinki.

Comment on David T. Llewellyn

Ralph P. Heinrich

David Llewellyn argues that technological innovation and deregulation are reducing barriers to entry in banking and are reducing the costs of market relative to bank finance. As a result, banks are facing increasing competitive pressures in their traditional lines of business. New entry by nonbank financial intermediaries and even by nonfinancial firms together with increased pressure from financial markets is driving structural change in the banking industry. Llewellyn's paper focuses on several ways in which traditional banks are responding to these pressures. They are cutting costs through outsourcing, unbundling of financial transactions and the deconstruction of the value chain, and they are scaling back traditional lines of business and instead expanding into new areas.

I find this argument broadly persuasive, and would like to raise some additional points that complement those made in the paper. My comments fall into four parts. The first part will look briefly at the consequences of disintermediation for the capacity of the financial system to monitor the use of financial resources by borrowers. The second part takes up the paper's discussion of the impact of technological innovation on scale and scope economies and hence on structural change in the banking industry itself. It points out that in addition, perhaps sometimes also in contrast to the competitive responses discussed in the paper, traditional banks are also responding to increased competitive pressure through consolidation (i.e., mergers between banks) and conglomeration (i.e., mergers with other financial firms). The third part asks about the motives for nonfinancial firms to enter the traditional banking business and offers an albeit speculative explanation based on the value of information as an input into the traditional businesses of the new entrants. The fourth part will touch upon some of the regulatory policy issues that present themselves in the face of structural change in the financial industry.

1.   Disintermediation and Monitored Finance

In the United States, banks have lost ground to other financial intermediaries and to markets in both business lending and consumer lending (Allen and Santomero

2001). Similarly, they have also lost ground on the liabilities side of their balance sheets to other financial intermediaries like pension, mutual, and money market funds. As argued by Llewellyn (2001), banks have been able to maintain their position as a percentage of GDP and as a share of total financial assets only by moving away from traditional deposit taking and lending and into trading and fee-generating lines of business. While the picture looks somewhat different for Germany, where banks have succeeded in maintaining their share in total financial liabilities of both the household and enterprise sectors, disintermediation has also gained ground in a number of other European countries like France and the United Kingdom.

These developments raise the important question whether competition from financial markets implies the demise of monitored finance. On the one hand, ex ante screening of borrower quality is increasingly replaced by credit-scoring techniques (Kroszner 1998). Moreover, with banks facing more competition, borrower-specific information becomes more dispersed, as each financial institution has unique information about a smaller subset of borrowers. This creates an inefficiency by reducing the screening ability of financial institutions (Marquez 2001). Finally, competition erodes informational rents banks have traditionally earned because through their monitoring they gained an informational advantage, locking their customers into captive relationships. On the other hand, information advantages not only constitute a source of rents, they also constitute a barrier to entry. Thus, banks may respond to increased potential competitive pressure by reinforcing their efforts to acquire and maintain borrower-specific information in an effort to shore up their core customer base against potential entrants. Thus, while some banks may move away from their traditional business, others may instead focus all the more on their core comparative advantage, namely monitored relationship lending, leaving arm's-length lending to the markets (Boot and Thakor 2000; Hauswald and Marquez 2000; Aoki and Dinc 2000).

2.   Structural Change in the Banking Industry: Consolidation and Conglomeration

The paper stresses that banks are losing business to financial markets and to nonfinancial firms entering the banking business. It also stresses that banks are getting out of traditional lines of business and are entering nontraditional lines. Finally, the paper claims that banks are splicing up the value chain, are unbundling financial services that used to be delivered together, and are sourcing out parts of these "deconstructed" services. A case in point would be loans that are originated by one financial institution, prefinanced by a second, repackaged and securitized by a third, and refinanced by a fourth. These developments might suggest that economies of scope and perhaps also economies of scale are declining in the traditional banking business, that the trend should go towards more specialized, tightly focused banks, and that banks should be losing in importance relative to financial markets.

While this may well be what is happening in parts of the industry, there are also some recent trends that point in a different direction. We have witnessed a wave of mergers and acquisitions (M&As) in both the U.S. and the European banking industries of late (ECB 2000; Berger 2000). The bulk of the activity involved consolidation, i.e., mergers between banks. But there is also evidence of – mostly bank-driven – conglomeration, i.e., of banks acquiring securities businesses or insurers. M&As appear to have been responsible at least in part for increased market concentration in a number of European countries. Apart from taking excess capacity out of the market, the mergers have been driven by the desire to realize economies of scale, e.g., by combining distribution networks or sharing the investment outlays for new technology. Moreover, conglomerate mergers have also aimed at diversifying risks, smoothing income volatility, and combining businesses with predominantly short-term liabilities (banks) with businesses with predominantly long-term liabilities (insurers). In a similar vein, conglomerate mergers have become attractive because technological innovation holds out promises of new ways of cross-selling and one-stop shopping. On balance, it thus seems that at least in some areas, technological innovation is raising rather than lowering economies of scale and scope in finance.

3. Entry of Nonfinancial Firms into Banking: Where Is the Competitive Advantage?

Why are nonfinancial firms entering traditional banking markets? It might be tempting to argue that they do so "because they can":

- They own brand names, branch networks, customer bases, and they have assembled information on their customers for purposes of inventory management and of designing marketing and pricing strategies
- Information is a public good, hence it is free once assembled, and so it can be used for additional business, such as personal financial services at no additional cost.

However, even if some nonfinancial firms do have these attributes, this can be no more than a necessary condition for market entry. In order for nonfinancial firms to make inroads in the market of traditional banks, they have to answer the question: what do nonfinancial firms have to offer that traditional banks do not have? Traditional banks have brand name capital, they have branch networks, they have customer bases, and they have information on customers. So on these counts, it is difficult to see how nonfinancial firms could have a comparative advantage over incumbent banks. To the contrary, incumbent banks certainly have a head start in that they know their business far better than any nonfinancial firm would. By the same token, the fact that the cost of providing certain financial services is reduced through technological innovation could explain successful entry by nonfinancial firms only if these cost savings were not available to the incumbent banks on the same terms.

One possible explanation how nonfinancial firms are able to compete, and the one favored by Llewellyn (in this volume), is that they cherry-pick only the most profitable financial services and thereby undermine any cross-subsidization possibly practiced by incumbents. However, it is far from clear that cherry-picking is necessarily a superior strategy in banking. Indeed, most theories of banking emphasize synergies between the different parts of the banking business (see, e.g., Freixas and Rochet 1997).

But at the same time, an alternative explanation suggests itself. Traditional banking theory argues that one reason why banks are offering deposits and payments services is to obtain information on customers, which is a highly valuable input into their lending business. Similarly, nonfinancial firms, such as supermarkets, may be entering financial services not so much because they have a genuine competitive advantage in them, but in order to obtain information on customers which is valuable for use in a different area of their business, namely the marketing of goods.

Technological innovation has drastically reduced the costs of assembling, storing, retrieving, and processing large amounts of data. This means that it has become much more economical to base competitive strategies on the analysis of vast amounts of micro data, and hence it has become much more attractive to search for creative ways of obtaining such data. Indeed, the marketing of customer databases assembled on the Internet has become a viable business in itself recently (Shapiro and Varian 1998). Offering financial services like payments services and consumer credit may be another way of assembling such databases.

When customers sign up for these services, they can be asked to provide information on things like age, address, income, and possibly other details not readily available otherwise. Moreover, by offering credit and payment services, retailers are able to match customers to individual purchases and hence to learn more about individual preferences. Thus, rather than targeting personal financial services as a new profitable business, retailers may be targeting it as a way to assemble more information on their customers, which will be used subsequently as a resource to generate higher profits in their traditional lines of business.

4.   Policy Issues

Structural change in the financial industry raises important issues for regulatory and supervisory policies. To the extent that nonbank financial firms will either merge with banks (conglomeration) or will enter the banking business, the borders between different segments of the financial industry will increasingly be blurred. This raises the issue of how to ensure a level regulatory playing field for all participants (ECB 2000). Similarly, one change that comes with a shift of banks from traditional lending to market trading and fee-based income is that financial institutions are getting more exposure to market risk as opposed to credit risk. This implies that financial intermediaries today are more likely than in the past to be adversely affected by crises originating in financial markets and vice versa.

This may call for a reform of regulatory structures. The two basic options are integrating the functions of different regulators into the hands of a single regulator, or coordinating the regulatory policies and actions of different regulators in ways that take account of the structural changes in the financial industry. Besides allowing an encompassing assessment of risks, integrated supervision might generate economies of scope and scale, and it might enhance transparency. However, excessive homogenization of regulation across activities with different risk profiles might also reduce the quality of supervision, and integration of supervisors would reduce the potential for regulatory competition. At the national level in Europe, several countries have moved towards integrating the supervision of different segments of the financial industry (banks, insurers, financial markets) into a single authority (Belaisch et al. 2001). However, empirical evidence on the success of alternative approaches to regulation is still missing.

In a similar vein, to the extent that nonfinancial firms enter parts of the banking business, the question will need to be addressed to what extent there are grounds for regulating these firms similarly to financial firms in general, and to banks in particular, or for reforming and possibly relaxing the regulation of traditional banks. On the one hand, if traditional regulatory policies are well-justified by market failures inherent in the banking business, then chances are that nonfinancial firms may suffer from the same potential market failures when entering the banking business. Hence, a case could be made for subjecting them to similar regulations. On the other hand, a careful examination of current regulatory policies might also reveal that maybe some of them are no longer necessary, in which case these policies should be dismantled in order to enable traditional banks to compete on a level playing field.

For instance, the fact that banks are increasingly able to repackage, securitize and resell their credits, thereby substantially increasing the liquidity of their assets and reducing the maturity mismatch characteristic of the traditional banking business, implies that regulation aimed at protecting depositors against liquidity risk may lose some of its justification in a new financial landscape.

Whether systemic risk will rise or decline is less clear. In particular, the implications of conglomerate risk for future regulation of the financial industry is an open question (Freedman 2000). On the one hand, conglomeration might reduce risk through diversification of earnings streams (Berger 2000). Recent simulations calibrated for the United States suggest that mergers between bank holdings and life insurance firms would lower conglomerate risk (Lown et al. 2000). On the other hand, a crisis hitting one part of the business of a financial conglomerate might spill over into other parts of its business in a sort of intrafirm contagion (Santomero and Eckels 2000). Similarly, if a safety net such as deposit insurance is extended to part of the business of a conglomerate, this might raise the incentive to take additional risks in other unregulated business areas. Boot and Schmeits (2000) show theoretically that the diversification effect of conglomeration tends to dominate if market discipline is weak. In any event, focusing on the *systemic* risk which firms engaged in providing financial services represent would mean that traditional distinctions between banks, insurers, and other financial firms would not necessarily form a sound basis for regulation in the future. A regulatory approach along these is being discussed in the United Kingdom (Richardson and Stephenson 2000).

References

Allen, F., and A. Santomero (2001). What Do Financial Intermediaries Do? *Journal of Banking and Finance* 25(2): 271–294.

Aoki, M., and S. Dinc (2000). Relational Financing As an Institution and Its Viability Under Competition. In M. Aoki and G. Saxonhouse (eds.), *Finance, Governance and Competitiveness in Japan*. Oxford: Oxford University Press.

Belaisch, A., L. Kodres, J. Levy, and A. Ubide (2001). Euro-Area Banking at the Crossroads. International Monetary Fund Working Paper 01/28. IMF, Washington, D.C.

Berger, A. (2000). The Integration of the Financial Services Industry: Where Are the Efficiencies? Finance and Economics Discussion Series 2000-36. Federal Reserve Board, Washington, D.C.

Boot, A., and A. Schmeits (2000). Market Discipline and Incentive Problems in Conglomerate Firms with Applications to Banking. *Journal of Financial Intermediation* 9(3): 240–273.

Boot, A., and A. Thakor (2000). Can Relationship Lending Survive Competition? *Journal of Finance* 55(2): 679–713.

ECB (European Central Bank) (2000). *Mergers and Acquisitions Involving the EU Banking Industry – Facts and Implications*. Frankfurt/M.: ECB.

Freedman, S. (2000). Regulating the Modern Financial Firm: Implications of Disintermediation and Conglomeration. Discussion Paper 2000-21. University of St. Gallen, Department of Economics, St. Gallen.

Freixas, X., and J. Rochet (1997). *Microeconomics of Banking*. Cambridge, Mass: MIT Press.

Hauswald, R., and R. Marquez (2000). Competition and Strategic Focus in Lending Relationships. Mimeo. Indiana University and University of Maryland.

Kroszner, R. (1998). The Political Economy of Banking and Financial Regulatory Reform in Emerging Markets. *Research in Financial Services: Private and Public Policy* 10 (1998): 33–51.

Llewellyn, D. (2002). Financial Intermediaries in the New Economy – Will Banks Lose Their Traditional Role? This volume.

Lown, C., C. Osler, P. Strahan, and A. Sufi (2000). The Changing Landscape of the Financial Services Industry: What Lies Ahead? *Economic Policy Review* 6(4): 39–54.

Marquez, R. (2001). Competition, Adverse Selection, and Information Dispersion in the Banking Industry. Mimeo. University of Maryland, College Park.

Richardson, J., and M. Stephenson (2000). Some Aspects of Regulatory Capital. Occasional Paper 7. Financial Services Authority, London.

Santomero, A., and D. Eckels (2000). The Determinants of Success in the New Financial Services Environment: Now that Firms Can Do Everything, What Should They Do and Why Should Regulators Care? *Economic Policy Review* 6(4): 11–23.

Shapiro, R., and H. Varian (1998). *Information Rules – A Strategic Guide to the Network Economy*. Cambridge, Mass: Harvard Business School Press.

LIST OF CONTRIBUTORS

NORBERT BERTHOLD
Professor of Economics, Universität Würzburg, Würzburg, Germany

MICHAEL BURDA
Professor of Economics, Humboldt-Universität zu Berlin, Berlin, Germany

RAINER FEHN
Lecturer, Economics Department, Universität Würzburg, Würzburg, Germany

DOMINIQUE FORAY
Principal Administrator, Centre for Educational Research and Innovation, OECD, Paris

RALPH P. HEINRICH
Financial Markets Research Area, Institute for World Economics, Kiel, Germany

PETER JOHNSTON
Directorate-General Information Society, European Commission, Brussels, Belgium

DALE W. JORGENSON
Frederic E. Abbe Professor of Economics, Harvard University, Cambridge, Mass., United States

DAVID T. LLEWELLYN
Professor of Money and Banking, Loughborough University, Leicestershire, United Kingdom

CATHERINE L. MANN
Senior Fellow, Institute for International Economics, Washington, D.C., United States

AADITYA MATTOO
Senior Economist, Development Research Group, The World Bank, Washington, D.C., United States

ELI M. SALZBERGER
Director, Center for the Study of Crime, Law and Society, The Law Faculty, University of Haifa, Haifa, Israel

LUDGER SCHUKNECHT
Principal Economist, Fiscal Policies Division, European Central Bank, Frankfurt am Main, Germany

JÜRGEN STEHN
Head of International Economics and Structural Change Research Group, Institute for World Economics, Kiel, Germany

RÜDIGER SOLTWEDEL
Head of Regional Economics Department, Institute for World Economics, Kiel, Germany

JÜRGEN STEHN
Head of International Economics and Structural Change Research Group, Institute for World Economics, Kiel, Germany

KEVIN STIROH
Research Officer, Federal Reserve Bank of New York, United States

Kiel Institute for World Economics

Symposia and Conference Proceedings

Horst Siebert, Editor

Towards a New Global Framework for High-Technology Competition
Tübingen 1997. 223 pages. Hardcover.

Quo Vadis Europe?
Tübingen 1997. 343 pages. Hardcover.

Structural Change and Labor Market Flexibility
Experience in Selected OECD Economies
Tübingen 1997. 292 pages. Hardcover.

Redesigning Social Security
Tübingen 1998. 387 pages. Hardcover.

Globalization and Labor
Tübingen 1999. 320 pages. Hardcover.

The Economics of International Environmental Problems
Tübingen 2000. 274 pages. Hardcover.

The World's New Financial Landscape: Challenges for Economic Policy
Berlin . Heidelberg 2001. 324 pages. Hardcover.

Economic Policy for Aging Societies
Berlin . Heidelberg 2002. 305 pages. Hardcover.

Economic Policy Issues of the New Economy
Berlin · Heidelberg 2002. 251 pages. Hardcover.

Tübingen: Mohr Siebeck (http://www.mohr.de)
Berlin · Heidelberg: Springer-Verlag (http://www.springer.de)